Offending Behaviour

for Roger
with great admiration
+ best wishes
for your series.

Philip

Offending Behaviour

Skills and stratagems for going straight

James McGuire and Philip Priestley

B T Batsford Ltd   London

© James McGuire and Philip Priestley 1985
First published 1985
Reprinted 1985, 1987, 1989

All rights reserved. No part of this publication
may be reproduced, in any form or by any means,
without permission from the Publisher

Typeset by Tek-Art Ltd, Kent
and printed in Great Britain by
Butler & Tanner Ltd
Frome, Somerset

Published by B.T. Batsford Ltd
4 Fitzhardinge Street, London W1H 0AH

British Library Cataloguing in Publication Data
McGuire, James
  Offending behaviour.
  1. Corrections
  I. Title   II. Priestley, Philip
  364.6   HV8665
ISBN 0 7134 4403 7

Contents

Acknowledgements

This book has its origins in a Home Office funded research project, undertaken between 1975 and 1978 in two prisons, Ranby and Ashwell, and in the Day Training Centre in Sheffield. Our first debt therefore is to the prison officers, probation staff, and co-researchers who worked with us on that project, and to the many offenders who took part. A single finding from the project, that men from Ranby prison who had worked on their own violent behaviour were subsequently less likely to be reconvicted of violence, provided the germ of the idea for the book.

For supplying, developing, and testing some of the ideas included here, we are indebted to Brenda Palmer of the south-east Probation Staff Development Unit, to David Binney, John Lazarus, Mary Watson, and all of the other officers who participated in the Unit's project on 'Offending'. Further ideas were contributed by Stewart Kemp, by Bill Mather, and by Audrey Murrell. Ann Reynolds read an earlier version of the text for us. For assistance in locating other kinds of materials, we thank David Crawford, Barbara Hudson, William Marshall, Raymond Novaco and Ian Robertson; the staff of Sheffield City Library, and of the libraries of Sheffield and Bristol Universities, University College London, Sheffield City Polytechnic, the Institute of Psychiatry, the Institute of Education, and the Cambridge Institute of Criminology. Our thanks also to Bill Mather and RAP for permission to reproduce the drawing on p. 195 and to Dr Anne Robinson for reading the manuscript. Responsibility for the final text is of course ours alone.

Offending Behaviour is intended not as a 'reading' book but as a working manual and sourcebook for those who deal with offenders on an everyday, face-to-face basis. We hope that it will help such workers to focus their efforts more directly on what people actually do when they commit offences, with individuals who would like to confront this problem in their lives. We hope too that it will stimulate such workers to carry out their own research in what is still largely unexplored and often difficult territory.

Part one
The offence

1 Responding to crime

It is very difficult to imagine a society without rules; societies rely for their existence on the maintenance of rules by their members. Such rules evolve in parallel with a society's history and character in other respects, and reflect some overall state of compromise between different pressures acting within it. Rules perform a number of vital functions for both the individual and the group. They act as a kind of social lubricant; by prescribing some kinds of behaviour and prohibiting others they make many daily decisions much easier, and relieve us of the burden of always having to think out things afresh; they help the majority who observe them feel that they 'belong'; and they bind citizens together in a collective identity within which they can find physical, emotional and moral security. Though rules may have many negative aspects, and many individuals have devoted their lives to trying to throw them off, it remains true that even the most permissive and libertarian visions of Utopia have carried some implications as to what is tolerable or acceptable and what is not.

But just as it is difficult to imagine a society with no rules, it is equally difficult to imagine one without individuals who break them. Ever since human beings assembled in groups there have been those who have disregarded the rules, have short-circuited them when their own interests have conflicted with the group's, or who as a result of carelessness, malice, disadvantaged position, or straightforward disagreement have failed to conform with their society's requirements of them. Even the pioneering Puritans, who set out for the New World to escape the squalor and vices of the old, within a few years found themselves engulfed in a crime-wave as painful and disruptive as any they had left behind (Erikson, 1966). In this sense, offenders would seem to create something of an insoluble dilemma for the society in which they live. Its members set up a system of rules, but then a number of the supposed partners to the agreement flagrantly violate them. This may not however be as inconvenient as it sounds. For the lawbreaker stands as a constant reminder to the rest of society of where its boundaries lie; the negative social behaviour of some individuals sets an example through which the positive social behaviour of others may be reinforced. Seen in this light, the procedures which a society has developed for coping with its offenders tell us a great deal about it; how cohesive is its institutional fabric; how contented or discontented are most of its citizens; whether its ideals are substantial or hollow. In this respect, the recent history of most nations, and certainly of those in the industrialized West, poses a major question-mark over their general state of moral, social, and organizational health.

The response a society makes to those who offend against it is the central subject of this book. In essence, the concern of the book is with the failure of our own society to develop a manner of dealing with offenders which is at one and the same time effective, rational and humane. This may seem like a tall order and in one sense it is. But a parallel can be drawn with many other problems which perplex us at the present time. We can send some of our fellow human beings to the moon; speak to others on the far side of the earth; harness energy in vast abundance; allow a thousand million citizens to watch one football match – or blow them all up. Yet we cannot solve more pressing, yet basically simpler problems about the distribution of food, the eradication of disease or just living together in peace. As regards responding to transgression, moreover, our inability to take useful action is especially puzzling: for most approaches to this problem address themselves to almost everything but the offending act. Herein in fact may lie the root of the problem. By looking at the offender's personality, his or her family background, education, work history, or various other personal data, attention is somehow distracted from the reason why this individual has come to the attention of the authorities – that he or she has broken the law. Some questions of a personal kind are useful and entirely legitimate; and discussion, however perfunctory, inevitably occurs at some stage about the actual circumstances of and motivations for the offence. The balance, however, seems all wrong; the offender is processed through the legal bureaucracy much as if this were an end in itself: the offence loses significance and is not long afterwards forgotten.

However, the last few years have witnessed a growth of interest in the idea of examining and tackling offending behaviour directly. This book is an attempt to draw together some of the concepts and methods in what seems like a long overdue departure. It looks at offenders' beliefs and values and how these may be related to their motivations to offend – or stop offending. It considers the possible role of self-perceptions in the manufacture of an 'offender' image. It discusses skills – such as resisting group pressure or controlling one's anger – which can be acquired by and may be useful for those trying to keep out of trouble. And it contains some exploration of the parts played by excitement, risk-taking, and faulty decision-making in certain kinds of offence activity. The book is intended, first and foremost, to act as a practical guide to those who work with offenders and who would like to approach offending behaviour more closely in their work. But it also contains some material that is 'background' – surveying the reasons why certain methods seem potentially useful; and other material that is speculative – pinpointing some directions which seem promising for future work. First of all however, we would like to set the overall aims of the book more firmly in their context.

Established reactions to offence behaviour

In all but the very simplest societies, in addition to the rules which govern day-to-day conduct, there also exists a further set of rules specifying the action to be taken when a member infringes the law. In most cases the operation of rules of law has come to be enshrined in a distinct group of institutions, accompanied by their own set of ceremonies and rituals, and administered by a specially appointed sub-group of citizens who are accorded elevated status as a result. This group of citizens is therefore allocated a great deal of influence. By common agreement they may literally have powers of life and death over other citizens. The most savage form of retaliation which a society can make against an offending member is to condemn him or her to death. This need not be done actively, as in judicial execution; but can be done passively by excluding the individual completely from continued membership of the society. In extreme circumstances, without companionship or any other form of solace, having lost all sense of personal identity or any purpose in living, the person may succumb to what is known as 'hex' or 'voodoo' death (Cannon, 1942, 1957).

Execution is the most severe end of a spectrum of responses to the offender which has as its unifying principle the inflicting of pain – the meting out of *punishment* to transgressors both as an attempt to control their future behaviour and as a signal to everyone else that the behaviour was proscribed. For centuries, punishment was the dominant if not the sole mode of dealing with offenders throughout Western Europe. The philosophy behind it was simple: that by being punished, the offender recompensed society – in a manner determined by society as appropriate – for the wrongdoing perpetrated against it. At about the turn of the eighteenth and nineteenth centuries, however, this philosophy changed in its object and manner of implementation, even if its insistence on the use of punishment remained the same. Its focus became the soul or mind of the offender rather than the body; it sought to punish by controlling the offender's actions, and the aim of punishment became the reform of the offender rather than the exacting of retribution (Foucault, 1979; Ignatieff, 1978). This system, with its prisons, its emphasis on discipline, and its striving to transform the personality of the offender, has stayed with us to the present day.

To characterize the contemporary practice of penology wholly in terms such as these would however be something of an unjust and unwarranted oversimplification. There is today a very wide range of means of 'disposal' of offenders against the law. In England and Wales alone one might cite a list including custody in its various forms – from Community Homes, Detention Centres, Youth Custody Centres, through to imprisonment; probation, licences, and various other forms of supervision; Day Centres, hostel residence, and other types of 'alternatives to prison'; Intermediate Treatment, an amorphous and still uncertain option for younger offenders; Community Service, centred on the concept of the offender's indirect reparation for the damage he/she has done; fines, cautioning, suspended sentences, binding over, and innumerable variations and combinations of all of these. Within these formal or legalistic categories, one might detect activities as diverse as job training, basic and higher education, character-building, groupwork, therapeutic communities, token economies, New Careers schemes, personal counselling, family therapy, and a host of specialized services for offenders with specific problems such as homelessness, alcoholism, or drug addiction. In the United States the list would be still more extensive, ranging from a variety of drug, electrical, or other behavioural therapies, to confrontation between younger and older offenders, to self-reliance training through participation in outdoor adventures, to decarceration. But however impressive and multiform this list may appear to be, the overwhelming majority of its constituent items can be subsumed, without much unfairness, under three broad headings.

1. *Punishment*. This remains the dominant mode of approach to offending behaviour, receiving the lion's share of penal budgets in most countries. It is still based for most people on the principle of retribution; the notion of 'just deserts' remains pre-eminent in the public mind; it is happily congruent with popular views of how to go about child-rearing and education; and it meets with the approval – perhaps not on a personal but on a more general level – of most offenders themselves. For penology, however, the aim of punishment is not now retributive. Its purpose is two-fold: to act as a deterrent, and to 'reform' the offender – although the fact that it is creditworthy with the electorate is also a point in its favour. Into this category come all forms of sentence which are based on depriving offenders of their freedom; the imposition of disciplinary codes or military-style timetables; and the forced extraction from offenders of sums of money or hours of unpaid or badly-paid work.

2. *Treatment*. Just as insanity was once viewed as possession by the devil but subsequently came to be seen as an illness; just as the 'disease' model came to replace the Manichean one, so too have medicine and psychiatry made inroads into the

standard view of offenders and of how they are best dealt with. The use of various kinds of 'treatment' – while rarely administered as sentences in themselves – has been gradually assimilated into the content of numerous penal measures over the course of the last thirty or forty years. The aim of treatment is 'rehabilitation'; it rests on the assumption that the offender is a sick, or damaged, or inadequate, or in some other way defective person; and that his or her defects can be remedied by the ministrations of psychiatrists, psychologists, group therapists, social workers, probation officers or counsellors of some other kind. The blight on the offenders's personality must be removed; following which he or she will no longer have a need to break the law, a desire to get even with society or to test authority to its limits. Into this class comes a considerable range of the products of psychologists and others – from drug therapies and behaviour modification to psychoanalytically-based casework, therapeutic communities and transactional analysis.

3. *Practical help*. A third approach to the handling of offenders tries to eschew both the manipulation of discomfort and the administration of therapy as means of inducing offenders to change. In some instances, in fact, it is undertaken without any actual interest in whether or not it affects individuals' patterns of offending. This is the furnishing of practical assistance with the problems – personal, financial, legal, or social – with which many offenders are beset. This approach has no underpinning philosophy nor any set of theories on which it is based, save that of providing for the welfare of a group which in many respects is given the lowest priority of any section of society. However, this approach is rooted in a number of assumptions rarely made explicit by its practitioners, which in some ways constitute both an account of the aetiology of crime and a programme for attempting to reduce it. 'Given that many offenders come from the economically and socially less advantaged segments of society, their transgressions are not uncommonly a result of the hardships they face. Help them to improve their lot in this respect, and they will be less likely to break the law. The implication is therefore that if individuals' everyday problems in relation to housing, work, family welfare, money management or other spheres of life are solved, their reasons for committing offences will have been removed and they will return to the ranks of the (supposed) law-abiding majority.' Into this realm fall many of the advice-giving functions of counselling as practised in the social work and probation services, rights advocacy, pre-release preparation of prisoners, or various remedial education schemes which operate in a number of penal settings both custodial and community-based.

Penal effectiveness

These, then, set out above in a somewhat rough-and-ready fashion, are the main types of response (Western) societies have made to the problem of offending behaviour. Punishment may be there because of fears of wholesale public protest were its use to be discontinued. Therapy may be there because its usage convinces some that penology has a sound scientific basis. Practical help may be given quite disinterestedly, or supplied because of pressure from within our confused mentality on the subject of offenders, to soften the blow of punitive treatments with a touch of humanitarian concern. But all of these approaches, openly or implicity, purport to be about the influencing of offenders as such; about reducing the frequency of crime or alleviating its severity; about reacting to offenders in a way that will actually make them less prone to offend. What is the fate of these approaches gauged in terms of their impact in this respect?

First punishment, with its twin intentions of reforming the present offender and deterring the one of the future. If punishment did reform, if it did deter, if it were 'economically preventive' of offences, to use Honderich's (1976) phrase, then it might be justified – properly and equally administered – as a suitable response to offending acts. On both of these criteria, however, punishment falls down. There is little evidence that it affects those to whom it is applied, at least in terms of their propensity to commit offences. Home Office figures (HMSO, 1969) show that, for offenders aged 17-20 and 21-29 sentenced to imprisonment for two years or less, 87% and 72% respectively will have been reconvicted within five years. For most offenders under 29, rates of recidivism are roughly the same regardless of the way they are dealt with by the courts. The weight of the evidence suggests that the more 'punishing' forms of sentence, including all forms of custody, are consistently *less* likely to result in changed behaviour than more lenient sentences of fines, discharge or probation.

With regard to deterrence, too, punishment seems to be a considerable failure. It is, after all, the basis on which the sentencing policies of most countries have rested since they were first consciously formulated. The era in which the modern prison was born and the foundations of present penal codes were being laid was one which presented a pattern of crime markedly different from the one with which most nations are confronted today. In terms of quantity, crime has shown dramatic increases over the last seventy years. Between 1900 and 1974 the number of indictable offences in England and Wales increased thirteen-fold (Radzinowicz and King, 1977). Crime, often assumed to be associated with poverty, actually declined during the depressed decades of the twenties and thirties; but in the years of growing affluence between 1955 and 1964 showed rates of increase (per 100,000 persons) of 70% in France, 54% in Holland, 44% in Sweden, and 40% in Italy (Radzinowicz and King, 1977). In 1981 the number of offences known to the police in England and Wales exceeded three million for the first time. In terms of severity too, crime seems to have assumed almost epidemic proportions. In the 19 years from the assassination of John F. Kennedy in 1963 till 1982, no fewer than 440,000 Americans were killed by gunfire in their own country – substantially more than were killed in the Vietnam war (*Guardian* 23/11/82). During all of this period, the use of imprisonment and the threat of the death penalty existed to deter Americans from committing homicide. Some limitations on the availability of firearms could hardly have been *less* effective. For most of the time since offences began to be recorded the prospect of punishment has lingered before all would-be law-breakers; its effects as a deterrent have yet to be felt by most. Those politicians and others who wish to see a return to harsher forms of punishment for their supposed deterrent effects seem unaware that even at points in the past when very harsh penalties have been readily available, the crime rate has gone on rising just the same.

Turning next to 'treatment', a roughly similar pattern emerges; though as we will see below the picture is not quite as bleak as is widely believed. Major reviews of the effectiveness of different sentencing policies and accompanying attempts at 'rehabilitation', measured by the yardstick of reductions in recidivism rates, have drawn uniformly negative conclusions. Bailey (1966), Davidson and Seidman (1974), Lipton, Martinson and Wilks (1975) in the United States, together with Brody (1976) in the United Kingdom have surveyed research in various parts of the penal field. In many cases the picture was confused by the methodological inadequacy of much of the work that had been undertaken; nevertheless their findings are almost wholly and depressingly pessimistic. The messages emanating from their work have come to pervade criminology and penology with a feeling that the attempt to alter criminality by almost *any* means is virtually futile.

Numerous innovations in probation methods; the use of therapeutic communities;

experiments with various kinds of alternatives to prison; intensive community-based treatment programmes; even the conversion of whole institutions to a particular manner of working, all seemed to these commentators to have failed in their intentions or not to have been designed or evaluated in such a way that any clear conclusions could be drawn. The inability of researchers to demonstrate positive outcomes from all this endeavour has led some writers to urge for the abandonment, or at least the demotion, of 'reducing crime' as a possible aim within probation work (Bottoms and McWilliams, 1979); and must make us sympathise with the resigned tones of Martinson (1974): 'It may be . . . that education at its best, or psychotherapy at its best, cannot overcome, or even appreciably reduce, the powerful tendency for offenders to continue in criminal behaviour' (*op. cit.*, 49).

The truth may however be slightly more complex than this, as a more recent survey by Blackburn (1980) revealed. Scrutinizing research on the effects of different forms of intervention, carried out since the early seventies, Blackburn showed that though the general weight of evidence indicated that criminality was 'insensitive to treatment', there have also been a few pieces of research which have produced success. Applying fairly strict criteria (e.g. clear definition of programme; use of replicable methods; inclusion of appropriate control group; minimum two-year follow-up) to a batch of research studies published between 1973 and 1978, Blackburn selected five pieces of work (from an initial list of forty) which satisfactorily met the required standards. The methods used in these projects ranged from social casework (Shaw, 1974; Sinclair, Shaw, and Troop, 1974) and transactional analysis (Jesness, 1975) to behaviour modification (Jesness, 1975) and social skills training (Sarason, 1978). *All* were successful in obtaining reduced recidivism rates amongst their treated groups as compared with controls (though in some cases attempts to replicate them failed; see Fowles (1978) who repeated the work of Shaw (1974)). Blackburn proposed amongst other things that different kinds of approach might work with different kinds of individual offenders; rather than comparing 'competing' methods for their overall effects, we should be trying to find out which are most likely to succeed with various kinds of people. In fact, some research using a 'differential treatment' paradigm, in which offenders are selected on the basis of personality type or other factors and assigned to therapies thought to be suitable to them, has yielded positive results (see Warren 1977; the study by Jesness referred to above; and Cavior and Schmidt (1978) though in this work effects were obtained with only one out of four sub-groups). This stratagem, admittedly, has not always been successful (Folkard, Smith, and Smith, 1976); but given its early promise, it is sad that it has not been exploited more vigorously and extensively.

While the bulk of the literature implies, then, that little can be done about offending; and though findings to the contrary may be relatively disparate and piecemeal, the possibility that some psychologically-based methods could affect this behaviour cannot be dismissed just yet. A second proposal made by Blackburn (1980) is endorsed in this book: that focusing our efforts directly on offence behaviour – which hardly anyone has attempted – might furnish yet more encouraging results.

The third type of general approach identified above for dealing with offenders was the giving of practical help. The effects of this are not easy to estimate. Advice-giving and allied forms of assistance tend to be part of most aspects of work with offenders. In so far as their effects are therefore entangled with those of other kinds of approach, very little can be said about their value as means of modifying offence behaviour. Looked at in this way, the rendering of practical help to offenders with their problems could be said to be no more effective than any of the other tactics we have been discussing.

Evidence on the usefulness of practical help *per se* for reducing recidivism points in a similar direction. Even if better able to find jobs, secure rights, manage their money, deal with officials, and solve various other difficulties, offenders may nevertheless be no less likely to get into trouble (Priestley et al., 1984). On the other hand, there is a small amount of evidence that, for juvenile offenders at least, programmes aimed at the fostering of educational and job-related skills may help to lower re-offending rates (Lipton, Martinson, and Wilks, 1975).

Alternative approaches

Given that the accumulated 'law-and-order' budgets of industrial countries represent a literally enormous sum of money, and given the amount of energy expended by those working in the penal field (an effort which, despite the lumbering inertia of the institutions involved, *has* inspired some very imaginative schemes), the net return on investment must, by any reckoning, be considered very poor indeed. Time after time, hope and enthusiasm have been channeled into novel programmes of one sort or another, only to record the same dismal results. Be that as it may, many individuals, who believe that some *constructive* approach to work with offenders in worth finding; and who are loath to support, actively or passively, the further burgeoning of a penal system built on punitive measures, remain reluctant to abandon the search for alternative methods of working. The purpose of this book is to describe some directions in which this search might continue – directions which partially overlap with work done in the past, but which also involve a slight change of orientation in terms of the way we look at offenders.

It is of course fairly easy to be critical of current practice in penology, and to dispute the value of what is being done, but considerably more difficult to prescribe courses of action which might secure results that have so frequently eluded us in the past. A constructive and effective response to the problem of offence behaviour would necessarily have many different ingredients; our aim here is to point towards what may be one of them – a focus upon what offenders have actually done to bring themselves to the attention of the law. To achieve this aim, two separate kinds of activity are pursued in the book.

First, there is a strong argument for attempting to do something about offence behaviour directly. This means working with offenders who themselves would like to change their own behaviour, and trying to help them accomplish this by the most appropriate line of attack. Several such 'lines' are included here, from a wide variety of options that might have been entertained. Our aim with regard to each of them is first, to consolidate ideas and methods in the light of work that has been done so far; and second, to explore other avenues which, on the face of it, look promising and potentially fruitful. All of this is tailored for work with individuals or small groups and the focus is on the beliefs, feelings and behaviour of the participants themselves.

Second, as much work in sociology and criminology has shown, offences are partly a product of the society in which they take place; society creates offences by defining them as such (Becker, 1963; Taylor, Walton and Young, 1973). This argument can of course only be carried so far; some behaviour will remain physically and morally offensive whatever its status in the eyes of the law. But to alter offence patterns may mean more than just working with offenders; it may call for social and political initiatives to adjust, perhaps even transform, the environment in which behaviour judged as 'criminal' occurs. Changes in the way offenders negotiate the law, changes in the law itself, changes in the way the penal system operates, must all be considered in any comprehensive attempt to affect offence behaviour.

To cover this ground, the book is divided into three parts.

Part 1 consists of this chapter and the next. The present chapter is designed to set the scene for the book as a whole; the second describes a number of methods for investigating offence behaviour – for looking closely at real offences and exploring them in detail.

Part 2 (chapters 3-7) forms the largest portion of the book, and illustrates methods for helping individual offenders assess and bring about changes in their own offence-related attitudes and behaviour. Several sorts of issues are considered in turn:

Beliefs and values A great deal has been written about delinquent or criminal 'sub-cultures', and while some offenders do hold views quite distant from those of 'straight' society, a much more common experience is of confusion, bewilderment, and mixed-up emotions and beliefs. It is however possible to help individuals clarify their attitudes and beliefs and even change them and some exercises for tackling this are presented in chapter 3.

Self-image Although the notion of a 'criminal identity' is a rather simplistic one, there is some evidence which suggests that many offenders do have a picture of themselves which contributes to their law-breaking behaviour. Offenders have been reported to be lacking in self-confidence and self-respect, and often anxious and uneasy in their dealings with others. Another way of helping them, therefore, could be based on the enhancement of their self-esteem.

Social skills Some individuals end up breaking the law because they react to particular social encounters in an inappropriate or stereotyped way. In addition, many offences are *joint* offences; they are partly instigated by group interaction and by the inability of some individuals to resist peer-group pressure. In both these cases people are lacking in certain social skills; and it has been shown that training in these skills (e.g. to become more assertive, or more flexible in our reactions) can help offenders to cope with people in ways that are more acceptable both to others and to themselves.

Self-control The issue of control is relevant to offending in two principal respects. First, some evidence indicates that many offenders' views about the world around them is characterised by fatalism: by a feeling that they are victims of circumstances or pawns of fate; that there is little they can do to alter their own lives. Second, some kinds of offences, notably those connected with addictions or with violence, may be the result of losses of control by individuals over very strong feelings or impulses. In both of these areas it has been shown that people are capable of change: their beliefs, feelings and behavioural failures of self-control can all be overcome through specific kinds of training methods.

Risk-taking and decision-making Most offences entail risks of some kind: of being caught, of things going wrong, of escalating into more serious incidents than planned, or of being in real physical danger. Many offenders on the other hand are very bad decision makers and are very poor at estimating the extent of such risks. A better appreciation of their chances of success or failure might genuinely deter some people from some kinds of criminal acts. Or improved decision-making skills might enable them to make a more realistic appraisal of the ramifications of 'trouble' in their lives.

Each chapter in this central section has a similar format. First, an opening statement explains the rationale for the inclusion of the topic; this is followed, where it proved possible and seemed potentially worthwhile, by a review of evidence concerning the relevance of the area to the problem of offence behaviour. The rest of the chapter then consists of methods and exercises for use by anyone working with offenders who would like to address offence behaviour directly.

Part 3 of the book involves a change of 'levels'. From looking at individual offence behaviour we move on to consider the relationships between the offender and society; whether offenders can learn to cope with the penal system in ways that are less injurious to their subsequent chances of staying out of trouble; or what, having fallen foul of the law, offenders might salvage from the situation so that it is not a wholly destructive experience. In the final chapter this issue is examined in the still wider context of whether there are changes which could be made in the judicial and penal systems which could themselves have direct effects on offence behaviour.

As regards the methods to be outlined in the book, some caveats may be in order. They will not be applicable, by any means, to all offenders; some will only be helpful for some individuals, and there will be other offenders – perhaps many – with whom nothing will work at all. But most important, the methods are intended, without exception, *only* for the use of those who are *willing* to employ them; who would like at least to examine (though preferably also take some action about) their own offence behaviour. All participation, in other words, should be on a *voluntary* basis.

In this connection, two other points should be added about the nature of the methods. First, all of them have the common feature that their aims, underlying principles, and the practicalities of their actual use can be relayed in straightforward non-technical language to the people who are likely to use them. Nothing in any exercise is so complex or esoteric that it cannot be grasped by most offenders. That an exercise can be clearly understood by someone who might want to use it is a crucial prerequisite of genuinely voluntary participation. Second, the methods share a further characteristic: to work, they must be placed under the control of those who are trying to change themselves. Their success depends absolutely on the exertions of their users. In this they are distinct from all species of psychotherapy which rely primarily on directions given by therapists; from the use of drugs or electric shocks; and from other institutional behaviour-change methods such as token economies (for a valuable review of some of these, see Nietzel (1979)). All of the latter hinge on the operation of forces *external to* the offender.

Lastly, as to the choice of topics which chapter headings represent, there is nothing precious or exclusive about the list itemized above. The areas we deal with have been pinpointed because of their apparent potential value for influencing offence behaviour. Other areas could doubtless have been covered with equal justification. Some of the methods included are backed up with strong evidence as to their utility in this respect. Others have no such backing as yet, and will have to be judged for the present in terms of their plausibility as ways of focussing on offence behaviour.

2 Exploring offence behaviour

The literature on criminology is large enough to fill several libraries; but what is known about offending behaviour – what actually goes on when a crime is being committed – could be encompassed in one or two volumes of no great length.

These disproportionate quantities of knowledge reflect the historic concerns of those who have made the study of crime their business. On the one hand there has been a macro-accounting tradition, fostered by the growth of the social sciences and a concern with measuring and counting, the better to control 'the movement of crime'; and on the other there has been a concern with the psychology of the individual offender, the better to 'cure' or reform him or her. Neither of these approaches is pointless; there are interesting things to be learned from both. But between them, and virtually lost to view in all but a few criminology texts, lies the criminal act proper, the *casus belli* in society's perpetual battle with one part of itself. The reasons for this neglect are complex, part of the history of ideas, and beyond the terms of reference of this essay. But it has two consequences of importance to what is being attempted here. One is the divorce it has created between what offenders actually *do* and what happens to them in court by way of sentence. There is a tariff, it is true, based on broad categories of offence and on the repetition of offences by the same offender, but there is no straightforward sense in which the 'punishment' can be seen to 'fit the crime' except in a few exemplary cases. A by-product of this process has been the progressive neglect and exclusion of the victim from legal proceedings. A second consequence has been the disregard of offence behaviour as a useful starting-point for post-sentence work with offenders. Both of these effects have been intensified by the 'treatment' orientation in penology, which starts and ends with the personality of the offender, and which sees the offence as no more than a superficial symptom of some underlying disease or disorder. By this view, the smallest and least serious offence could betoken the most profound psychological difficulty, and warrant the extensive incarceration of the individual offender for treatment purposes.

The approach adopted in this book starts with the offence as a *reason* for society's interfering in the life and liberty of the offender, rather than as a symptom of anything else. It starts with the offence behaviour as something which needs to be dealt with directly, openly and honestly with as many as possible of those offenders who wish to change what they do and in ways that will remove them from the uncomfortable grip of the criminal law.

The worker who seeks to explore actual offending behaviour enters into virgin territory charted only by a few previous explorers; the literature consists of some biographical descriptions and some participant observer studies (e.g., Patrick (1973)), plus one or two systematic analyses. The best posture to adopt therefore is that of experimenter. In this field anyone who collects twenty or more first hand descriptions of offences in the words of those who have committed them has something worthy of publication. Since most of this work remains to be done, some parts of the present book, including some of the methods outlined here for collecting details of offences, must remain rather speculative. More data, and the experience of gathering it, will almost certainly suggest to workers some different directions for subsequent work to the ones indicated below.

> BEFORE BEGINNING ANY EXERCISES DESIGNED TO ELICIT INFORMATION ABOUT OFFENCE BEHAVIOUR IT IS ESSENTIAL TO ESTABLISH VERY CLEAR AGREEMENT WITH OFFENDERS ABOUT THE CONDITIONS UNDER WHICH YOU ARE WORKING. THESE SHOULD INCLUDE ABSOLUTE CONFIDENTIALITY AND A GUARANTEE THAT THE WORKER WILL NOT ENTER DETAILS OF OFFENCES DISCLOSED ON ANY OFFICIAL FILES, AND WILL NOT DIVULGE INFORMATION TO THIRD PARTIES EXCEPT WITH THE EXPRESS PERMISSION OF THE PERSON CONCERNED.

If you can't give assurances like these, and keep them, then you should not attempt any of the exercises in this chapter.

Criminal records: an informal survey

If you are working with convicted offenders, many of them will be only too familiar with the CRO format – the record kept by the Criminal Records Office – originally as typewritten lists held in individual folders but increasingly computerised and available to the beat policeman within seconds of reporting the name of a suspect over his radio. The CRO record is what the police read out in court before sentence is passed. Its basic format is as follows:

JOHN SMITH d.o.b. 15.12.50

Date	Court	Offence	Sentence
21.9.71	Bristol Crown Court	Theft in Dwelling	6 mos impr.
13.5.72	Thornbury Mag. Court	Theft	£20 fine
1.2.73	Southampton Crown Court	Indecent Assault	2 yrs impr.

The number of offences recorded on the CRO computer/file is almost certainly a serious under-estimate of reality in most cases, and is occasionally wrong in detail; i.e. it omits offences, adds extraneous ones, or records convictions for offences of which people are clearly innocent.

A quick way of assessing more accurately the criminal involvement of the people with whom you are working is to display a list of offences:

TRAFFIC	BREACH OF THE PEACE
THEFT	DRUNKENNESS
BREAKING AND ENTERING	POSSESS DRUGS
FRAUD	VIOLENCE
CRIMINAL DAMAGE	SEX

Read out each category and add a few words of explanation if that seems necessary, for example:
'THEFT means taking anything that doesn't belong to you, with the intention of permanently depriving the owner of it – that is never giving it back. It includes taking bits and pieces home from work or college; using the phone at work for personal calls – "theft of electricity"; keeping things you find, not giving back excess change to shop-keepers, etc.'

'FRAUD includes travelling on the tube or the bus without a ticket and not paying, or paying for a shorter journey, when you get to the other end; filling in fallacious expenses claims, etc. etc.'

'BREAKING AND ENTERING sounds fearsome, but the act of turning a doorknob and pushing the door open can be interpreted as this offence so long as the intent to steal is present.'

'VIOLENCE includes hitting anybody whatsoever for any reason whatsoever, even your own children.'

A quick poll can be taken by reading out each category and asking all those present who have ever committed that sort of offence to raise their right hands. (In some groups it is easier to ask for a show of hands from those who have *never* committed the offence.) Count the hands and enter the total on a large sheet. Repeat the procedure for all other items on the list.

For a more private survey, distribute prepared sheets with the categories typed on them and invite each participant *either* to place a tick or a cross against the offences, *or* to estimate the number of times he/she has committed that particular act. If the group has very criminal members, limit the time period to 'last year' or 'last month', or even 'this week'.

Collect the results and combine them in totals on the sheet. They will be revealing, to say the least. Discuss the patterns that emerge, the contrast with official records and the implications for individuals and for society as a whole, e.g., if everyone commits offences, why is it that some people get into trouble and others don't? Is that just a function of bad luck, of police practice, of the scale or intensity of law-breaking by particular people? Are some laws bad laws? It can also be a good idea for staff members to complete this exercise alongside the group and to disclose their own criminal records. This will help to dispel any sense of self-righteousness on the part of the staff and dissolve, or begin to dissolve, the line that exists between 'us' and 'them', or 'you' and 'them'.

Just to prove the point, here are the results of this exercise carried out with a number of serving probation officers:-

Probation officers admitting the commission of offences (N=202)

Offence	%
Theft	98.50
Traffic	97.53
Fraud	72.28
Excise (smuggling)	66.34
Breach of peace	61.88
Drunkenness	59.41
Violence	50.99
Criminal damage	49.51
Possess drugs	38.12
Breaking and entering	36.63
Sex	6.44

Figures like these are a salutary reminder that offending behaviour is also normal behaviour, but there is in most people's definitions a cut-off point beyond which fiddling and 'doing what everyone else does' becomes *real* crime. You should discuss with individuals or group members exactly were they think this point lies.

Analysing offences: the 5-WH

A logical progression from this is to examine some actual offences people have committed and see what can be learnt from them. This will both produce more information and should encourage offenders to think about their own behaviour and how it might be modified. A fairly simple strategy can be adopted for this purpose. It involves what is sometimes known as a *situational analysis* of an offence; which despite its technical ring can in fact be undertaken using a 'do-it-yourself' device called the '5-WH'.

This exercise can be carried out either by you, working with one person, or by dividing the members of a group into pairs. The objective is to interview someone about an offence revealed during the 'Criminal Records' survey, in order to find out as much about it by answering the questions:

WHO?
WHAT?
WHEN?
WHERE?
WHY?
and
HOW?

Interviewers should try to obtain as exhaustive replies as they can to each of these

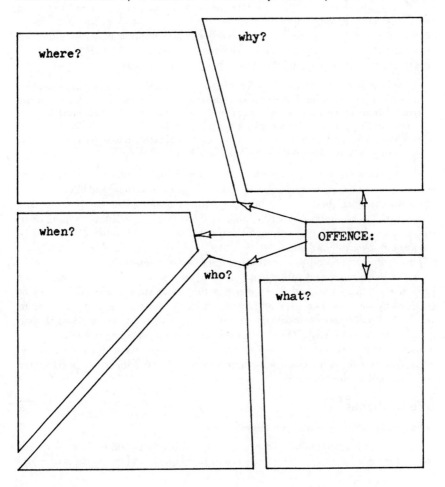

questions, by generating different sorts of things to ask; for example under the 'Who?' heading might be 'Who was with you?'; 'Who suggested committing the offence?'; 'Who did what?'; 'Whom do you think is affected by what you did?'; and people's responses to these questions could be recorded on a ready-made sheet similar to the one shown on p. 25.

If you are doing the interview yourself the questions to ask may be obvious. With some groups the idea of conducting such an interview may be an alien one and you may have to spend some time just developing a list of questions which should then be left displayed prominently on the wall. The 'How?' question can be aimed either at the *modus operandi* or at change (e.g., 'How could it all have been different?'; 'How could you avoid this next time?'). If the exercise is done in a group, some feedback should be obtained from the interview pairs. With both individuals and groups, the analysis should be repeated for a number of offences to ascertain whether there is any underlying pattern or set of common factors at work.

Telling the story

As an alternative to the analytical approach of the exercise just described, narrative accounts of offences can be elicited by skilful interviewing; either in a one-to-one situation or, with the consent of the interviewee, in front of a group of his/her peers. The aim is to secure as full a story as possible, given the nature and complexity of the offence, whether solo or in the company of others, and within the limitations imposed by the language at the disposal of the raconteur. The role of the interviewer should be kept to a minimum, starting off the proceedings in a general way:

> 'I want you to tell the story of this offence in your own words, taking as long as you like, starting at the beginning and going on to the end. I'm interested in anything you can remember about the incident – who was there, who said what, why it happened, who did what, what happened just before, during and just after the actual offence took place, what you were feeling as time went on, and what other people seemed to be feeling. Anything you want to say in other words. What's the first thing you remember?'

For the remainder of the story the interviewer should restrict his/her activity to encouraging the flow of words, nodding and smiling as appropriate and helping things along with leading questions and prompts if things begin to flag, e.g. 'tell me more about that', 'what happened then?' – and clarifying points which are not quite clear, e.g. 'who was it said that?' 'I thought he'd gone home by this time?' 'What was he holding out towards you?' etc.

The results can be simply observed and discussed or thought about; or they can be audio- or video-taped and subsequently transcribed (or not – a time consuming and expensive business this); or, as happens at the police station, the offence can be recorded by someone long-hand and handed back to the person as a statement to be signed. A friendly ex-policeman might be able to help with the correct style and format for this part of an exercise. The finished product becomes the property of the person whose story it tells. But the point of doing it is to raise issues for reflection and discussion either in an interview or a group. Several stories together could be compared and discussed by their authors.

Offence diaries

Offence diaries can be kept in a number of ways.

1. The diary of a particular offence can be traced over a period of days, especially where it involved prior interaction between its participants and the taking of decisions

at contingent points.

2. Numbers of offences can be plotted on a longer term diary where the interest lies not so much in the particular offence as in the patterns that emerge over a period. This might consist of cryptic entries for days of the week representing the commission of particular offences.

3. Alternatively, where offences are committed frequently, the diary form can be divided into columns representing the 5-WH questions, and entries made as appropriate.

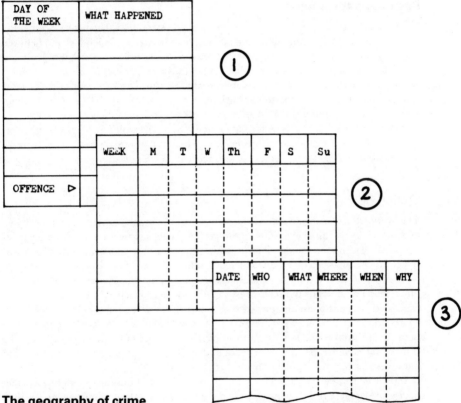

The geography of crime

Secure a large map of the area in which most of the offenders with whom you are working live. This could be a photocopy of the *Ordnance Survey* six-inch map – depending on local circumstances you may need several sheets. In the case of new estates you may have to draw your own, or get those taking part to draw one.

Individuals or groups then mark on these maps, with crosses or flags or pins, the locations of their various nefarious deeds. The markers or flags can be colour-coded to represent different sorts of offences; *red* for violence, *blue* for property; *green* for damage, *black* for drunkenness; *white* for fraud, *rainbow* for drugs. The resulting patterns can form the basis for discussion; identifying locations, or types of location, where specific types of offence are more likely to occur – and why; measuring distances between home and the site of offence commission (in their study of crime in Sheffield, Baldwin and Bottoms (1976) found that distance travelled to the scene of the crime increased dramatically with age, and that the youngest offenders committed a high proportion of their offences within a mile of their homes); looking at types of housing and the rateable values that distinguish the domiciles of the offenders from the places where they commit their offences; and so on.

If individuals are shy of putting their marks on a map in public, it can be left on display together with a supply of markers or stickers or flags, so that entries can be made at any time and without witnesses. This may lead to some over-representation of offence numbers but the general relationships are unlikely to be too seriously distorted for the map to serve its intended purpose.

Recreating the offence

In order to examine more closely the patterns of interaction that take place before, during and after the commission of an offence, both between co-offenders and between offenders and their victims, it is essential to re-create as fully as possible at least one example (and preferably more – if time and enthusiasm permit) of an actual offence. We have looked at ways of doing this anecdotally, eliciting key features of offence events through questioning on a one-to-one basis, or in group discussions. A much more vivid, if more time-consuming way of depicting events is to re-enact them on videotape – or simply as observed roleplays. A format for doing this, here called an 'Action Replay', is presented below. The format is a general one which can also cover non-offence aspects of behaviour that concern offenders and their fellow-offenders, or offenders and their families.

'Action Replays'

The overall aim of using an *Action Replay* is to help individuals learn from their own past experience, by asking them to do two things: first, to look closely at one of their offences and analyse it in as much detail as possible; and second, to think carefully about how the event chosen could be made to turn out differently next time around.

To run an Action Replay, people are invited to imagine that they are going to direct a film about an incident – in this case an offence – in their own lives. The exercise can be explained in terms of an analogy with the more familiar 'action replays' of television sports broadcasts, where we see, for example, how a goal was scored in a football game because of mistakes made by a team's defenders. In the same way, we can examine things that have happened to ourselves and so be better prepared next time we find ourselves in a parallel set of circumstances.

Individuals select one offence which they would like to use for this purpose, and devise a roleplay, preferably not lasting more than three or four minutes, which is then enacted and recorded on video, thus showing how the pattern of events unfolded. To help them do this thoroughly they are asked to follow this sequence, based loosely on a modified version of the '5-WH', and to make preparatory notes about each item:

1. TITLE. If it seems appropriate and participants can think of one, the tape can be given a title, which can even be displayed before the action begins.
2. WHEN and WHERE the incident took place; the date, time of day, and location, perhaps also giving some thought to what individuals were doing at the time, e.g. had they just started in a job? just left prison? recently had an argument at home? – or any other information that might seem relevant.
3. WHO was involved. People can be asked to give quite detailed consideration to this, perhaps to compile brief character sketches of each of the 'actors', and to record them in a set of boxes (here allowing for 'self' and up to seven others):

Me			

Obviously, vignettes of this kind will take up more space than suggeted here. Each of them can cover a number of points, for example: age, sex, occupation, and social standing of the people present; some estimate of how well known they were to the individual whose Action Replay this is; a brief description of their physical appearance; a short statement of the sorts of people they were, in as far as this was known to the individual concerned; together with his or her surmise of their states of mind, motives, and intentions at the time. For these later items, if individuals find this difficult, they could be supplied with a makeshift checklist of adjectives (e.g. *anxious, angry, depressed, singleminded, uncaring,* etc.) and asked to mark off those which apply in each case. The result of all this should be a fairly full description of the personalities involved, which might in itself point to the root cause of the incident, or might yield ideas for circumventing it in the future.

4. WHAT exactly happened. Next, individuals turn their attention to the events themselves, and continuing to picture themselves as film directors for this purpose, try to produce as realistic an account as possible of what occurred. The categories shown below

TIME	ACTION What went on	SCRIPT What was said	STATES OF MIND What people thought and felt

can be used for this; though it is unlikely people will be able to reproduce accurately everything that was said, they should aim to be as faithful as they can to the real thing. Depending on the general nature and scale of the incident depicted, the number of parts, and other factors, individuals will need variable numbers of sheets set out like the one shown above. In fact, the entire Action Replay format is probably best presented in a specially-prepared booklet (say on duplicated A4 paper) for participants to fill in.

By the time individuals have completed these activities – which overall might take most of a morning or afternoon – they should have before them a reasonably exhaustive analysis of one 'critical incident' in their lives. They will then be in a position to assign roles, rehearse, and play the action through, recording it on video as they do so. Action Replays are best used in small groups, but they can if necessary be done by one offender and one worker to enact two-person situations. Videotape is not absolutely essential, as the action could be played 'live', but the exercise is most useful when recorded so that the finished product can be replayed to whatever audience seems suitable.

Using an Action Replay

Once individuals have their cameos ready for viewing, they should then address themselves to two more fundamental questions (again borrowed from the '5-WH' scheme): WHY did this offence occur? and HOW could I have acted in order to make things happen differently? To make this as penetrating as possible, videotapes can be stopped at various points for the action to be explained – by posing questions such as

'What is really happening at this moment?'
'What is going on in so-and-so's head?'
'Why did I/he/she say this or that?'

But the point is not merely to *understand* what was going on; it is to use the simulated event to search for *alternative ways* of dealing with whatever happened. Crucial points in the script can be identified, the tape played up to that point and then stopped, and further questions asked, e.g.

'What else could I have done here?'
'What would have happened if . . . .?'
'How did the way that was said lead on to what happened next?'
'What could someone say instead of that?'
'Is the outcome of the whole incident obvious or inevitable by this point?'
'When is the last exit point that someone could realistically have taken from the escalation of events (towards the offence)?'

– all couched, of course, in language familiar to the participants. The answers to these and other questions should be discussed for as long as seems useful, drawing on the ideas of as many people as possible, with the emphasis all the time on *different* ways of behaving and of looking ahead to see what is coming so that evasive action can be taken sooner rather than later – effectively rather than ineffectively.

When positive alternatives are identified, whether of things to do or things to say, these can be role-played by the original actors, or by substitutes, to see if they work in practice. The aim of all this activity is to provide, for the offender concerned, and for group members who share similar experiences, a glimpse of other possibilities, other ways of acting and reacting which lead to different conclusions, i.e. *not* to the inevitable commission of an offence.

When what look like useful things to do have been identified and thoroughly tur[n?] over, the whole episode can be re-recorded and shown back to demonstrate a diffe[rent?] and happier ending.

Seriousness of offences

Ask individuals or groups to make a list of offences arranged in order of seriousness – most serious at the top and least serious at the bottom. Pursue the differences and the similarities in individual lists. What do they reveal about the underlying values of the people concerned? Does violence or property head the list? Where do sexual offences come? Do personal victims count for more than insitutional ones? Next, display this random-order list of offences on a board or sheet of paper:

Exceeding the speed limit	Theft from parents
Obstructing railway line	Air rifle uncovered
Assault occasioning actual bodily harm	Taking a vehicle
Burglary	Theft of 50p from a house
Breach of the peace	Carrying an unauthorized passenger
No motor cycle insurance	Theft from a shop
Arson	Criminal damage – to value £5
Indecent assault	Theft of £10 from a house

Ask members to select the four most serious and the four most trivial offences from the list. Combine their choices to produce three sub-lists – most serious, in-between, and most trival. When policemen, magistrates, social workers and probation officers were asked to do this exercise, they chose: (1) offences against the person as the most serious; (2) offences against property as of intermediate seriousness; and (3) breaches of regulations as most trivial (Priestley, Fears and Fuller, 1976).

Discuss the differences between the individual ratings and between the group perception and that of the professionals.

Counting the cost

Of all the arguments in favour of crime, those which assert it to be a profitable occupation are the ones most often and furthest removed from reality. For all but a tiny fraction in the ranks of the criminal army, crime simply does not pay.

If you are working with self-confessed thieves i.e., property offenders, put the proposition to the test by arranging for them to make an inventory of their life-time spoils from the game, together with their approximate value at second-hand prices, or the money actually stolen or received in return for stolen goods, e.g.

Cash	£5
Transistor	£9
Car-radio	£10
Records	£3
......	
......	

In another column add up the penalties incurred for criminal behaviour: fines, compensation orders, community service, time spent in probation or social services offices or on remand in custody or in children's homes or in detention centre or borstal or prison or hospital. In a third column can be entered less tangible but sometimes more terrible forms of retribution: being unable to get a job because of a criminal record; anxiety and misery caused to self and relatives by being caught; appearing in court, and being sent down; time lost at school; relationships severed and put asunder; marriages broken; children neglected; depression; homelessness, etc. An attempt might be made to put some monetary values against some of these items. Finally the columns should be added up on the CREDIT and DEBIT sides and the balance struck between them. Anyone in credit at the end of this exercise has *either* hardly ever been caught, *or* has been exceedingly lucky, *or* is a brilliant professional criminal of the kind very little is known about about because they hardly ever come to official notice.

Measuring motivation to change

Collecting information about offence behaviour may serve no purpose whatsoever unless the person concerned wishes to do something about changing it. Our experience is that a significant proportion of offenders *would* like to change their behaviour, even though they may lack the means for doing so, that some are not sure, and that some have no intention whatever of deviating from the paths they appear to have chosen for themselves. No precise proportions can be put on the sizes of these three groups, but some effort to distinguish between them is essential for workers about to embark on a programme of activities devoted to offending behaviour.

A force-field analysis

Form two equally sized groups. Ask the first group to discuss and agree between themselves the TEN MOST ATTRACTIVE REASONS they can think of for getting involved in COMMITTING OFFENCES. Ask the second group to discuss and agree amongst themselves the TEN MOST ATTRACTIVE REASONS for NOT getting involved in COMMITTING OFFENCES. (If it seems useful, the CREDIT and DEBIT items from the previous exercise maybe used instead; or the two columns can simply be headed 'FOR' and 'AGAINST' crime; as illustrated below.)

Prepare some large sheets – say A1 size – with ten lines drawn on them and ask someone in each group to enter the ten reasons (not necessarily in order of importance) one per line. When they are full put them on the wall side by side.

FOR CRIME	AGAINST CRIME
SHOWING OFF	The worry
GIRLS LOOK AT YOU	GETTING NICKED
The excitement	Sitting in a cell
Feel good.	LOSING FRIENDS
Financial benefits	POLICE AGGRO
THE LAUGHS	Paying fines
	PARENTS UPSET

1. Discuss the two lists and the items on them.

2. Invite participants to give scores 1-5 to each item, where 1 means they do not find that a very convincing reason and 5 means they find it very convincing and 2, 3 and 4 lie in between those two extremes. Adding all the scores for both lists produces two scores, one in favour of committing offences and the other against. The gap (and its direction) between these two scores invites further examination and discussion.

3. Individual participants can add to each column items of their own devising, or replace the whole list, so that the resulting scores are entirely a reflection of their own beliefs and attitudes.

An interview

The subtleties of motivation may however evade merely mechanical methods of assessment: they must in some cases be pursued with equally subtle questioning conducted by a skilled interviewer. The focus of such an interview should be on the balance of advantage which the individual perceives in continuing to offend *versus* giving it up. Professional criminals are much more likely to make a rational calculus about such matters, but younger or less reflective people will need assistance to assess the quality of the arguments for and against, and where useful, to quantify the strength of their commitment to one side or the other.

The interviewer should seek to elicit first of all the nature of the rewards or satisfactions which accrue to the person committing the offences. These will vary according to the nature of the offence and the characteristics of the offender. They may be financial or emotional; they may be purely personal or related to the person's group memberships. They may in some instances be utterly inexplicable or beyond acknowledgement, in which case the direct question 'would you like to change your behaviour?' may be the only tactic worth trying.

Having formed some impression of the rewards of crime, as perceived by the criminal, the interviewer should next attempt some estimate of the costs of giving it up. These might include: loss of self-esteem; of standing with friends; the absence of excitement in an otherwise drab existence. Whatever they are, they should be weighed against the positive incentives to going straight; which might be the departure of hassle and aggravation from their lives, the restoration of family relationships, and the regard of non-criminal elements in the immediate environment.

The values to be attached to all these terms in the equation are clearly problematical, but the upshot of the interview should be a rough-and-ready assessment of motivation as falling into one or other of the three categories suggested above – namely 'motivated to change', 'uncertain' and 'not motivated to change'. Members of the first two groups should be invited without hesitation to take part in *offending behaviour* programmes, but those in the third category should be considered only if their presence is *not* likely to infect others in a group with an unwillingness to participate fully.

Part two
Working with individuals

3 Values, beliefs and crime

'Why do people commit crimes?' is a question that has been asked with increasing frequency and intensity in industrialized societies over the past two centuries. The answers it has received, none of them wholly convincing or enduring, constitute one strand of the subject matter of criminology. The list of those who have offered explanations of criminality is a long one – theologians, philosophers, sociologists, psychiatrists, psychologists, biologists, political scientists. Their discourse has taken place not in a theoretical vacuum, but in a world where ideas have been translated into concrete penal policies; all to a chorus of distant shouts and cries from a more popular, and populist, debate about what is nowadays termed law and order.

Before the middle of the eighteenth century a quest for the causes of crime would have seemed unintelligible. Crime was looked on as a sort of natural phenomenon, a feature of the social landscape dating from time immemorial, and immune as a mountain range to change at the hands of mere mortals. Insofar as any thought was given to the individual aetiology of crime it was couched in a religious terminology of sin and guilt, but with little real conviction, since the lower orders from which the bulk of criminals were drawn were seen neither as members of the polity nor of polite society, where religious beliefs might have some implications for personal conduct. The growth of rationalist ideas and the concept of the individual as someone with rights and responsibilities led to the formation of a utilitarian philosophy which looked on crime as something of a puzzle – how could men, in a world where reason was supposed to be sovereign, act against their own best interests by acting against those of others? The cause of it could only lie in ignorance – once the paths of righteousness were pointed out no rational man could fail to be convinced of the need to follow them. Two keys were proposed to open these doors of understanding in men's minds. The first of them was universal education. And for those who failed to respond to elementary tuition, the penitentiary was evolved, an even harder school where instruction, reflection and repentance were to work miracles of rationality in all but the absolutely irredeemable. Robert Owen's *New View of Society* (Owen, 1816), inspired by his work at New Lanark, embodies the first remedy. The second is expressed in the writings of Jeremy Bentham, and in innumerable Victorian prison buildings throughout the British Isles (Bentham, 1791). It is a curious footnote to the history of these ideas that when they met in practice in 1842, in the newly built model penitentiary at Pentonville, they were proved wrong by the fact that a large majority of the first one thousand convicts to endure its novel regime had some previous experience of basic education (Kingsmill, 1854).

Following the failure of the penitentiary experiment effectively to reform offenders, new theories and new penal practices were put forward. One way of classifying these arguments is to locate them at different points along a line representing the degree of *personal responsibility* which offenders are deemed to possess for their offensive acts. The criminal law itself defines one end of this continuum, rooted in an assumption that blame for offences can be justly allocated to particular individuals. It makes exceptions – rather grudging ones admittedly – on grounds of age and manifest mental disorder. Otherwise, those found guilty of an offence are thought fit to face whatever punishment the courts decide to impose on them. Utilitarian philosophy fitted perfectly into this scheme of things. But nearly all subsequent notions lie towards the other end of the line, tending to deny or discount the role of personal responsibility in the commission of criminal acts. A number of overlapping and conflicting positions can be discerned in this 'determinist' camp. *Biological* theories have assumed a variety of forms. Lombroso thought that criminals were not necessarily responsible for what they did, since they represented a strain of genetic morbidity in the general population, evolutionary throwbacks with poorly developed intellectual and moral senses – in other words *moral defectives* (Lombroso, 1895). The signs of this condition were to be seen in distinct physical attributes, most importantly the brain, the skull and the facial features, but also in bodily development. These notions found ready echoes in the eugenicist movements set up to improve the racial stock of newly modern societies (Chesterton, 1922).

Remnants of the theory linger on in the anthropometrical work of Sheldon and others (Sheldon, 1949; Glueck and Glueck, 1950), who have claimed that criminality is correlated with body-build. Other embers have been fanned into heated controversy around Eysenck's theories of extraversion and conditionability (Eysenck, 1964), and the discovery of chromosome abnormalities in some violent offenders raised momentary hope in the breasts of seekers after truly 'scientific' explanations of law-breaking (Jacobs, Brunton, Melville, Brittain and McClement, 1965).

Psychological determinists, for their part, have taken the view that delinquent behaviour is the result of psychological processes and pressures over which the individual offender can have little or no control. These may be thought, in the classical Freudian formulation, to have biological roots, but the most widespread modern versions of them suppose that deprivations and disturbances in the child's early emotional life pre-dispose it to anti-social behaviour in later life, including the commission of crimes (Bowlby, 1946). The extreme case, by this theory, is the production of the 'affectionless' or 'psychopathic' personality, a guilt-free individual capable of the most horrific acts against other human beings, and incapable of learning from experience to modify that behaviour (Whiteley, n.d.). The hallmark of this whole approach is that it treats the offender as psychologically sick and in need of prolonged (and often problematic) psychotherapy (Smith, 1933).

An altogether more pervasive school of thought relates the incidence of individual delinquency to the wider conditions of the society in which it takes place. The simplest statements of this *social* determinism draw an analogy with 'public health' measures which progressively reduced disease and physical disability in populations by improving the environment, eradicating poverty, and dispelling ignorance. Criminals, by this view, are simply the symptoms of poor social conditions; remove the conditions and crime will abate and eventually disappear. Meanwhile the individual offender cannot be held at all responsible for the conditions which have produced him or her. The fact that recent material progress has been accompanied, not by decreases, but by increases in levels of crime has dented the self-confidence with which claims of this sort have habitually been made. And it has led to the emergence of a position which may be roughly described as *political* determinism.

Whilst broadly accepting the social determinist position, the political standpoint insists that general material progress masks the continued existence of specific inequalities in modern societies; relative inequalities of income and opportunity, power and status which fuel a continuing and escalating crime rate (Cloward and Ohlin, 1960). For some of these critics the answer to the problem is not material progress under the present order, but a social revolution in which wealth and power and opportunity are all more equally distributed. The radical nature of this programme has so far protected it from any possibility of empirical test (Mathiesen, 1974). Failing the appearance of the revolution, the political theory makes few suggestions as to what its adherents should do either to pass the time or to hasten the day when society shall be turned upside down.

A variation on the political theme is articulated in 'labelling' theory, the idea that 'crime' is a product of processes of social construction which select certain forms of behaviour (typically lower class) for censure and repression so as to promote social cohesion in the majority group (Erikson, 1966). This theory not only tends to deny the responsibility of the offender for an offence, it positively encourages, in the hands of its uncritical enthusiasts, a 'romantic' view of the offender as hero, as a rebel against the social order, a Robin Hood figure in some cases, dedicated to the re-distribution of ill-gotten wealth in a rotten world (Becker, 1963).

Beyond this point the search for the causes of crime becomes less revealing about the values and beliefs of investigators and rather more inquisitive about those of the individual offender. In part, it is now argued, offenders commit offences because they belong to families, peer-groups, sub-cultures or communities in which the ruling norms and values of the dominant culture are set aside or modified so as to accommodate, and in some cases to actively encourage, the perpetration of delinquent acts (Miller, 1958; Whyte, 1943). Thus the street values of a 'tough' housing estate may positively support the idea that vandalism and gang-fights are 'good things' and status goes to those who live out these ideals in their personal conduct. Nor should it be assumed that these are 'anti-social' values, merely cocking a snook at conventional morality or expressing something sometimes referred to as 'anti-authority' sentiment. Many of the tenets of such codes – 'Stand up for yourself.' 'Be tough.' 'Be smart.' 'Help your mates in fights.' – are straight quotations from the ethics of the dominant culture but bent towards illegitimate ends. They act as functional adaptations to the environments in which they flourish and form a cohesive antithesis to the values of the wider society which plays host to their deviant subscribers.

Virtually all of these theoretical statements tend to deny the responsibility of the offender for his or her offence behaviour: the causes are held to lie beyond the individual in the wider environment – familial, social, cultural and political. The cures for these conditions, according to the theories, must lie in social or political action rather than in work with individual offenders. The approach adopted in this book does not deny the importance of many of the social and political factors reportedly associated with criminal behaviour, and a later chapter addresses some of these issues directly, but it *does* assert the value and validity of work with individual offenders. Unassisted common-sense suggests that individuals are never entirely at the mercy of the forces that help shape their attitudes and values and behaviour. In virtually every situation there are choices to be made, and the fact that they are habitually made in a particular way does not mean that they *must* be made in that way. Something of these possibilities can be glimpsed in the statistical findings which are normally used to demonstrate relationships between factors like poverty and deprivation and criminal behaviour. In their book *The Delinquent Way of Life*, for example, West and Farrington quote figures to demonstrate a connection between drinking and criminal behaviour in a sample of London youths (West and Farrington, 1977). (The percentages in this table are taken from West and Farrington (1977); the numbers and the chi-square are our calculations).

	Drink 20+ pints per week		Drink less than than 20 pints per week	
	No.	%	No.	%
Delinquent	46	46.9	55	18.9
Non-delinquent	52	53.1	236	81.1

Chi-square = 29.95; d.f. = 1; p< .001

These figures are statistically significant, i.e. would occur by chance on less than one occasion in a thousand. They would be accepted by most people as evidence of some sort of connection between the two phenomena, but closer scrutiny can also reveal a different side to the story; namely that rather more than half the heavy drinkers do not become detected delinquents, and that conversely, rather more than half the delinquents are not heavy drinkers. It is through that gap in the figures, through that window of chance *and* choice, that this book seeks to hand methods and materials to the people who inhabit the 'wrong' boxes of the tables, in the hope that they can use them to break out of the circumstances, both social and personal, in which they find themselves imprisoned.

The exercises in this chapter are designed to help individuals and groups look at and make explicit some of the values they hold which are relevant to their offending behaviour; and to help *those who wish to do so* to change or modify some of them sufficiently to reduce the likelihood of their contributing to future delinquent acts.

Eliciting values

The first of the exercises in this section are intended to draw out of offenders, not all of whom will be all that articulate, some account of the reasons and rationalizations they give for the offences they commit, together with some more general rules that govern their behaviour. They do not represent a suggested curriculum to be applied in the order in which they appear; workers will want to select from them those they wish to use; will have to change and adapt them to meet local peculiarities and the specific needs of individual offenders; and will add to them items of their own devising, as well as ones from other sources. None of them is an end in itself; the purpose of all of them is to provoke thought and conversation and to raise the possibility of change.

A word of warning may be appropriate at this point. Discussion of values with offenders is often fraught with a double difficulty. What is the worker to do if group members deliver themselves of views – say of a sexist or racist or fascist nature – which are both personally abhorrent and alien to the spirit of what is being attempted? Should the worker speak out, or keep silent? Is it possible to dissent from the views of group members without appearing to pre-judge lots of issues, and without creating the impression that the worker has all the answers? *We* have no easy answers to the question, but it is linked with a second difficulty, namely that group discussion of members' values *can* become a platform from which deviant notions are declaimed and reinforced. Two suggestions: (1) workers should make it clear that their purpose in discussing values is not simply to permit the airing and confirmation of prejudice and anti-social attitudes – just the reverse, that is to find ways of looking differently and more constructively at the world; (2) workers should reflect, in their dealings between themselves and with their offenders, an alternative and positive set of values of their own. No suggestion should be made that the workers' attitudes are the only possible ones for offenders to adopt, but they should provide an acceptable model of beliefs and behaviour in action.

How far would you go?

Give each person a copy of the following list of offences which are roughly rank ordered in terms of 'seriousness' – he/she should go down the list putting a tick beside each offence he/she would be likely to commit. Discuss and compare different people's responses.

Parking bike illegally	Enter shop illegally
Theft of police notice	Steal goods from shop to value £20
Theft of dog food	Steal goods from shop to value £200
Giving false name	Handle stolen video recorders
Driving with bald tyres	Attack person in a group and steal wallet
Ignoring speed limits	Take part in gang affray
Breach of the peace	Kick policeman in groin
Drunk and disorderly	Steal car
Smash window of house	Pass false check worth £1,000
Punch someone	Beat up old age pensioner, and steal belongings from home
Possess cannabis	Stab someone
Theft of raincoat	Rob bank at gunpoint
Smash shop window	Shoot someone on a 'contract'

Temptations

The 'temptations' listed in the box on p. 42 are best typewritten onto separate cards which can be shuffled and dealt out at random to the assembled members of a group. Each person in turn reads out a dilemma and makes a response. Alternatively, distribute the entire sheet with the instructions shown. The objective in either case is to invite group members' views on the rights and wrongs in any given situation (and in addition to individual reactions, you could also take a group vote on each one); and to see whether any general or underlying moral rules can be abstracted from the series of decisions made. The ten examples shown here would be best suited to use with younger age-groups; other items would have to be devised for older ages or for exploring other areas of judgment and belief.

Who would you steal from?

Give each person a sheet with a blank set of concentric circles on it. Inside each circle the name of a person should be entered – the most intimate and the most liked at the centre and the most distant and least liked at the edge. If necessary, personal names can be replaced with the categories, e.g. brother, mother, best friend, mate, boyfriend, neighbour, someone you know by sight, complete stranger.

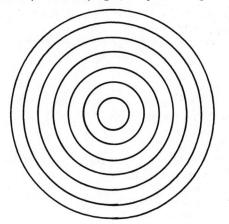

Think about some of the situations described below and about how you would deal with them.

(1) You are playing cards for money, with someone who's not very good. You are sure you could get away with cheating. Would you do it?

(2) You are in a small shop, standing at the counter, when the shopkeeper goes into a back room. There is no-one else in the shop. Would you take anything?

(3) You find £5 lying in the street. Would you hand it in to the police? Would your answer be different if it was £1? £20? £100?.

(4) A friend has lent you some records but seems to have forgotten doing so. Someone else you know offers to buy one from you, thinking it is yours. Would you sell?

(5) Someone you don't like very much has been accused of stealing. You are asked whether you saw him/her do it. You didn't see anything, but you've recently had a fight with the person; what would you say?

(6) You find a briefcase or bag that someone has left on a bus. Would you: (a) hand it to the conductor; (b) take it home; (c) take it to where you could empty it; (d) ignore it; (e) mention it to someone else; (f) if none of these, what would you do?

(7) A friend has lent you £5. He/she comes up to you and says, 'Can I have my three pounds back?' and seems to have forgotten lending you five. Would you remind him/her?

(8) You are given the wrong change in a shop - a pound too much in fact. Would you point it out?

(9) You borrow some tapes from a friend to take to a party. Everyone at the party thinks they are really good and that it was you who made them up. Would you take the credit or say it was your friend who had made them?

(10) A window has been broken and two of your friends are blaming someone whom they don't like. They ask you to back them up. You've got nothing against the person they are accusing. What would you do?

Starting from the ouside, the decision has to be made whether you would steal something from that person. If the answer is 'NO' the circle can be left blank; if the answer is 'YES' the circle can be coloured in – say in red. Discuss the results. The exercise can be extended by changing the instructions; for example:

● WOULD YOU STEAL FROM THIS PERSON
    a. If you were certain of not being caught?
    b. If there was a chance of being caught?

● WOULD YOU STEAL FROM THIS PERSON
    a. Something of sentimental value only?
    b. Something worth 50 pence?
    c. Something worth more than £50?

● WOULD YOU STEAL FROM THIS PERSON
    a. If he/she had just done you a favour?
    b. If you had just had an argument with him/her?
    c. If he/she had stolen from you in the past?

Alternatively, within each circle, a number of individuals could be specified who were either *liked* or *disliked*; or the probability of stealing from someone in each ring could be expressed in percentage terms.

Discuss the results. Are there common features in the replies of group members? Are any individuals exempt from victimization at their hands? Who and why? What conditions make it more rather than less likely that someone is seen as a legitimate target?

Heroes and villains

Invite the members of the group to think of people who fall into four categories:

ADMIRED/DESPISED × CRIMINAL/NON-CRIMINAL.

	ADMIRE	DESPISE
CRIMINAL		
NON-CRIMINAL		

These can be entered on individual sheets or on a composite wall chart as above. Discuss the reasons for the inclusion of certain criminals and non-criminals on each side of the ADMIRE/DESPISE line. Are the admired qualities the same for both categories of people? Could the admired people ever do anything to remove them from their pedestals? Could the despised ever do anything to redeem themselves in the eyes of their despisers?

The axes on the diagram can also be used to plot chosen people at different points on each dimension, e.g. from highly admired to highly despised; and extremely criminal to absolutely non-criminal.

'My ten commandments'

This exercise can be done individually or in small groups; the task is that of devising a short list of the rules by which the participants attempt to order their lives and everyday behaviour – 'my ten commandments'. It is not necessary to insist on ten; a few more, or less would do. It may help some individuals/groups to have available copies of the biblical ten commandments and also some examples of more secular rules, e.g.:

I should try to be kind to animals.
Old and weak people deserve decent treatment.
Taking things from your friends is wrong.
Do not spit in the street.
People should not criticize others without knowing all the facts.
Violence is alright in self-defence.
It is a good thing to be generous.
Etc. etc. etc. etc. etc. . . .

Use the results to work out an agreed set of moral rules, and discuss their validity both for the members of the group and for the wider society. How far do they reflect conventional values, and where do they diverge?

There may be differences between say, boys' and girls' lists, between younger and older people, between the more and the less criminally sophisticated, between offenders of different kinds, e.g., violence/property/drugs.

Desert island rules – OK?

Divide a larger group into smaller ones – say three/four members each. Tell each group that its plane has come down in the sea and they are the only survivors, who have swum to an uninhabited but fruitful tropical island nearby. Starting from scratch they have to build a society on the island and as a first step they must set out some simple rules of conduct. These might or might not extend to economic organization, the distribution of rewards, and so on; or they may remain at the level of personal moral rules. One group of prisoners set this task decided that their first priority was to build a wood and bamboo prison at one end of the island to hold those men who broke the rules – as yet unformulated!

Hang 'em and flog 'em

In the earlier part of the nineteenth century it was commonplace for quite minor offences to attract the death penalty – sometimes 'mercifully' transmuted into sentences of transportation for life; and for lesser crimes it was not unusual for a short sentence of imprisonment to be accompanied by a number of lashes with the 'cat' or the birch.

The death penalty is still technically possible for offences of treason and 'arson in Her Majesty's Dockyards'. If hanging and flogging were to be brought back, for what offences would the members of your group like to see them used? Offenders are notoriously punitive in their general attitudes, keen to see draconian penalties visited upon the wicked, so long as they are not included in that number.

Capital punishment debate

Organize two teams to debate the proposal that 'Hanging should be brought back'. Allow time for preparation and suggest that a proposer and seconder be nominated to speak from both sides. Run the debate for as long as seems useful and then discuss the arguments that have been deployed on both sides. Alternatively, re-run the debate, this time with all the protagonists on the opposite side of the argument.

Reasons for offending

Informal theories of crime are to be seen in the excuses which people make for their bad behaviour. They know that what they have done is illegal, or harmful, or at the least looked on with some displeasure by others, but they attempt to explain it away when challenged, by offering defences and rationalizations. Divide the group into smaller sub-groups and assign to each of these an offence category, e.g.

Theft
Shoplifting
Burglary
Damage
Violence
Sex

Ask them to think of as many excuses as they can which might be used by someone caught committing an offence of that sort. One member of the group should write down all the excuses on a large sheet. Allow ten minutes for this, then ask each team to display the results of their deliberations.

These can be discussed, and an attempt can be made to classify the responses. Some common categories of excuses for offences are:

1. NEED – I was hungry, cold, broke . . .
2. GAIN – I was short of money to go out with . . .
3. EXCITEMENT – You should have seen us going round corners! . . .
4. RETALIATION – He started it . . .
5. ACCIDENTAL – I didn't mean to do it . . .
6. IMPULSE – I don't know what came over me . . .
7. HATRED – Those bastards, I just hate the sight of them . . .
8. INEXPLICABLE – Dunno. Just happened, that's all . . .

Techniques of neutralization

Gresham Sykes and David Matza (Sykes and Matza, 1957) contend that offenders customarily seek to 'neutralize' the seriousness of their offences by using one or more kinds of rationalization. They distinguish five such strategies:

DENIAL OF RESPONSIBILITY – It was an accident; it was someone else.
DENIAL OF INJURY – Nobody got hurt; they were insured.
DENIAL OF VICTIM – They were rich/insured; those bastards deserve it.
CONDEMNING THE CONDEMNERS – All coppers are bent: the law is fixed.
APPEAL TO HIGHER LOYALTIES – I was only helping a friend in a jam.

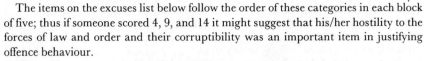

The items on the excuses list below follow the order of these categories in each block of five; thus if someone scored 4, 9, and 14 it might suggest that his/her hostility to the forces of law and order and their corruptibility was an important item in justifying offence behaviour.

The pattern of choices might form the basis of individual interviews or of a group discussion in which the categories are made clear and examined.

Excuses

Here are some excuses. Put a tick against any of them that you would use yourself, if you had been caught for committing an offence.

1. It was an accident.
2. Nobody got hurt.
3. They kept needling me, what did they expect?
4. I'm not the only one; there are plenty of bent coppers.
5. I owed my friends a favour, you can't welch on them.
6. It was the others who did the job, I just hung about outside.
7. It was just scrap; they were going to throw it away anyway.
8. Queers deserve everything they get.
9. The law is there to protect the rich against the poor.
10. Anybody who insults my football team is asking for it.
11. If they had done what we said they wouldn't have got hurt.
12. Most people are insured against theft; they don't care.
13. Rich people can afford to lose a few of their things.
14. Nearly everybody fiddles things at work, they can't complain.
15. Anything that hurts the upper classes is a good thing.

Pleas of mitigation

Excuses are not the prerogative of the offenders; more sophisticated versions of them are frequently to be heard in court on the lips of defending lawyers. These pleas of mitigation also often contain 'theories' of delinquency, sometimes at an implicit and unacknowledged level, sometimes lightly veiled in acceptable legal rhetoric, and sometimes quite explicitly. Offenders themselves sometimes present quite articulated accounts of their own, both verbally and in written forms and these *apologia* reveal both an intuitive awareness of what courts might find acceptable, *and* something about the underlying belief structures of their authors.

Ask participants to form pairs and take in turn an offence in which one of them has been involved. His/her partner assumes the role of defence lawyer and together they work out a plea of mitigation which can be delivered in not more than two minutes, packing in as much information and as many mitigating factors as possible. After a suitable interval for preparation and/or rehearsal, these pleas are then presented verbally by the 'defence lawyer' to the rest of the group, representing 'the court, the bench, or the judge'. At the end of the plea each case is judged, on a show of hands, as to whether the sentence should be lenient one or a severe one. The procedure is repeated until pleas have been made for everyone present. Draw out the major points in the presentations, common themes, good ideas, turns of phrase – things that brought tears to the eyes of the bench and those that aroused derision – and also matters of presentation, what was it that distinguished the better from the worse, the more effective from the less?

Prosecuting counsel

It is not permissible, in English or Scots law, for the prosecution to call for the imposition of specific sentences, as happens in some Continental codes. Ask your group to imagine that the law has been changed so that the prosecution – the police or a solicitor in the lower courts; barristers in the higher ones – can put forward their suggestions for sentence at the end of a trial. Supply the group with current cases clipped from the national or local press *with the sentence blanked out or cut off* and ask them to formulate demands for minimum sentences, together with the arguments they would use in court to justify their particular submissions.

The causes of crime (a slow-motion debate)

Divide the participants into two equally sized groups, located in separate rooms, or in a room where it is not possible for them to overhear what the others are saying. Explain to the groups that they are going to have an argument or debate by telegram. The topic to be debated is 'The causes of crime'. One group is given the job of arguing from the position that crime is something that is 'in the blood' of the offender; some individuals are born bad, and whatever you do to them they will always remain so. The other group is given the job of arguing from the position that people commit offences because of the way they have been brought up and the various pressures on them from family, friends and society.

Each group has ten minutes to discuss and agree an opening statement, which should be short enough to be written on a sheet of paper by one of the group members, in the form of a 'telegram' to be sent to the other group. The telegrams are then exchanged; if necessary the messenger who delivers the message may be asked to explain briefly anything that is not clear.

The teams then consider the opening statement of their adversaries and discuss and agree a reply to it; between five and ten minutes could be allowed for this. The number of exchanges will depend on the response of the groups to the exercise, but the exercise can be concluded by re-assembling both groups in one room to thrash out any unresolved issues between them.

With larger or more sophisticated groups, several positions could be allocated to separate teams; genetic causes, psychological causes, social causes, political factors, etc.

Changing values

It is not difficult to think up endless devices for eliciting and making explicit the motives and rationalizations of some deviant members of society, but where these values lead to directly harmful and indefensible behaviour – raping women, assaulting innocent bystanders, stealing from the poor – the point, – as Marx remarked in a different context, is not simply to understand them, but to change them, or try to.

For this arduous task history has furnished us with many illustrations of failure and few, if any, promising precedents on which to build programmes of rational activity with offenders. The problem is one of 'socialization after childhood', a phrase used by Brim and Wheeler (1966) to describe some of the difficulties that attend all attempts at adult re-socialisation. According to them:

> There are three things a person requires before he is able to perform satisfactorily in a role. He must know what is expected of him (both in behaviour and in values), must be able to meet the role requirements and must desire to practise the behaviour and pursue the appropriate ends. It can be said that the purposes of socialization are to give a person knowledge, ability and motivation.

They combine these elements in the following table:

	Behaviour	Values
Knowledge	A	B
Ability	C	D
Motivation	E	F

Brim and Wheeler argue that many forms of adult socialization, e.g. into occupations, tend to be restricted to overt aspects of role behaviour: instructing them in what is required and providing training to upgrade performance (cells A, B, C and D) but tending to avoid fundamental questions of motivation or of deviant values (cells E and F).

It is to precisely this area that a part at least of any effort to bring about changes in offending behaviour must be addressed. There is no single way of doing this, and no way known to man that is also acceptable to liberal or humanist thought, of altering someone's attitudes or values against his or her will. If change is to take place at all it has to be with the informed consent and active co-operation of the person concerned. Gaining that consent is one of the issues that has confronted the development of moral education in schools. There, it has sometimes been dealt with by a sleight of hand which seeks to disguise what is being attempted as games or puzzles devoid of moral significance. Such an approach will not wash with offenders, especially sophisticated ones, whose antennae can detect stealthy piety a mile away.

At a formal level, it is possible to distinguish a number of models for moral education (Hersh et al. 1980). Among them are *values clarification* which seeks to promote greater understanding of moral issues and the standards by which they are judged and decided – an essentially pedagogic approach to the problem. *Cognitive moral development* is a more ambitious strategy in which individuals are provided with experiences and tasks designed to develop the complexity and sophistication of their moral reasoning. A third and more widespread model of moral education uses *social action* as a vehicle for fostering altruistic feeling in students. The materials in this chapter make use of the first and third of these models; the exercises above on 'eliciting values' are essentially discussion and reflection based, and there are suggestions below for community action. To them are added three further strategies: they involve (a) the use of role-play, role-reversal and other social skills techniques; (b) the direct challenging of anti-social attitudes; and (c) confrontation with the consequences of offending behaviour in the person of the victim.

Role reversal

There is some evidence that role reversal can bring about changes in the views of those who engage in it; and specifically that extremist but unconsidered views can be moderated by having to take the role of someone who takes an opposing view (Culbertson, 1957). Some roles which offenders might usefully attempt:

'You are the secretary of a football club towards the bottom of the third division. You have just appointed an ambitious new manager who wants to play lively and attractive football to bigger and bigger crowds so that he can use the gate money to deal in the transfer market and offer higher wages to better players. The only way to get a bigger crowd is to attract a family audience with wives and children. They will not come if there is violence on the terraces. Your team does well in the FA cup and is through to the fifth round. You draw a First Division side for a home game. There is a large crowd and the television cameras are there for 'Match of the Day'. Some of the younger supporters behind the home goal are in a boisterous mood. Before the match begins you take the microphone and talk to them over the Tannoy.'

'Your super-duper portable stereo transistor radio/record player/cassette deck has been taken. Someone says he saw Ronnie going off with it from the club the night before. Just then Ronnie rings up to say he has been told that you know he has got the machine, and he wants to apologize.'

'You are in the army serving in the Falklands. Your mother writes to you to say that the bloke she was living with has left her, taking a lot of her things, and beating her up quite badly before he went. You write a letter to her, and one to her bloke; both of them will be seen by the army censor who will refuse to send any direct threats or obscenities through the post.'

'Your job is to visit people who have just been burgled. You go to see an elderly couple whose house has been broken into and badly damaged; lots of things have been taken, and a lot of mess made by whoever did it. They are both in tears and don't know what to do. Your job is to help them.'

'You have lost a five pound note from your pocket. You walk back the way you have just come across a park. At the place where you bent down to lace up your boot, you see someone pick something off the floor. You ask the person if it is a five pound note. The person laughs at you.'

These are simply examples. The best role-plays to use for this purpose are ones that come from the experience of the offenders with whom you are working; reflecting their own views and the real-life situations in which they are likely to express them in words or deeds. Some of the role-plays can be done as two-handers, with the worker or another group member playing the role of the offender; or, where appropriate, more people can take part. The essential point is for the offender to take the role most diametrically opposed to the one he or she normally takes, and to play it enthusiastically.

'Taking the perspective of the other'

The ability to 'take the role of the other' is one of the foundations of moral maturity. An inability to do so may be at the root of some offending behaviour. Chandler's work with 'egocentric' offenders (Chandler, 1973; see p. 91) suggests that there are benefits to be gained by running role-play sessions in which the individual offender is required to play in turn each part in the same scene. A simple format for doing this is suggested here:

Divide larger groups into smaller ones of not more than four to six members. Ask each group to think of an incident or scene in which one or more of them has been involved; it could be a funny incident, or an embarrassing one, or simply a scene from everyday life which is of interest or concern to the people involved. *Only one rule should apply to the choice of topic: No outlandish or fantastic scenes drawn from televison or the cinema or detective stories or science fiction.* In essence the stories or scenes should be as near to the everyday lives of the participants as they can contrive.

The parts in the scene can be initially allocated at random. One member may act as the 'director' of the scene but should occupy one of the roles as well. Everyone in the group should have a part in the proceedings. The scene is rehearsed and then recorded on videotape. The finished product is then looked at critically so that the next 'take' will represent an improvement on it. Successive versions of the same scene are filmed, each time with each of the participants in a fresh role. Each time, the finished film is reviewed and discussed before the next version is recorded. A final session reviews all the tapes and discusses what has emerged from the experience of taking *all* the parts in a single scene.

In the original experiment each of these sessions lasted three hours, and took place once a week for a total of ten sessions.

Modelling

Social learning theory argues persuasively for the importance of 'models' in the acquisition of basic attitudes and behaviour (Bandura and Walters 1967). Anti-social tendencies may be due to the absence of appropriate models or to the presence of inappropriate ones. Angry parents are likely to raise angry children; children who have never seen altruistic behaviour practised are unlikely to reproduce it in their own interactions with others. Like the connection between drink and crime, these are of course only approximate causes and they do not *determine* subsequent performance. But the strength of the underlying learning mechanisms means that they can be pressed into service for pro-social purposes at later stages in life than childhood.

We have already suggested that those who work with offenders can model appropriate attitudes and behaviour both towards each other and towards their charges. This need not mean a self-conscious and artificial assumption of perfection – just the expression of common decencies such as respect for other people, honesty and straightforwardness in their dealings with them, and good humour. More explicit forms of modelling, in role-plays and on videotape, can be supplied by staff, by admired outsiders, by other members of groups or their predecessors in previous proceedings, and by individual offenders for themselves.

Whoever does it, the aim is to set up situations in which the 'model' expresses or gives evidence of a desired attitude, e.g., altruism, generosity, tolerance; or acts in a way which reflects these and other virtues. The situations depicted in these role-plays should be sufficiently realistic for offenders to accept them as relevant to their own lives, e.g.:

Talking to a friend in trouble	Being asked to donate to a charity
Visiting a relative	Deciding what to do with a windfall
Being asked for help	Dealing with someone injured in a car crash
Talking to a stranger on a bus	Visiting someone in hospital

These are only suggestions. The best situations are those identified by individuals or group members as ones in which they would be likely to participate, and in which the positive attitudes are ones they genuinely admire or aspire to – or at the very least which they would not be ashamed to be seen expressing in words or deeds. With individuals who have a pronounced public image as 'hard' or 'mean', the first forays into these delicate areas might have to be taken in one-to-one sessions. It may also be necessary to start with unequivocally suitable targets for the 'desirable' behaviour – someone you fancy for instance, or an admired personality, an older family member you like and respect, or someone so dependent on others as to command universal sympathy, e.g., a terminally ill child, an old person who falls over in the street . . .

The point of all these exercises is to portray behaviour in which 'helpful' or other positive sentiments are expressed, and seen to be expressed, by a range of people with whom the offender can identify. The final stage in the process is 'self-modelling' where videotapes are made and played back of the individual him- or herself engaging in the behaviour in question.

Contesting values

Using material gathered during earlier exercises such as the 'Force-field' on crime, 'Excuses' or 'Ten commandments' ask for a volunteer to put up one of his or her anti-social values or beliefs for general attack. The volunteer should be able to formulate a general proposition; e.g. 'It's alright to attack Pakistanis because they're over here pinching our jobs or our women.' OR 'What's wrong with breaking up a phone box if you get the change out of the box?' OR 'You should get the boot in first before the other person.'

Write the proposition up, then give the rest of the group ten minutes or so to come up with all the possible arguments they can think of against this proposition, and of ways to present them as forcefully as possible, and to make fun of anyone who holds that particular point of view. Arrange the chairs so that the 'defendant' is in the hot seat, the focus of everyone's attention, and let the proceedings begin. The audience should attack the defendant with every verbal means at its disposal. The accused can defend his/her point of view, but must listen to the ripostes from the group and attempt to deal with them rationally, i.e., not by showering abuse on, or offering violence to, those who make them. Let this proceed for as long as seems useful, but not longer than ten minutes, and much shorter than that if fisticuffs threaten to replace the spoken word. An extension of this exercise is for the 'defendant' to vacate the 'dock' where his/her place is taken by someone willing to take up the cudgels in defence of the same proposition. The erstwhile defendant now joins the attack, as vigorously as possible, on his/her previous position.

Offenders and their victims

At the heart of legal and penal proceedings in the Anglo-Norman tradition there is a profound paradox. The trial itself is hedged about with devices for ascertaining that the accused actually did what the charges allege – in cases of reasonable doubt juries are urged to acquit rather than convict. Exceptions are made for extreme youth; children under the age of seven were historically held to be incapable of forming a criminal intent (the doctrine of *doli incapax*); and obvious degrees of mental disorder (codified in the M'Naghten rules) disqualified offenders so afflicted from bearing full responsibility for their actions. Otherwise the convicted offender is pronounced fit to receive whatever punishment the courts see fit to administer. There is, in other words, a scrupulous concern to determine the personal *responsibility* of the offender for the offence. But what follows, by way of retribution and even of reform, tends to regard the offender as essentially *irresponsible*, to be treated as an object on which pain and suffering and deprivation (and sometimes 're-education') are to be visited in quantities supposedly calculated to equate with the damage done to society either generally or in the person of the individual crime victim. The whole transaction is sometimes characterized as the offender 'paying his debt to society'.

There are many consequences of these curious arrangements, but for present purposes, the most important is the fact that the offender is denied any real opportunity for assuming proper responsibility for his or her own behaviour. Once it has been channeled into the courts, the offence becomes a public property whose title can be redeemed only by symbolic repayments in a currency of loss and suffering to be undergone by the offender. Thus dispossessed, he feels absolved of all further interest in his 'case' and concerned only with enduring the deprivations imposed on him as a sentence of the court. This fundamental irresponsibility can only intensify the already poor picture of him or herself held by many an offender. 'We have all done something really bad,' as one life-sentence prisoner put it, 'Now we would like to do something good, but no one will let us.'

The restoration of a true sense of responsibility for all one's actions, good or bad, is fundamental to the dignity and self-esteem of the individual. This is not to deny the fact that offences thrive in certain social conditions for which individual offenders can bear no part of the blame. But to treat offenders as the blind end products of social forces over which they can exert no control is to condemn them to eternal damnation, and is a counsel of despair. One antidote to this form of 'treatment' is to make it possible for offenders to assume some responsibility for the damage they have done to others or their interests, and to play some part in making good that damage – by arranging for restitution, reparation, or reconciliation to take place (Galaway and Hudson, 1978; Goldstein, 1974).

The victim experience

One way of introducing a victim perspective into work with offenders is to spend some time looking at the experience of being victimized. This can be done by examining particular offences committed by someone with whom you are working and by attempting to reconstruct parallel accounts of the events from both sides – the offender's version, and that of the victim. If it is possible, an actual account by the victim in question – in writing, on video or audio tape, or in person – is better than an imagined one. But just to imagine how it felt to be on the receiving end can be a useful experience for some offenders. Alternatively, it is more than likely that offenders themselves have more than once in their lives been the victims of offences committed by others; they will have had things stolen from them or damaged; some of them will have been criminally assaulted by relatives or 'friends' or strangers. This exploration of the victim experience should not be undertaken in a spirit of 'rubbing their noses in it', nor with the question in mind, 'How would you like it if . . .' to which a great many delinquents have early acquired immune responses.

Compensating victims

Two kinds of schemes exist in this country to meet the needs of the victim: the Criminal Injuries Compensation Board (CICB), set up in 1964 to award cash compensation to the victims of certain categories of violent crime (CICB, 1982); and victim support schemes, dating from 1974, which offer practical and emotional assistance to recent victims of property and/or violent offences (NAVSS, 1981). Many offenders will know little if anything of the working of either of these schemes. This exercise is intended to raise the issue of *the victim* in general terms.

Present one or more of the following cases to a group; either in writing or verbally, and invite them to sit as the CICB to determine the amount of any cash award they think appropriate for the injuries, distress etc.

CASE 1: A widow aged 67 – partially paralysed after a stroke – spoken to by some youths in a car. One of them grabbed her handbag and she was dragged along the pavement, bumping into the car. She let go of the bag which contained £70 in banknotes. Treated as an out-patient for 13 days for shock, cuts and bruises (CICB 1981).

CASE 2: 16 year old school girl walking home. Approached by another girl who caught hold of her hair and bit off the lower portion of her left ear lobe. Taken to hospital, given general anaesthetic and the ear trimmed and stitched (CICB 1982).

CASE 3: Girl aged 19 – engaged to be married – attacked by a stranger with a brick. She is now spastic in all four limbs; takes three or four minutes to walk a dozen feet; speech also affected. Must live in a protected environment (CICB 1981).

CASE 4: Young man, 21, playing cricket for a local cricket team. The bowler asked him to move in from deep square but he refused. Later, in the changing room the bowler punched him about the head and face. Severe fractures of the bone above the left eye. Off work for two weeks; headache, blurred vision and dizzy spells which lasted for some time (CICB 1982).

CASE 5: 28 year old married woman asleep in bed – husband away on business. Disturbed by intruder in a black hood and speaking with a Bradford accent. She thought he was the Yorkshire Ripper. Made to walk round the house whilst he took articles of value. Made to lie on the bed and tied up. Man went downstairs and came back with a knife. After pacing up and down he said he was leaving and threw the knife on the bed so that she could cut herself free (CICB 1982).

If there are enough people present it is interesting to have more than one group deliberate and decide on amounts of compensation. Discuss the amounts that are eventually awarded, and the reasons for them; on what grounds some are larger than others; and how the injuries or distress were quantified in cash terms.

The actual awards given in these cases, by members of the Criminal Injuries Compensation Board, were:

CASE 1	£500
CASE 2	£1,750
CASE 3	£102,180
CASE 4	£1,002
CASE 5	£1,000

All of these cases are taken from the reports of the CICB for 1981 and 1982, and the values of the awards reflect then-current prices. Look at, and talk about, the differences between the figures reached by group members compared with those of the official agency.

The Board also publishes general guidelines to the amounts of compensation thought suitable for different kinds of injury, for example:

	£
Undisplaced nasal fracture	375
Displaced nasal fracture	625
Wired jaw	1,200
Rape (leading to no serious physical or psychological damage)	2,250
Laparotomy following stomach wound	1,500
Loss of two front upper teeth with plate inserted	1,000
Loss of two front upper teeth fixed bridge inserted	850
Male scar (unmarried man aged 20). Scar running approximately from the join of the lobe of the left ear and face across the cheek to the left corner of the mouth	4,000

Female scar (unmarried woman aged 20). Scar running
   approximately from left corner of the mouth backwards
   diagonally downwards, ending just underneath jaw bone   6,500
Loss of vision in one eye   10,000
Total loss of vision   45,000
Total loss of hearing (young man of 25)   27,500 (CICB 1982)

This list can be given out, *minus* the suggested money values, to see what figures would strike group members as fair and reasonable. Another aspect of the Board's policy of interest to offenders is the fact that applications for compensation may be and frequently are dismissed on the grounds that the person's character or way of life has contributed to the commission of the offence(s) against them, or that they do not deserve compensation.

Making amends

Apologizing

In families, amongst friends, at work, and in other face-to-face situations, the commonly accepted way of dealing with acts that harm others is for the person at fault to apologize – that is to accept responsibility for what has happened and to express some regret at the consequences. The apology does not have to be all that heartfelt for it to be acceptable, and there is a degree of convention about the forms of words that are suitable for use on such occasions. Some people cannot however bring themselves to apologize for anything they have done, however damaging it may be to others, and whether they are near and dear, or remote and unrelated. It *is* possible however to apologize with dignity, without grovelling or creeping, or acknowledging personal weakness, and offenders can be encouraged to do so.

Reparation and restitution

More practical steps may be taken in some cases to repair the tangible damage done by an offence: mending broken windows and doors, replacing stolen objects, or paying for new ones. Even if these repayments are of token proportions only, they emphasize a sense of responsibility on the part of the offender, and defuse to some extent the justifiable anger of the victim at his/her loss (Harding, 1982).

Conciliation

In some offences, notably those involving violence or sexual assault, the damage is not to property but to persons and therefore far more difficult to put right. In the case of severe mental trauma, the damage may be eternally irreparable. The idea, therefore, of arranging some kind of meeting between erstwhile victim and offender to discuss what happened between them may be something from which workers in the offender field will instinctively shrink. But many violent and sexual offences are in fact continuations by other means of previously existing relationships in families, between friends and acquaintances, and lovers. In not a few cases the victims and the offenders have to go on living, if not together, then at least in close proximity to each other. It makes sense in some such instances to think in terms of meetings which explore the events in question and attempt, should it prove feasible, some measure of conciliation between the parties (Hudson and Galaway, 1980).

As with apologizing, and to some extent with restitution, some offenders may find all this too painful to think of and to take part in; but the point of proposing it is not to inflict punitive suffering on them, but to help them accept as much responsibility as possible for who they are and what they have done, and to put them in charge of efforts to come to terms with the consequences of their past actions. Not to offer such an opportunity is to deny to the individual some part of his or her responsibility and his or her self-esteem as a self-willed and self-governing person in his or her own right.

IT SHOULD BE STRESSED THAT VICTIM-OFFENDER MEETINGS ARE LADEN WITH POTENTIAL DIFFICULTIES AND SHOULD NEVER BE UNDERTAKEN WITHOUT DEEP PREVIOUS THOUGHT AND PREPARATION, NOR WITHOUT THE INFORMED AND WILLING CONSENT OF *BOTH* PARTIES.

Symbolic reparation

Where there are no personal victims to a crime – as in shoplifting from a chain-store, or damaging a street sign, or being drunk and disorderly – but where the offender would like to make some sort of amends, symbolic reparation can be effected through the undertaking of voluntary community service, or the offering of services to victims other than one's own.

Community action

The pioneering exposition of social education via community action was made by Richard Hauser in this country (Hauser and Hauser, 1962). His ideas were put into practice in Wandsworth prison where they led to the formation of Recidivists Anonymous, and in many schools. Like many other new departures in penal practice the Wandsworth experiment failed to survive, but the notion has taken root in education that thinking about other people's problems and doing something about them is a good way of encouraging both the growth of altruistic sentiment, and the skills to put it into practice.

The basis of the approach is that the group in question should explore its immediate social environment in search of difficulties or problems or needs that might be remedied by local action of a finite nature, i.e., not requiring major societal change. The problems cannot be predicted in advance of the work that discovers them, but hypothetical examples might be the resiting of a bus-stop to make it more convenient for a larger number of its users; the installation of a pedestrian crossing; the designation of streets as play areas barred to traffic; the redesign of communal housing features; the repair or decoration of community facilities; agitation for better transport or lower fares for poor people. Offenders might come up with more specific projects of their own. Morris and Fanny Eisenstein worked with young people from Harlem and the Bronx during the 1960s on projects of their own devising. These included lobbying the New York State legislature for a change in the law to permit funding of further projects similar to their own, and the unionization of schools which they attended. British workers may shrink from what appear to them to be political activities incompatible with their continued employment by agencies of the state or the local authority. But less overtly difficult projects might be sought in the specific problems encountered by offenders as a consequence of conviction, and in some cases, incarceration. They include accommodation and jobs for offenders, and plotting free or extremely cheap leisure amenities.

4 Status and self-esteem

The ethos of our society is a very competitive one, and seems to become more so year by year. The pressure is on people to succeed, and to display their success through (sometimes conspicuous) consumption of material goods or the adoption of particular life-styles. Like other competitions, this one too creates winners and losers. It is scarcely surprising that a proportion of those who cannot attain conventional success by legitimate means should choose to pursue it through alternative channels. Offenders, and certainly those who are apprehended and milled through the grindstones of justice, are generally losers in this contest. If we subscribe to the rules of the race and the picture we have of ourselves is reflected, at least in part, through our final standing in it, then those who come at the back are liable to end up with a rather low opinion of themselves.

This chapter is about self-image and status in the eyes of others, about the possibility that offending acts may be partly the result of a lack of self-respect on the part of those who commit them. If this were the case, and if the means were available to help such individuals to see themselves in a better light – surely a worthwhile enough goal in itself – then perhaps this upgrading of self-image might have an additional pay-off in a reduced tendency to break the law.

The notion that an individual's level of self-esteem or self-respect may be in some way bound up with a propensity to offend may seem an odd one to many people. Offenders' attitudes to themselves have however formed a link in a chain of reasoning put forward by a number of social scientists in their attempts to account for criminal behaviour. This chain has taken a number of different forms; the exact part played in it by self-image is something on which not everyone is agreed. Here are some of the most common proposals.

- One possibility is that people with low self-esteem tend to become offenders because they don't value themselves, don't care what happens to them and are unconcerned about the consequences of getting into trouble.

- An alternative explanation may be that criminal activity is another route to the success denied some individuals by 'straight' society; by succeeding at crime they can recover some of their lost self-respect by virtue of the success itself and the (presumed) accompanying material gains.

- Again, some people – adolescents in particular – may commit offences because they will lose status in the eyes of their friends and other associates if they don't – their self-respect is conditional upon the approval of others.

- A quite different viewpoint is that the poor self-image of some offenders is a product of the fact that they have been identified as such. The mere act of 'labelling' an individual as 'deviant' ascribes to him or her a lowly status and leads to a questioning of self-worth.

● Associated with the last view, the legal processing and perhaps institutionalization of law-breakers brings about a gradual wearing-down of self-respect and may further reinforce the feeling of being an outcast, with the result that the offender has even less regard for the values and rules of 'mainstream' society.

To try to sort out which if any of these views is 'correct' would be a more or less impossible task. They may all apply in different ways to different individual offenders. For present purposes it matters little which view of the role of self-esteem we choose to espouse. However, in this chapter we do want to endorse the suggestion that the way offenders see themselves *is* in some cases initimately connected with their breaking the law. Changing the way they see themselves might then be one path to helping them modify their offence behaviour.

It may be worth emphasizing at this point that the notion that low self-esteem may be somehow connected with offending acts is not in itself a deterministic one. People with low self-esteem will not necessarily become offenders, nor will all offenders be found to have low self-esteem. It may however be a pre-disposing factor for some individuals which under certain circumstances cements them into position on the wrong side of the law. Or it may, as indicated in the above list of possibilities, be a product of the way they have been dealt with by the legal and penal processes.

Most of this chapter is taken up with exercises for helping people to appraise the value they put on themselves and the judgments they pass on themselves, and for attempting to transform their views into something a bit more positive and less self-deprecating. First however, we would like to scrutinize in more depth the idea that law-breakers have a poorer self-image than those who conform.

The self-esteem of offenders

The view that a negative self-image may contribute in some way to deviant behaviour is a long-standing one in criminology. Cohen (1955) forwarded the idea that, within delinquent gangs, individuals achieved high status, with its associated rewards, through the commission of offences and that this served to keep the group together as a gang. Becker (1963), working from a quite different point of view, proposed that deviant acts were those which were labelled as such; but that the labelling process conferred a certain identity and value upon individuals, with concomitant effects in terms of the way they perceived themselves. Hewitt (1970) and Kaplan (1975) have elaborated entire theories of deviant behaviour with the self-esteem 'motive' (the notion that individuals seek to preserve or enhance positive self-attitudes) as a core concept. Such suggestions are potentially very fertile in that they link together psychological variables – the personality and self-perceptions of the offender, with sociological ones – the rules and expectations of the group and the relationship between these and society as a whole.

How much evidence is there that offenders have low self-esteem? It cannot of course be shown conclusively that all offenders have a negative self-image; it is unlikely that we could find anything which all offenders have in common other than the fact that they have been so defined by the law. However several pieces of work suggest that a negative self-attitude may be a feature of the psychological make-up of many offenders.

Deitz (1969) compared the self-perceptions of a group of 40 delinquent boys aged between 14 and 18 with those of a group of non-delinquents of similar age, and matched on various social background characteristics. To do this he used a series of rating scales (the *Semantic Differential*) on which individuals were asked to describe themselves using pairs of adjectives which are the opposite of each other; such as 'strong – weak' or 'valuable – worthless'. They were asked to undertake these ratings in a number of ways, first describing themselves – 'Me as I really am' – then 'Me as I would like to be', and also to rate themselves as they thought they were perceived by each of their parents. Although on basic self-concept there were no significant differences between the two groups, the discrepancy betwen 'actual' and 'ideal' self was significantly larger for the delinquents than for the non-delinquents; the former were, in other words, significantly less self-accepting. Offenders also believed themselves to be less accurately perceived – more often misunderstood – by their parents than did members of the non-offender group.

The same kind of self-rating measure was used by Eitzen (1976) in a comparison between the self-images of 16 delinquent boys in a community home and those of 82 boys from a local high school. The delinquent boys took a much more negative view of themselves – differences in self-ratings between the two groups were highly significant. Their ratings of how they were seen by teachers and by their mothers were also consistently less favourable than those of non-delinquents, but no such differences emerged when the boys were asked to rate themselves as seen by their friends.

A parallel finding to this last one was obtained by Thompson (1974), using the same methods with a sample of 500 first- and fourth-year pupils in British secondary schools. While no differences were detected between delinquents and others in overall self-evaluation, the former – together with members of a group designated as 'maladjusted' – rated themselves as less 'successful' and less 'good' as seen by others. At the fourth-form level, offenders rated themselves poorly as seen by adults – teachers and parents – and seemed to regard themselves as undervalued by them. Only their friends were seen to value them appropriately. These distinctions did not appear with 'well-adjusted' pupils, leading Thompson to the conclusion that the delinquents were '. . . peer rather than adult oriented' (Thompson, *op. cit.*, 46). In addition, delinquents thought of themselves as consistently more 'hard', 'cruel', and 'dirty' than well-adjusted pupils, typecasting themselves thoroughly in terms of '. . . the traditional tough "bad boy" image' (*ibid.*, 47). That young offenders should see themselves as less successful in school has some basis in empirical fact. Douglas, Ross, and Simpson (1968) for example, found that delinquent boys performed less well than non-delinquents on most ability tests, and had poorer records of attendance at school. The image of the delinquent as a 'low achiever' in school is pervasive enough to make some non-delinquent children who are not doing well at school believe that others perceive them as delinquents (Frease, 1973).

A different kind of method from the above was used by Ziller and his associates (Ziller, 1973). These workers used a specially-constructed task in which individuals were asked to rank-order a series of people (e.g. 'yourself', 'a teacher', 'a friend' etc.) in a row of blank circles. The placing of 'self' in this exercise was found to be a useful measure of self-esteem. The task was given to a group of 'problem' children (30 boys and 27 girls) in a state institution, and their scores compared with those of a matched group of 57 children from a local school. The problem group consisted mainly of delinquents, though unfortunately for our purposes it also contained a number of children with other problems of a psychiatric nature. However, differences between the two groups were found to be significant, with the 'problem' group manifesting lower self-esteem than the 'normals'.

Findings in agreement with all of the foregoing were also obtained by Scarpitti (1965), by Sumpter (1972), and by Mulligan (1979), though it should be borne in mind that in most of these studies the lower self-esteem of offender groups could have been due to the fact that they were in institutions.

An alternative approach to the role of self-esteem in fostering offence behaviour

...ight be to ask: is there something about the self-image of *non-offenders* which protects them from getting into trouble? Reckless and his colleagues attempted to understand delinquency-proneness in relation to the way young people see themselves, proposing that higher self-esteem in some way acted as an *insulator* against the commission of delinquent acts. In a sequence of studies extending over several years, these workers explored the way in which groups of young people saw themselves and were seen by others (Dinitz, Reckless and Kay, 1958; Dinitz, Scarpitti and Reckless, 1962; Reckless, Dinitz and Kay, 1957; Reckless, Dinitz and Murray, 1956; Scarpitti, Murray, Dinitz and Reckless, 1960). The basic strategy of this research involved asking teachers in a number of schools to nominate pupils from their classes whom they would designate as 'good' boys on the one hand – boys whom they believed would be unlikely ever to get into trouble with the police – and on the other, 'bad' boys whom the teachers reckoned would be much more likely to get into such trouble. A number of comparisons were then made between the two groups, using psychological tests, rating scales, interviews with the boys' mothers, and checks in police files to see how many of the boys in each group actually did commit offences. As many of the boys as possible were followed up after a four-year period, covering their age span from 12 to 16, and similar kinds of information gathered about them at the older age-level. The nominated 'good' boys saw themselves as less likely to get into trouble than did the 'bad' boys; their mothers and teachers accorded with these judgments; and the boys differed also in the way they believed their teachers and parents saw them. Furthermore, by the age of 16, whereas only four of the 103 'good' boys traced had actually been in trouble (and once each only), 39 per cent of the 'bad' boys had been in frequent and serious trouble.

Unfortunately, this research incorporated no direct measure of self-esteem, and the evidence that the way the boys saw themselves was any kind of determining factor in whether or not they had contact with the police is wholly indirect. The research has been subjected to strong criticism on methodological grounds by Tangri and Schwartz (1967). That self-evaluations may have played an important part in delinquency-proneness is however suggested by the results of Schwartz and Tangri (1965) who made a direct comparison, using the familiar self-rating scales, between 'good' and 'bad' boys (as listed by their teachers) from a single school in a high-delinquency area of Detroit. The good boys had on average a significantly more positive self-concept than did the bad boys; they believed others saw them in a more positive light than did the bad boys; and there were greater inconsistencies for the bad boys amongst the ways they believed they were perceived by other people (teachers, mother, and friends) than was the case for the good boys.

A different method of assessing self-image was used by Roberts (1972) in her work with 143 girls in Arohata, New Zealand's only borstal for females. She used the 'Who am I?' sentence completion test (Bugental and Zelen, 1950; Kuhn and McPartland, 1954). This consists simply of asking individuals to complete a sentence beginning 'I am . . .' in their own words, up to 20 times, saying something different in each case. The responses made by the girls were used by Roberts in conjunction with interviews in a wider-ranging study of personal development and the impact of borstal on it, but as part of this she classified the test responses according to the *quality* of self-concept manifested by each girl. Self-concepts were categorized as *good, doubtful,* or *poor.* For example, the following self-description produced by one girl was rated *good:*

I am (girl's name).
I am a European.
I am 20 years old.
I am an unmarried mother.

I am not a mean girl.
I share my things to other people.
I hate two-faced people.
I love music.
I like knitting.
I like children.
I am now over six months pregnant.
I like to have friends.
I come from an unhappy home.
I like writing to friends.

Another girl in contrast received a self-image rating as *poor:*

I am (girl's name).
I am 17 years old.
I am a heathen and a hypocrite.
I have brown hair.
I am 4 ft 11½".
I am useless.
I am the most disliked girl here.
I am a liar and a trouble maker.
I prefer girls to boys.
I hope to carry on a career in criminology.
I hate discipline.

Each girl's set of replies, then, was classified according to apparent level of self-esteem. The test was also administered to a 'control' group of girls in schools and at work throughout New Zealand (all the girls, including the borstal group, were in the 16-20 age range). Although she does not adduce statistical evidence for the control group, Roberts asserts that '. . . none of them would have been rated "poor", and only a few would have been rated "doubtful" ' (1972, 26). On the other hand 24 of the 143 borstal girls were rated as poor (17 per cent) and a further 60 (42 per cent) were rated as doubtful. 'There is an indication then, in this assessment, that one of the major differences between borstal and non-borstal girls lies in their image of themselves' (Roberts, *op. cit.*, 27), and this seems predominantly to derive from differences in level of self-esteem.

Various other pieces of evidence suggest that a negative self-image may be characteristic of individuals who commit specific types of offence, or whose behaviour exhibits patterns often related to offending. Amongst drug addicts, for example, Kaplan and Meyerowitz (1970) found self-devaluing replies to be much more common than amongst 'normals', on a series of self-report questionnaires and rating scales (the addicts involved, 300 in all, had recently been released from prison or hospital, and may have been going through difficult times, but were not at the time taking drugs). Amongst alcoholics, Berg (1971) found significantly larger discrepancies between 'real' and 'ideal' self-ratings than amongst a comparison group of social drinkers. In addition Williams (1965), working with an American college population, found excessive drinking to be more common amongst those who expressed 'self-rejecting' attitudes on a specially designed adjective checklist (a form of questionnaire in which you are asked to describe yourself by choosing from amongst a provided set of adjectives). For sex offenders, Williams (n.d.) and Marshall, Christie and Lanthier (1979) found a tendency towards lower self-esteem than amongst non-offender groups. While Marshall et al. found this to be the case for paedophiles only, Williams found that both rapists and paedophiles had significantly lower self-esteem than other non-sexual offenders in a Canadian penitentiary – a result which might well be expected in view of the execration felt towards sex offenders by other prisoner groups (Priestley, 1980).

Finally, there is considerable evidence that some types of violent offenders engage in aggressive acts at least partly as a means of overcoming doubts about themselves in other respects. Toch (1969) undertook an in-depth study of the motivations of 69 violent men in prisons or on parole in California. On the basis of interviews and detailed analysis of the accounts men gave of violent incidents in which they had been involved, Toch drew up a typology of violent offenders which reflected the dominant themes they used in explaining their own violent tendencies. The largest single group to emerge from this, encompassing 28 (40 per cent) of the sample, was that of the 'self-image compensator'. A further ten men (15 per cent of the group) acted violently, mainly to defend the reputations they had acquired for hardness. For these men then, aggression was '. . . a form of retribution against people who, the person feels, have cast aspersions on his self-image' or it acted as ' . . . a demonstration of worth, by people whose self-definition places emphasis on toughness and status' (Toch, 1969, 176). For a majority of this group then, committing violent acts was in some way bound up with a lack of self-esteem or feelings of self-doubt. Confirmation that there exists some link between low self-esteem on the one hand and aggression and hostility on the other has come from a number of other reports (Green and Murray, 1973; Rosenbaum and de Charms, 1960; Worchel, 1960). Low self-esteem, therefore, may not be associated only with apparently meek, withdrawn, or self-effacing individuals, but also with those whose social behaviour takes quite the opposite form in aggressiveness, forcefulness, and assault.

Self-esteem and offence behaviour

Overall then, though it cannot be shown unequivocally that offenders are dogged by low opinions of themselves, there is sufficient evidence to indicate that this is a promising area for work. It may for some people at least be very closely associated with their motivations to offend (or at least, *not* to abide by the rules). But why should this be so? At the beginning of this chapter a number of possible connections between self-esteem and offending behaviour were mapped out. Each of these is probably partially valid in that it accounts for the behaviour of some offenders, or explains one portion of the reasons why people offend. It may be useful to set out a hypothetical chain of causes and effects which draws all of these possibilities together.

First, if individuals fail to do well by the standards of a group to which they belong, they tend eventually to reject the standards of that group. For example, Sherwood (1965) showed that when people were given positive evaluations by a group the membership of which was important to them, they endorsed the norms of the group; when they were given negative evaluations, they discounted the group norms. Other evidence bearing on this point has been surveyed by Kaplan (1975). The principal source of evaluations for most of us as we grow up is our parents; and there is evidence that the links between low adolescent self-esteem and delinquency are stronger the less supportive are an individual's parents (Jensen, 1973). Turning to a more public domain, offenders tend to perform less well than average in the sphere which is taken as a primary yardstick of success in our society: academic achievement (Douglas, Ross, and Simpson, 1968; Prentice and Kelly, 1963). If the social disadvantages under which many adolescents labour are taken into account, their chances of doing well at school are almost bound to be low. Faced with negative information about themselves from both home and school, a natural course of action for many young people is to turn their backs on the origin of the unwelcome news, and *discard* the rules and values of the society which has put them in this disillusioning position.

Second, there is evidence to suggest that, as adolescents move onward fr
early teenage years, they become progressively more attuned to their peers rat
to adults as a source of values and personal nourishment. This has been im
research on self-perception using rating scales, questionnaires, and other m
(Rosenberg, 1965; Thompson, 1972) and has also emerged from wider-rangir
on adolescent attitudes based on interviews (Kitwood, 1980). Comfort and solace for
those who have dispensed with 'straight' values might, then, be found amongst people
of the same age who have arrived at the same point in their feelings towards others
(Hewitt, 1970; Mulligan, 1979).

Third, within groups so formed, offending may provide an alternative means of
building a more positive self-image: for the further young people proceed in the
direction of offending and absorption of delinquent values, the more their sense of
positive self-evaluation appears to be restored. Hall (1966) found support for this point
in a study of boys aged between 14 and 16; some self-reported delinquents, some on
probation, and some placed in an institution. Using interviews and attitude scales, Hall
found that there was a marked association between attachment to delinquent values
('immersion in the delinquent subculture') on the one hand, and more positive self-
image on the other. Thus offending behaviour becomes *rewarding* – not just materially
(probably a minimal advantage for most young offenders), but psychologically, by
endowing individuals with acceptance and status. Self-esteem can, in other words, be
recouped through the commission of delinquent acts.

Finally, once individuals in this position become adjudicated as delinquents, other
mechanisms of labelling, stigmatising and so on come into play. That so-and-so is
expected to re-offend becomes more or less a self-fulfilling prophecy, which seen from
within so-and-so's framework of values, is a good thing in any case; his entrapment
within a delinquent way of looking at the world is now complete.

This hypothetical cycle of events is intended to illustrate how low self-esteem may be
a factor in engendering offences or offence-related behaviour. Even a relatively brief
decline in self-evaluation can make people more willing to 'break the rules'. Evidence
on this latter point comes from laboratory experiments in which short-term changes
(upwards or downwards) in self-esteem have been artificially induced amongst
different groups (e.g., by giving false feedback about performance on a test). For
example Aronson and Metee (1968) and Graf (1971) working with college students,
and Fry (1975) working with seven-year-old children, found 'resistance to temptation'
drastically reduced amongst individuals temporarily given negative feelings about
themselves (they were more likely to cheat at cards, or play with forbidden toys, and so
on). If such results seem a long way removed from the settings in which real offences are
committed, the results of Roberts's (1972) work with New Zealand borstal girls,
outlined earlier, may anchor them more firmly in the outside world. Roberts kept track
of the girls' progress for a year after they left borstal; and at that point, whereas only
32.2 per cent of the 'good self-image' group had been reconvicted, the corresponding
figure for the 'poor' group was 75 per cent (the proportions given custodial sentences
were respectively 18.6 per cent and 62.5 per cent). The girls' pictures of themselves
seemed to play a decisive part in shaping their criminal careers. Findings essentially
similar to these have also been reported by Bennett (1974) and Joplin (1972).

Taking all of the preceding evidence together, we can conclude that something about
an individual's self-worth may be very significant in affecting whether or not he or she
gets into trouble to begin with; and may subsequently be crucial in deciding whether he
or she adopts a 'criminal identity' (or in less dramatic tones, becomes a recidivist).

To help offenders alter their visions of themselves may therefore be one route towards helping them stop committing offences. The remainder of this chapter describes methods for exploring and acting upon this possibility. First some exercises are outlined for enabling individuals to look at themselves, specifically in relation to the value they place on themselves. Then, some other exercises are described for helping them to *change* the way they look at themselves. Obviously, there are no secret formulae or miracle-cure ways of doing this; you cannot just throw a switch and be confronted, effortlessly with a completely new version of yourself; but self-esteem can be changed, by deliberate, conscious effort, and the methods surveyed below can be used to encourage and sustain this process.

Self-assessment

Almost all attempts to help people solve problems with which they are confronted involve some kind of change in the way they see themselves. Some types of 'deep' psychotherapy aim at a total restructuring of the individual personality; but even the more 'superficial' forms of therapy assume some change of awareness; people's behaviour cannot be modified without allowing or encouraging them to perceive that this is what is going on. Just to achieve one goal you have never accomplished before, no matter how trifling, results in a recognition that you could do it again if required. Education and even job training rest upon the same basis. To the extent that any of these enterprises succeeds it could be said to do so through changing an individual's self-image. 'I know something I didn't know yesterday; feel differently about something; am able to do something I couldn't do before.'

The focus in the exercises which follow is on self-esteem. 'Self-esteem' does not mean conceit, or pomposity, or being very self-conscious of your own presence or importance. It simply means valuing yourself, in the way you value others; considering yourself worthwhile; recognizing that you are a unique individual and that you count just as much as anybody else. A person with high self-esteem is not by virtue of the fact big-headed, arrogant, or smug. On the other hand a person with low self-esteem may be very unhappy, oppressed with self-doubts, lacking in confidence, and unable to get much satisfaction out of life as a result. The first group of exercises here is designed to explore this aspect of an individual's self-image.

The 'Who am I?' test

To call this exercise a test is probably not very accurate, since like the other suggestions here it is designed for *self*-assessment. The information it yields is not, in other words, to be taken away and mulled over by workers: it is for participants' own use in the process of self-appraisal and personal change.

All that is required is that an individual should try to complete the sentence beginning 'I am . . .' as many times as possible up to a maximum of 20 (though if it seems possible and useful this ceiling could be set higher). The resulting sentences can be written down, recorded on audio- or video-tape, or just spoken to you or someone else to write down. Some examples produced by girls in borstal in New Zealand were given earlier.

When this has been done, the finished sentences can be used in several ways. First, they can be divided up into positive and negative: those which by and large say something good about an individual, and those which are derogatory or critical. The balance between the two will serve as a rough index of relative level of self-esteem, and if you are working in a group you could invite members to compare their scores. Alternatively, the sentences could be judged on an impressionistic basis: when you have gone through someone's sentences, what is the general feeling you are left with?

Secondly, working with an individual, you could review what he or she has said, and use this as a basis for a more thorough exploration of his or her self-image. Why has this person said these things about him or herself? How does he/she feel about different things that have emerged? Are those things which the individual fundamentally believes or things other people have said? Which of them if any could be changed and how?

The Self-esteem Scale

The 'Who am I?' exercise represents a fairly loose and unstructured way of approaching the issue of self-esteem. A less flexible, but nevertheless useful instrument for doing the same thing is the *Self-esteem Scale* which is set out below.

This scale comes from the work of Rosenberg (1965) on the self-perceptions and social development of adolescents, and can also, like the previous exercise, be used either to yield a simple score, or as the starting-point for an interview. What individuals have to do is to put a tick or cross in a box opposite each item, denoting their degree of agreement with each statement in turn. Each item can then be given a score between 1 and 4. In each case, the higher score represents a higher level of self-esteem; however the order alternates over the ten items, with the first item being scored 4-3-2-1, the second 1-2-3-4, and so on.

Rosenberg Self-esteem Scale

	Strongly agree	Agree	Disagree	Strongly disagree
1. On the whole, I am satisfied with myself.				
2. At times I think I am no good at all.				
3. I feel that I have a number of good qualities.				
4. I feel I do not have much to be proud of.				
5. I am able to do things as well as most other people.				
6. I certainly feel useless at times.				
7. I feel that I am a person of worth, at least on an equal plane with others.				
8. I wish I could have more respect for myself.				
9. I take a positive attitude toward myself.				
10. All in all, I am inclined to feel that I am a failure.				

To obtain the 'self-esteem score' all you have to do is add up the scores over the ten items as a whole. Scores will therefore vary between 10 and 40. Once again, it is interesting if you are working with a group to invite participants to compare their scores, and discuss some of the reasons for the differences which appear. Alternatively, and especially if an individual has a low score (say less than 20), this could act as a take-off point for an interview, peer interview, or small group discussion designed to probe an individual's feelings and beliefs about him- or herself in more depth. Clearly, with someone whose self-esteem is very low or who is very lacking in self-confidence, it would be best to do this on a one-to-one basis. The object of such an interview is to help people understand themselves better by asking them why they had placed themselves at particular points on each scale item; and perhaps to describe those aspects of themselves or those events in their experience which had led them to respond in the way they had done.

Adjective checklist

A third method which can be used to explore self-image and in particular self-esteem is to ask people to describe themselves in terms of a pre-arranged list of words like the one shown below. This is an *adjective checklist* and like other checklists it is used simply by asking people to go through and tick off whichever adjectives they think apply to them. You can ask them to mark off any number, or to choose a fixed number, say 20 out of the 60 in the list. Once again, a crude score can be derived from this: the list consists of 30 (what would generally be regarded as) positive words and 30 negative ones, alternating with each other. People can then be asked to count up their positive (odd-numbered) and negative (even-numbered) choices and see how many of each there are. And as before, the results and their general reactions to them can be used as the substance of an interview, peer interview, or small group discussion.

Adjective checklist

1. Good-humoured	21. Attractive	41. Worth knowing
2. Unfriendly	22. Unsuccessful at	42. Inferior
3. Loyal	anything	43. Outgoing
4. Boring	23. Warm	44. Jealous
5. Reliable	24. Not worth knowing	45. Independent
6. Nasty	25. Open-minded	46. Difficult to get on
7. Kind	26. Lonely	with
.8 Dishonest	27. Hard-working	47. Worthwhile
9. Good-tempered	28. Uncaring	48. Dependent
10. Unattractive	29. Easy to get on with	49. Easy-going
11. Happy	30. Hot-headed	50. Up-tight
12. Cold	31. Honest	51. Straight with people
13. Helpful	32. Aggressive	52. Unhappy
14. Narrow-minded	33. Caring	53. Popular
15. Successful at some	34. Disloyal	54. Screwed up
things	35. Cool-headed	55. Friendly
16. Lazy	36. Unstable	56. Unreliable
17. Interesting	37. Fond of people	57. Organized
18. Selfish	38. Depressed	58. Devious
19. Good at making	39. Pleasant	59. Able to cope
decisions	40. Unpopular	60. Unpleasant
20. Greedy		

Self-ideal discrepancy

A less direct, but equally thought-provoking assessment of an individual's self-esteem can be obtained by asking the question: how close are you to being the person you would really like to be? In some of the research quoted earlier, this was the strategy which was used. Unless you are working with saints or very satisfied sinners you will almost certainly find that most people would like to change themselves in some respect; they would like to be cleverer, tougher, less impulsive, more outgoing, better at telling jokes than they are at the moment. Not that you will necessarily be able to help them change in all these directions; but the degree of difference between the way they think they *are* and the way they *would like to be* may be some measure of their self-acceptance, their level of contentment with themselves. Just to discuss this with someone will be a valuable undertaking in itself. But the job can be made more structured, and entertaining, by using self-rating scales on which individuals are asked to place themselves at a point between two opposed adjectives such as 'anxious – calm' or 'timid – aggressive'. First, individuals are asked to suggest such adjectives, to generate a list of the words they might use when describing other people. Next, these are arranged into sets of opposites like the examples just given. People are then asked to complete two sets of ratings on the scales so formed: portraying themselves as they are at the moment ('me as I am') and as their ideal selves ('me as I would really like to be'). Comparisons between the two sets of ratings can then be made; any substantial differences noted and discussed; and if you use numbered rating scales, a difference score can be calculated by adding up the numerical differences between the ratings over all the scales. The size of this score may be taken as a reflection of the discrepancy between someone's 'actual' and 'ideal' self.

Personal ladder scales

Self-esteem can also be measured by asking individuals to place themselves on a ten-step ladder, the top of which represents 'the best possible life' and the bottom 'the worst possible'. The position they mark between these points represents an approximate

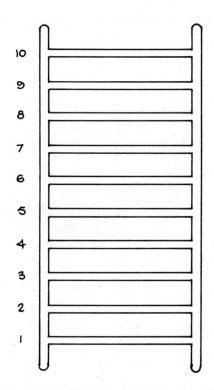

index of their satisfaction with life, which will obviously overlap with how good they are feeling about themselves. Individual positions can be compared with group averages, and also with the results of an international survey carried out by the Gallup organisation (Watts and Free, 1978). In this research, samples of people in 60 nations throughout the world were asked to complete a personal ladder scale like the one shown above. They were asked to do this in three ways: (a) for their *present* position between 'best' and 'worst'; (b) thinking of a point five years in the *past*; and (c) thinking of a time five years in the *future*. Some of the average scores which appeared, which might (for their sheer interest value) be worth setting out for people to see if you are working in a group, are shown in the accompanying table for various regions of the world.

Average scores on ladder scales in various parts of the world

	Past	Present	Future
United Kingdom	6.0	6.8	7.3
United States	6.0	6.7	7.5
Western Europe	5.7	6.3	6.8
Scandinavia	6.7	7.6	7.7
Latin America	5.0	6.0	7.9
India	3.9	3.4	3.4

Low scores, either for whole groups or for individuals within them, may indicate a mixture of things worth pursuing in further discussion or possibly role-play, most importantly perhaps to distinguish an objectively unsatisfactory state of affairs in someone's life from a blighted perception of the world, of the person him- or herself, or of other people.

Ladder scales can also be used to keep a record of any changes in self-image and self-esteem over an extended period, as expressed in terms of felt satisfaction with one's life. If they are to be used in this way, the date of each completion should be recorded beside the 'score'; successive entries for one person could even be plotted in the form of a graph to illuminate changes over time.

Circles exercise

The exercises we have looked at so far, as methods of helping people to scrutinize their attitudes towards themselves, all have one thing in common: they make no immediate reference to interpersonal relations or to the 'significant others' in someone's life. Almost inevitably of course, people *will* allude to others who are important to them, who play key parts in their lives, and with whom they are likely to compare themselves. This exercise and the next two direct attention towards the social aspect of people's feelings about themselves: how they judge themselves alongside others, the extent to which they rely on others for valuations of themselves, and the reasons they give for assuming themselves to have more or less merit that other individuals.

In the research carried out by Ziller (1973) and his colleagues, mentioned earlier, self-esteem was measured using a series of circles arranged in a horizontal line as shown

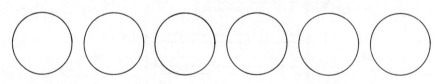

here. Respondents were given a list of six names, e.g.

Someone you know who is a good athlete	Someone who knows a great deal
Someone you know who is popular	Yourself
Someone you know who is funny	Someone you know who is unhappy
or,	
Someone you know who is cruel	A policeman
A judge	Yourself
A housewife	Your sister or someone who is most like a sister

They were then asked to assign each person (represented by an initial) to a circle. In fact, individuals were asked to do this with six sets of names in turn. A person's self-esteem score was taken to be the average position of 'yourself' over the six sets, counting from lowest to highest status. Curiously, Ziller and other workers repeatedly found there was a marked tendency for individuals, when doing this exercise, to place the highest-status person on the left and the lowest on the right. This does not always happen, however, and you need to check when working out a score which direction an individual is using. In doing this test, people are making some kind of statement about how they see themselves in relation to others, and once again this represents a point of departure for further discussion.

Group status

If you are working with younger offenders, the likelihood is that many of them will belong to larger groupings – will have sets of friends or acquaintances, people whom they spend time with, talk to about things, and perhaps get into trouble with. It will be worthwhile to obtain some estimate from individuals, and invite them to take stock of, their perceived positioning within the various groups of which they are members. Most juvenile crime is, as we will see in chapter five, committed in groups. Very often, young people are drawn into this via a network of personal and power relations within the group. The 'followers' go along because they are dominated by the leader; swept along by the contagious enthusiasm – or overwhelmed by the naked pressure – of other members. The 'leader' goes along to preserve his or her place in the group, to be seen taking initiatives and giving the group things to do. All are locked together in a nexus of affiliations and expectations. For most groups of course such structuring may be very loose or very unclear. To highlight the group relations as a source of pressure can be a revelation for 'leaders' and 'followers' alike.

One method is to ask people to draw a diagram showing the relations in their group of friends. This can be cast in the form of a pyramid to show a hierarchy of different levels of status; or could be a kind of map of patterns of relationships, showing who is the most popular person, etc., as in a sociogram. Most important however, individuals must be asked to identify their own location within this – what is their status relative to others, how do they see themselves stationed in their scheme of things? Such an exercise could be carried out with the actual members of a living group; but given that the system of power and influence within the group might distort what emerged, it might be best to try this with just one person at a time. Once more, this exercise will prove most fruitful if it is followed up with discussion of why individuals see others as being above them or below them in the 'social ordering' of their group.

Reputations

In his work with violent offenders, Toch (1969) found a certain number of men who engaged in violence principally to maintain reputations they had earned for themselves – a syndrome Toch called 'rep defending'. Such individuals felt 'socially obliged' to act violently; and some would do so when people expected it of them, even when they actually felt reluctant themselves. (For others, of course, matters were never complicated by such inhibitions.) But it is not just in regard to violence that people may feel they have reputations to sustain. Getting away with any offence; stealing faster or more expensive cars; pulling off a bigger con-trick, can all endow individuals with a notoriety which they may parade before others quite unashamedly. Within institutions, such reputations may consolidate individuals' positions in the top echelons of an inmate subculture (Schrag, 1954).

For other offenders, a desire to be in the top flight, to gain infamy, to establish themselves in these positions may be a major motivating force. If you are working with such a person, ask exactly how he or she would like to be known. What would he/she like others to think of him/her; to see written in the newspapers or broadcast on the television or radio; to hear said in court? For some people status derives from these kinds of reports; or more informally, from the kinds of things that are said about them amongst people of their own age. This can be approached indirectly by asking people to describe themselves as if they were someone else – by asking them to comment on things they had done as if they were news reporters, for example; or by giving them a list of adjectives or phrases (like the list on page 64) and asking them which they would like other people to use when thinking of or describing them. The outcomes of these sorts of exercise should then be used as before to discuss with an individual the extent to which, and the reasons why, these things matter to him or her.

Altering self-esteem

The suggestions and exercises which have been set out so far have the common aim of providing a mechanism by which offerenders' attention may be directed, if it seems appropriate, towards their perceptions of themselves, their valuations of themselves, and the possible relations between this and their offence behaviour. We are not proposing that all of these exercises should be used with any one individual or group; as with the materials in other chapters of this book, workers will have to choose, on the strength of their own experience and knowledge of the persons they are working with, whichever of the items seem most suitable to them. But if a negative self-evaluation does appear to be the root of the problem, or at least part of it, the worker will naturally want to take some kind of action that might be useful for assisting people towards a healthier or more positive appreciation of themselves.

It is a commonplace that some offenders 'grow out' of their delinquency; becoming older and wiser perhaps; getting married or having children; acquiring and keeping some kind of job; moving elsewhere; ceasing to mix with a particular group or gang; developing some kind of passionate interest. These transitions are related both to changing relationships in the real world, and the changes in self perception or self-image. But they are also *unreflective* and *unself-willed* changes which attract the generic title of 'growing up', 'getting older', or 'maturing'. Though they are the products of decisions people have made about their lives, these are not first and foremost decisions about personal change as such. This section raises the general question of what, if anything, can be done to make some of these processes more self-conscious; more under the control of the person to whom they happen; and how, if possible, they can be made to happen sooner rather than later.

Counselling

In large measure, helping those who have low self-esteem to take a more approving view of themselves may be very much a question of approach. Self-critical or self-effacing, withdrawn or perhaps depressed, unconfident or disorganized individuals obviously need to be handled with considerable care. Some form of counselling will be an essential requirement if you are working with someone in this frame of mind.

The ingredients of successful counselling have proven very elusive despite the expenditure of prodigious effort on the part of those who would like to understand it better. Some years ago Rogers (1957) proposed that there were three indispensable features of effective counselling and psychotherapy: (a) that the counsellor should appear *genuine* or authentic to the individual he/she was trying to help; (b) that the helper should exhibit warmth and respect or *positive regard* for the individual; and (c) that the helper should experience a certain degree of *empathy* towards the individual and attempt to see things from his or her point of view. Although substantial quantities of research have failed to show that these are the necessary and sufficient conditions of counselling that Rogers (who was trying to stimulate research) hypothesized them to be, they do seem to be worthwhile constituents of any bid to help someone with a problem such as a poor self-image. Indeed they may be more important in this context than in most other areas of counselling. Giving mild encouragement, emphasizing good points, and in general trying to give a boost to an individual's self-confidence, will be valuable strategies in this encounter. Obviously, none of these things need be done in an exaggerated or unrealistic manner, but simply in such a way that they convey a positive message to someone who from most other sources may be receiving only negative reports.

All the exercises in the previous section can be used to commence a counselling session along these lines; all the exercises in this section are additional tools for achieving the same end, for giving extra impetus to the basic helping process.

There is, unfortunately, no single piece of research which has shown that a change in self-esteem resulted in a subsequent change in an individual's offending behaviour. There are separate batches of evidence showing that self-esteem can be changed, and that improvements in self-image may go hand-in-hand with reductions in anti-social behaviour. The link between the two must remain for the time being a matter of speculation. The exercises below are based on evidence as far as possible; some, however, seem self-evidently useful things to do.

Developing awareness

One course of action to take with an individual whose self-estimation is low is to aid him or her in the discovery of good things about him- or herself. Just looking and focusing on the positive side, and bringing it more fully into view, can be a very productive and revealing experience.

Good points

Most people are more than familiar with their faults and weaknesses, and if asked to talk about them could probably produce enough material to fill a book or make a documentary programme for television. Thinking about good points is less easy, and talking about them to others is generally frowned upon as if it were arrogance or rodomontade. It is however worth asking people to try to find some of their good points; to make a list of them if possible; and to concentrate on thinking about the better side of themselves whenever they are assailed by negative feelings. If you are working with a group you could ask each member to describe his or her good points to everyone else; alternatively, each person records a talk on his or her good points on video – or work in pairs and describe each other's; the whole series then being played back for review and group discussion.

Good experiences

When some people look into the past, their minds tend to dwell on the unfortunate and unhappy events in their experience. Like pondering over personal faults, this can be a habit of thought which if well-established can blind an individual to the more positive side of things. This exercise is an attempt to reverse the process. Members of a group are asked to work in pairs and to interview each other about one good experience they have had, which was the result of something they had done and which they felt pleased with, satisfied about, or proud of afterwards. Examples: doing someone a favour; doing a piece of work well; achieving something that required a bit of effort; learning how to do something; organizing and going on a holiday or a day trip. If they are happy to do so, the members of each pair then describe their partner's experience to the rest of the group.

Life-space exercise

As a combination and extension of the two preceding exercises, invite individuals to make as thorough a review as possible of their past experience and present position. The aim is to make an inventory, as comprehensive as possible, of all the positive features of their lives: to map out their 'life-spaces', to use a term coined by Lewin (1951). They must marshal, from even the remotest corners of their lives, as much evidence as possible that they are as good as anyone else and have something to offer themselves, other people and the world. Their attention can be directed in turn towards different spheres, e.g.

> *Personal:* general state of health, fitness, and appearance;
>   character, habits, beliefs, attitudes;
>   fantasies, hopes, ambitions, aspirations;
> *Social:* family life and relations;
>   friendships – personal relationships outside the family;
> *Activities:* school; things they learned, enjoyed, achieved, were interested in;
>   work; all the jobs they have had, skills they have accumulated;
>   spare time; all hobbies, sports, interests they have tried;
> *Circumstances:* all advantages of their present living conditions, finances, etc;
> *Other events and experiences:* unique or unusual things that have occurred in their lives.

If the objective of selecting positive items from these various realms of an individual's make-up is adhered to, most people – even those who normally regard themselves as inferior, inadequate, or mediocre – will arrive at the end of their exhaustive inquiry with a list of affirmatives about themselves which will almost certainly contain a quota of points which they had previously more or less forgotten.

Using other people

Asking people to search for the more positive side of themselves, an activity to which they may be rather unaccustomed, is one way of increasing their self-awareness. If you are working with a group, another avenue is opened up via the feedback that people can be given by others.

Testimonials

Offenders are used to being 'bad news'. All the bad things about them are repeatedly rehearsed in social work investigations and reports, during court proceedings, and in their dealings with many others outside these official contexts.

One way of counteracting this constant barrage of bad news is to help in the collection of 'good news'; and one way of doing this is to solicit what middle class people call 'testimonials' from significant figures in the offender's environment. These might include employers, friends, relatives, project workers, club leaders, shopkeepers, neighbours, workmates, or fellow members of the group with which you are working. Such testimonials need not be lengthy or beautifully written but need only mention some of the strengths or abilities or virtues of the person about whom they are written.

They can be collated and kept in a file together with written accounts of some of the self-awareness exercises described in the last section.

Photo album

Many projects, and particularly those working with children and young adults, make special efforts to record in photographic form some of the activities (both outdoor and indoor) which they undertake, and to display the results prominently on the wall or in exhibitions. Part of the aim of this is to provide a permanent record of participation and pleasure of the type which many people find enshrined in the family photograph album, but which those from institutional or some family backgrounds might never otherwise enjoy. A secondary aim may be to enliven group proceedings and create a sense of occasion in the way the presence of a camera so often does; or to 'make a fuss' of people by giving them a kind of attention they may not have had in the past. The business of expanding self-awareness, developing confidence, and discovering different facets of someone's life can be made more vivid by this means. People are asked to make a collection – from home, school, work or elsewhere – of any snapshots of themselves or of people and places known to them. These could be combined with others, taken during the course of your work with them, to form a photographic addendum to the other materials they have gathered concerning themselves.

'This is your life'

A more elaborate and time-consuming version of the previous exercise is to research and make, as professionally as possible, a videotape equivalent of the programme 'This is your Life' for someone. This can be done not as in the studio format, but as a series of interviews with key people in the subject's life, all talking about him or her, and connected together with a narrative commentary. To do this well, several people would have to work on it as a team; an appropriate strategy if you are working with a group will be to ask them to contribute to the making of each other's life-stories in turn. It might even be possible to secure the services of a local television or radio person to do the commentary – provided you have reasonable technical facilities, a well-written script, and do not ask too often.

'Positive strokes'

If people are working together as a group for some time, they will obviously get to know each other to some extent. At this stage try introducing a game in which each can receive some positive feedback from the rest (assuming, that is, that the group atmosphere is in general a healthy one!). 'Positive strokes', based on some of the ideas of Berne (1968), is an opportunity for people to give each other compliments. But to save the embarrassment likely to accompany such an ordinarily taboo undertaking, the compliments can be given anonymously.

Each person is allocated a piece of paper; and every other group member in turn is invited to write something complimentary about that person on it, folding the paper over each time so that people can't see each other's comments. Every individual then ends up with a sheet containing some form of praise from all or most other members of the group. There is not unnaturally one absolutely inviolable rule: *only positive* comments should be written down. If you think some members may be unable to resist the temptation to make personal criticisms or just ventilate some of their own bad feelings, two variations on the exercise may be used instead. One is to take all the pieces of paper away and rewrite them with any unseemly comments edited out; this may seem dishonest and paternalistic, but weak egos may sometimes have to be given protection. Alternatively, one person at a time steps outside the room while other group members openly compile a set of compliments, which are then written down and given to the individual as before. A third option is of course to avoid the exercise altogether; but given the congenial impact that this game usually has on people, it would be a pity to have to resort to this.

The exercises we have looked at so far in this chapter could all be broadly characterized as having the general aim of 'building people up', 'repairing deflated self-images', or 'seeing yourself in a better light'. To accomplish this they have relied for the most part on fairly direct methods which involve individuals, working on their own or in small groups, in a comparatively straightforward process of self-discovery. In the remainder of the chapter, some more complex strategies are described which will almost certainly call for longer-term work, and which draw on more elaborate techniques of counselling and training.

The rational-emotive approach

The field of psychotherapy is currently replete with theories about the origins of human emotional problems. There are literally dozens of different points of view, each proposing separate accounts (sometimes overlapping, sometimes in conflict) of how problems develop, and each prescribing specific therapeutic procedures commensurate with its underlying principles. But according to Ellis (1962), while many of these approaches put forward quite plausible suggestions as to how emotional disturbances arise, none gives any consideration to the question of how such disturbances are *maintained*. To say for example that an individual suffers from feelings of guilt, shame or rejection because of particular childhood experiences (assuming for the moment that this were the case) does not explain why these feelings persist into adulthood, when the individual's circumstances are entirely different, and in the face of considerable evidence that it would be better for the individual *not* to feel that way. Nor does it explain why, even when individuals have (by means of psychotherapy) gained complete insight into the roots of their troubles, that these troubles nevertheless refuse to go away. To Ellis, both of these conundrums can be made intelligible by examining what individuals tell themselves about their difficulties. The human capacity for language and for internal speech means that (amongst other things) we can keep feelings of distress alive long after the situation which first evoked those feelings has passed into history. This is precisely what goes on in the case not only of many affective disorders, but also in many other experiences which are part of normal everyday life. People are prone, says Ellis, to 'self-sabotage' their own interests. In fact, in instance after instance, people build up quite irrational beliefs about themselves, other people, and the world. The job of the counsellor may be to help them pin down, confront and rid themselves of such beliefs and of the tendency to indulge in self-defeating self-talk.

It is possible that a negative self-image may be sustained by just such processes as these. The form of therapy which Ellis (1962) developed to help individuals with these problems is called *Rational-Emotive Therapy*. Essentially, this consists of *challenging* people's beliefs about themselves and asking them to *justify* the things they say about or to themselves. For example, a person may say that he is worthless, or a failure, because his marriage has broken down; because he has not done well in school; because he cannot get a job of a certain kind, or any job at all. Given these statements, Ellis would ask the person concerned to prove that these things showed he was worthless. No-one of course, can do this; the fact that you have failed at things and even done some quite nasty things does not prove that you are worthless. Yet people have been taught, as

Ellis says, to like themselves if they succeed at things and dislike themselves if they fail. This is one of the irrational ideas to which Ellis believes many of us are susceptible: the notion that to be worthwhile, individuals have to be adequate, competent, and successful in the things they do. Of course, *not* being so will be painful and may be difficult to accept: but it does not mean that we stand condemned, that our lives are hardly worth living, or that we might as well go and do other nasty things because we are no use to anyone anyway.

The first step in the rational-emotive approach is to explain to individuals the basic ideas which underlie it – to present them with a framework which will allow them both to choose whether or not they would like to use the method, and empower them to put it into effect should they wish to do so. This framework can be depicted as a five-stage sequence; the first three stages correspond to Ellis's view of the emotions:

A = Activating events or circumstances
B = Beliefs or mental organization which determine how the event is perceived
C = Consequences in terms of the feelings and behaviour of the individual

The key element in all this for Ellis is the set of beliefs within which the person interprets what has happened to him or her. The emotions experienced are a direct result of these beliefs, *not* of the external events. If the beliefs are rational, the feelings will be in a manageable proportion to the initial events, and the individual will still be able to function in a healthy manner. If on the other hand they are irrational, the resultant feelings may be excessive, unbalanced and possibly damaging for the individual. Rational-emotive therapy attempts to remedy this by tackling the beliefs and assumptions of the individual in two further stages:

D = Detecting or discriminating the individual's beliefs and self-statements
E = Effects on the individual of replacing these with more rational ones

Having used this simple ABCDE mnemonic to expound to someone the rationale of the approach, the next step is to help individuals to uncover the irrational nature of some of their beliefs, by demonstrating that some of the conclusions they have reached about themselves are not supported by evidence. Having persuaded them that this is so, or at least having sown the seeds of doubt in their minds, the next task is to encourage them to think about some of the things they say to themselves to shore up these beliefs. They need, in other words, to pinpoint exactly the words, phrases and sentences which are repeated over and over inside their heads whenever they are feeling bad about themselves. The objective then becomes to *change* the content of these messages; to find new, and more rational kinds of self-statements which bear a closer relation to the realities of the situation the individual is facing.

For example, suppose that, following the break-up of a relationship, an individual is feeling very depressed and self-accusing about the reasons for the split. The person may say inwardly 'I'm hopeless at relationships; nobody could live with me anyway. I'm a sick, useless idiot' – or words to that effect. Under such circumstances, inevitably feeling very unhappy, some people *do* torment themselves endlessly and almost overwhelm themselves with grief or debilitating self-pity. The rational-emotive strategy in this instance would consist of granting, first of all, that the individual feels very hurt and may indeed have behaved badly in the relationship; second, showing him or her that this can in no way prove that he/she is worthless or impossible to live with; third, helping the individual identify some of the painful ruminations which keep the process of self-condemnation alive; and fourth, substituting for these a number of more positive and realistic thoughts or images to summon when self-destructive thoughts on the offensive. Over the ensuing days, weeks, or months, the individual must then to use these new self-statements in an effort to adopt a more resilient self-image; acknowledging his or her loss of the relationship and the reasons for it, but nevertheless coping with life and anticipating that future relationships may turn out to be quite different.

Self-esteem and self-control

Rational-emotive therapy focuses on introspections, the things people say to themselves about themselves, as the master-key to many forms of personal change and the solution of many emotional and behavioural problems. As such it has been called a form of 'cognitive therapy' since it relies on the individual's *cognitions* or self-statements to engender change. A similar emphasis can be found in a related form of helping known as *self-control training*. We will be looking at this more closely in chapter six when we come to consider offences which are in some sense a product of an individual's lack of self-control (e.g. violence, drunkenness, or compulsive theft). But this kind of training has also been used with the problem of low self-esteem, and a number of exercises can be suggested along these lines.

Thought stopping

As the name implies, 'thought stopping' means trying to halt unwanted strings of thought by saying 'stop' to yourself whenever such strings begin to appear. All of us do this to a certain extent when we start to follow a chain of thought which we know to be unproductive: we tell ourselves to 'forget it' and think about something else. Sometimes, of course, this can be very difficult and we may need help to accomplish it; but if individuals are plagued by recurrent negative thoughts about themselves such a method might be used to help them resist them. However, since this procedure has been used primarily with obsessive or repetitive patterns of thought, it is described more fully in chapter six (page 141).

Positive intervention

A more common problem of those whose self-esteem is low is that they rarely think positive things about themselves. 'Positive intervention' is thought stopping in reverse; here, individuals try not to cancel out negative thoughts but to promote positive ones. For this to work, individuals must first identify some quite mundane piece of their own behaviour which occurs quite frequently, such as glancing at one's watch, looking out of the window, or switching on an electrical appliance. Individuals then try to 'schedule' positive self-statements by linking them as often as possible to these events; that is, every time you look at your watch (or whatever) you consciously make yourself think positive statements about yourself. This requires some initial practice over a fixed period, say a couple of sessions, during which individuals will forget to do it some of the time; but if they can make themselves keep at it evidence suggests that it can be an effective means of helping people feel better about themselves. The technique has been used successfully as part of treatment for those suffering from depression (Jackson, 1972; Todd, 1972) or who view themselves in an excessively self-critical way (Hannum, Thoresen, and Hubbard, 1974).

Graded achievements

People often feel bad about themselves because of an inability, real or apparent, to get certain kinds of things done. Low self-esteem may go hand in hand with a feeling of loss of self-control. Under these circumstances, it is possible to assist people in the gradual re-building of the sense that they can do things by themselves – with concomitant bonuses for their evaluations of themselves. Another exercise which has been used in the treatment of depression might be valuable here. If individuals feel that their capacity to 'get things done' is impaired, their sense of well-being is bound to suffer. They may come to feel that they cannot do even the smallest things. In this case, they can be presented with a list of tasks carefully graded in terms of difficulty. Even the simplest jobs can be broken down into smaller parts, and arranged into a progression so that individuals can tackle them in more easily achieved steps. If a series of such tasks of steadily increasing difficulty is prepared, so that the gap between one step and the next is relatively small, individuals can accomplish each in such a way that they are soon doing things which they would earlier have considered beyond them. The positive feedback which this brings gives encouragement to individuals and helps restore their self-esteem. Obviously, any set of tasks of this kind must be tailored exactly to the needs of those who are in this position.

Such a series of assigned tasks was used successfully by Loeb, Feshbach, Beck, and Wolf (1964) in helping to develop increased self-esteem and a more optimistic outlook amongst groups of depressed psychiatric patients.

Self-reward

The effects of each of the three preceding exercises (and indeed of all self-control training methods, as we shall see in chapter six) can be enhanced if they are allied to a system in which individuals monitor and reward themselves in accordance with their own progress. The successful usage of any of the methods should be something of a reward in itself, in so far as individuals will have thereby achieved something – like simply feeling less fed up with themselves – that is (presumably) instrinsically worthwhile. On top of this, however, people can also add further rewards of their own choosing as direct incentives to their own efforts. If someone manages to get through a day without feeling negative about him or herself, for example; or completes a pre-arranged number of graded tasks, then he or she should 'celebrate' in some way, however small. Rewards may consist of anything from a cup of tea, to buying something, to going for an evening out – entirely dependent on the preferences of the individual. If you are working with someone in this position try to plan a pattern of self-rewards with the individual in advance, in conjunction with the other self-control exercises or tasks which he or she has agreed to use. Task and self-reward can even be intimately combined: for example, people pick some event which they would like to happen, and set out to *make it happen*.

Apart from their 'reinforcing' effect, self-monitoring and self-reward can also be very useful as markers of the kinds and pace of changes which individuals are going through.

External rewards

Most people cannot go on giving themselves rewards in a vacuum, however. They must also receive assurances from other people that they are going in the right direction – that the progress they believe they are making is visible to other people. The importance of this should be self-evident enough, but it has been underlined by case-study reports of work with child and adolescent offenders. Wahler and Pollio (1968) worked with an extremely disruptive eight-year-old boy over a series of twenty-four sessions each lasting twenty minutes. The sessions consisted mainly of behaviour therapy but strong emphasis was given to the adoption of a warm, open attitude to the boy, the use of praise and the development of his relationships with others. By the end of the sessions his behaviour and attitudes had been almost totally transformed. Staats nd Butterfield (1965) used an even more direct form of reward with an extremely eprived, very anti-social fourteen-year-old delinquent: the boy was taught to read using a specially prepared set of remedial materials and given coloured tokens, which he could exchange for small amounts of money, according to his progress. Over a ten-month period the boy's reading age doubled; he became much less aggressive, more sociable, and performed much better in school. Clearly, the importance of encouragement, praise and reward as part of any programme for engendering personal change cannot be underestimated.

'Re-attribution training'

Rational-emotive therapy, self-control training, and several of the other methods we have discussed in this chapter as possible routes to the enhancement of self-esteem all rely at some point on changing the self-statements which mediate people's overall feelings about themselves as human beings. One other more speculative suggestion will be made in this connection, which stems from some work carried out by Ickes and Layden (1978) on depression. These workers devised a questionnaire for assessing the extent to which people believe that the good things and bad things in their lives are the result of their own actions or of external ungovernable factors. Ickes and Layden found differences in this respect between people low and high in self-esteem. While the former tended to blame themselves for bad outcomes to events and attributed good outcomes to factors beyond their control, the latter saw good things as a product of their own efforts and bad results as the fault of external conditions. The two groups differed in 'attribution style', i.e. the manner in which they ascribed causes to different sources within themselves or in the world outside.

On the basis of this finding, Ickes and Layden set out to help depressed, low-self-esteem individuals to alter their 'attributional style', by training them to impute to external sources the reasons for some of their difficulties, using self-verbalizations of the kind that might be deployed in rational-emotive therapy. Unfortunately, they could not make this work in practice; nevertheless some of the individuals with whom they worked did manage to do it and for them this was accompanied by an increase in self-esteem.

Though somewhat tentative, these results indicate that it may be worth exploring with individuals what *they* see as the origins of the good and bad features of their lives. As an exercise, they could be asked (via an interview or in direct pencil-and-paper form) to fill out a table like the one shown below.

The contents of the table are then examined closely and individuals are asked to give reasons why they have inserted specific items in a given quadrant. If you are working with a group, comparisons can be made between different members' perspectives on where different items belong. As a possible avenue to change, individuals may be asked if there are any 'good things' which they can bring more under their own control, i.e. move from the lower to the upper half of the box. Or, are there any items in the 'bad' category which they see as results of their own actions but which really belong in the lower right-hand square? Obviously, some people's judgments on all of these issues may be absolutely accurate and there may be nothing that can be done to change them. For others, however, their feelings of lack of worth may derive from a mistaken interpretation of the causes of their problems; discussion, counselling, and perhaps the development of new self-statements, may assist them in the construction of a more balanced perception of themselves.

	Good things in my life	Bad things in my life
Which are a result of my own actions:		
Which are a result of things outside my control:		

'Vocationally oriented therapy'

Managing to solve a real-life problem is obviously something that will give a person a boost – especially if this has come about largely as a result of his or her own efforts. Surveys show that offenders report a wide range of real-life difficulties of both a practical and personal nature: to do with work, accommodation, and money; family, marital, or other interpersonal predicaments; securing rights and dealing in general with the official world; drink, ill-health, physical appearance, the stigma of a criminal record, emotional instability, and many more (Holborn, 1975; Priestley et al., 1984). Whether helping offenders with problems like these will also help them to stay out of trouble is, as we saw in chapter one, not yet clear. While a few pieces of work have reported good results in this respect, the majority have reported the opposite. It seems likely that a conjoint attempt to offer offenders help with their problems *and* alter their offence behaviour promises the best chance of success.

It can however be clearly demonstrated that some kinds of practically-oriented work can increase offenders' self-esteem, and reduce their aggressiveness. Shore and his associates (Shore, Massimo, and Mack, 1965; Shore, Massimo, and Ricks, 1965) undertook a programme of 'vocationally oriented therapy' with groups of boys aged between fifteen and seventeen who had dropped out of school as a result of learning difficulties or anti-social behaviour. The main emphasis of this programme was not on psychotherapy as such, but on employment counselling, remedial education, the development of job search skills, and solving problems encountered at work. The programme was spread out in sessions, timetabled in a very flexible way, over a ten-month period; the boys were compared with a control group who did not take part in the programme, and the entire sample was monitored initially over the ten months in terms of both psychological test performance and overt behaviour. Differences between the 'experimental' and 'untreated' groups were significant; and, of particular conce here, the trainee group showed improvement in both self-image and observed behaviour as rated by two independent judges. Best of all, these benefits appeared to be very durable: substantial differences between the two groups in employment history and numbers of arrests were still in evidence at the time of a long-term follow up carried out *fifteen years* after the commencement of the research (Shore and Massimo, 1979).

Given current economic conditions, of course, jobs and reasonable incomes are liable to remain elusive if not completely unattainable objectives for most offenders. The provision of any programme geared towards job search may seem like a total irrelevance to many people. Allowing this, it may nevertheless be that a series of sessions angled at other sorts of problems, and encompassing some work on self-image and some on offending, could still be worthwhile and might have positive pay-offs in terms of all three areas.

Self-esteem and social behaviour

The final possibility for altering self-esteem which we would like to explore in this chapter is that of improving people's ability to interact with others – what is known as *social skills training*. As we shall see in the next chapter this training can be shown to have a direct effect on offending behaviour; for the moment however our interest is confined to its possible impact on an individual's self-confidence and self-esteem.

Street interviews

Most forms and applications of social skills training rely for their effectiveness on a battery of specific techniques and on the component of repetition or practice which is essential for the acquisition of any skill. One exercise which can, by contrast, be very immediate in its effects is the conducting of video-recorded street interviews with members of the public. Most of us are familiar with the kind of *vox populi* spot interview which forms part of many current affairs and other 'topical' programmes on television. Given access to a portable video-tape machine, this can be the basis of a very entertaining and productive exercise should you happen to be working with a group.

The mechanics of such an exercise are fairly simple. Group members first of all choose a topic on which they would like to survey public opinion; attitudes to offenders say, or some controversial local issue, or an item from the news. They then compile, through discussion, a list of possible questions to ask; these can be written up on a board or flip-chart initially and later transferred to a clip-board for easy use in the street. The group then goes into a nearby street or public park which will be busy enough to supply a reasonably steady stream of interviewees. To keep unwanted traffic and other noise to a minimum, a hand-held extension microphone will prove indispensable. Group members can take turns to operate the camera – which should if possible be set up on a tripod – and to ask questions of the local citizenry. As many as possible should be encouraged to try the latter role, for this is the one which involves the 'social skill' element of interacting with other people. Most people become quite excited by the idea of appearing on the street with a television camera; and in this way the exercise can be a valuable one for bringing shyer or less confident group members out of themselves. It is in this respect that the benefits to self-esteem can be seen. When a number of interviews have been recorded, the group returns to base to play back the products of its work. The experience of seeing themselves talk to, and ask questions of, complete strangers can be a very exhilarating and ego-boosting one for many people.

Helping skills

One of the principal areas in which social skills and allied methods have been applied is in the training of interviewers, counsellors, para-medical staff, teachers, and other groups whose job it is to work with people and help them with some of their problems (Brown, 1975; Ivey and Authier, 1978; Priestley and McGuire, 1983). Trainees for these occupations are asked to roleplay situations in which they are working with other people; their behaviour is video-recorded, analysed and assessed; the pros and cons of different strategies for helping people are discussed; and individuals practise, with the aid of roleplay and video-recording, the various constituents of helping skill such as expressing support, asking questions or giving advice. There is no reason why exercises such as these should be the exclusive preserve of trainees for the 'professional' helping role. For the first person most people turn to when they need help is a close friend or relative.

Some skills training in the area of helping skills could be advantageous for many individuals who will never undertake such an activity in a paid capacity. But just as important as this, the process of helping others can be a very positive one for would-be helpers themselves. Again therefore, if you are working with a small group and have a video machine available, a few sessions devoted to the business of how to help others will be very worthwhile and may have favourable effects on the self-image of group members with low opinions of themselves. The exercises undertaken need not be of a very elaborate order; just looking at how to respond to friends in need; what are good things to say and what is best not said; which kinds of advice might be most appropriate for different kinds of problem – these and similar kinds of question could be considered in turn. The value of training some groups of offenders to work with their less able peers has been amply demonstrated in some work reported by Vriend (1969).

Social training in general

For the most part, social skills training is designed to help people improve their interactive skills – their competence in dealing with others. Its principal focus therefore is on behaviour, on the things people say and do, and training is usually evaluated in relation to changes in overt behaviour. Some pieces of research have nevertheless shown that improvements in social skills amongst offenders are accompanied by changes in self-perceptions and self-esteem. Research results in this vein have been reported by Crawford and Allen (1979), by Gordon and Williams (1977), and by Spence and Spence (1980) amongst others. The means by which these changes were accomplished were through exercises such as role-play, modelling, and other techniques of social training, which have been developed to assist those who lack social skills of one sort or another. It is to this kind of training and its bearing on offence behaviour that we now turn.

5 Training in social skills

The criminological literature is long on description (e.g. the criminal statistics, portraits of the 'typical' offender), and full of analysis (e.g. theories about crime, polemics on how to define it), but it tends to fall short on practical suggestions as to what the worker in the delinquency field can do about the phenomena it has captured in its many abstracts and elaborate hypotheses.

One of the starting-points for the materials in this book in general, and in this chapter in particular, is a recognition that

offending behaviour = human behaviour = social behaviour

It is true that some forms of offending behaviour appear to be almost entirely self-generating, i.e. arising from within the offender's own thought processes and virtually without reference to others, but a great many offences take place in a clearly social context. They are, in other words, the product of *interaction* between two or more people; between co-offenders or between offenders and their victims.

The direction any interaction takes depends on a very large number of variables: such as the relationship between the people involved, their ages, cultural origins, family backgrounds, social class, personal motives, feelings, attitudes and many more. But a factor which has received increasing attention in recent years is the idea that, when two individuals meet, the course their interaction takes is influenced in part by what are now customarily called their *social skills:* the appropriateness and effectiveness of their behaviour in relation to one another. The reason for the growth of interest in this particular point is the proposal that some forms of problematic behaviour may be explicable in terms of a *lack* or *breakdown* of social skills amongst those who exhibit them; and further, that the problem behaviour might be rectified were the individuals given help to bring their social skills onto an equal footing with others.

The possibility that these proposals might be applicable to offending behaviour, and might thereby yield a strategy for use by those working with it, is the organizing theme of this chapter. The aims of the chapter are to outline 'social skills' methods and review some of the uses to which they have been put with offenders; and to present some applications of these methods to two areas of offending behaviour – joint offences of any kind and how to avoid becoming involved in them; and violent encounters with others.

The nature of social skills training

One of the reasons why some people find the idea of a 'social skill' initially difficult to grasp is the fact that in ordinary, everyday social intercourse, these skills are almost invisible. They are so built into our expectations about communicating with one another that they form part of the 'taken-for-granted' backdrop against which other, more important aspects of our interpersonal lives are acted out. We go about our daily business – talking, listening, looking and smiling at each other, gesticulating, using facial expressions, summoning all our past experience and awareness of our own culture to put messages across to our peers – yet we seldom consider what a well-co-ordinated, finely-tuned performance this all is. Only in certain circumstances does the nature and importance of interactive skill become evident. When someone fails to look us in the face, or says something in a tone of voice that is not matched with the accompanying words, we feel that something has gone substantially wrong. The most exaggerated version of this occurs in some kinds of psychiatric illness, in which a patient's social behaviour may become markedly non-conforming, to the extent that he or she appears almost cut off from the shared world of others. It was in this sphere, in fact, that the possibility of social *training* was first opened up; the idea that there might be a way of helping individuals to improve their relationships with others through exercises explicitly designed to develop interactive skill.

In this respect, those workers who imagined that such training would be possible and might have beneficial effects were guided by a specific approach to human development known as 'social learning theory' (Bandura, 1977). This is a variant form of behaviourism which, though drawing on some 'learning theory' principles, ascribes much more importance than does classical behaviourism to 'mental' or 'cognitive' processes. According to this approach, social development is best understood in terms of 'observational' learning. The cerebral capacity of our species means that unlike many other animals, we do not have to experience rewards and punishments directly in order to learn; we can note how others fare in a situation and copy their behaviour, or not, as desired. This is more or less what happens as children grow up; they learn, they become human beings and members of their parents' society by watching what goes on around them and then trying it out for themselves.

Of course, the precise details of how all this happens are as yet unclear; but one or two points are of special note in the present context. One is that the preceding sketch related to 'normal' development, and in an imperfect world a number of things are likely to go wrong with this process. For example, individuals may never have the opportunity to learn certain things; their social behaviour later in life may then show a 'deficit' of certain kinds of skill. Or again, individuals may be exposed to behaviour which is itself wounding, or maladaptive, or out of adjustment with the norm in some way; as adults they may then be likely to manifest these kinds of behaviour themselves. The roots of many kinds of psychiatric disturbance, as well as some of the types of 'deviant' behaviour we call 'crime', have been attributed to faulty learning processes such as these.

An even more crucial point of relevance for present purposes, however, is the contention of this school of thought that these kinds of damage can be repaired. By giving people training – 'social skills training' – they can overcome the disadvantages which their experience has visited upon them, much as someone who did not learn to read and write at school can go to remedial literacy classes and eventually catch up with others. The solution will not, in the main, be as straightforward as this; for here we are dealing with patterns of behaviour which may have afflicted individuals' lives, not to mention the lives of others, to a considerable extent and over a long period of time.

The principle, however, is the same; and in fact a useful comparison can be made between training designed to enhance social skills, and the time-honoured procedures individuals go through when they want to learn mechanical or 'motor' skills (Argyle, 1969). If we want to learn how to operate a piece of industrial machinery, for example, an instructor first tells us what to do; then demonstrates the machine for us; asks us to try it ourselves; and gives us some comments on how well we are doing as we go along.

Translated into the domain of interaction training, this means that it consists basically of the following four elements:

- *Instructions* – individuals are given a basic understanding of a social encounter, and if necessary some suggestions of things to say or do that will help them cope with it satisfactorily

- *Modelling* – the social skill equivalent of demonstration; if instructions are not enough, someone *shows* the individual what he or she would do in the encounter, i.e. supplies a concrete example of behaviour that can be copied.

- *Role-play practice* – individuals then try this out for themselves in artificially set-up scenes (role-plays) in which they can try the new behaviour without fear of real-life 'disaster' if they get things wrong

- *Feedback* – by listening to the advice of others, viewing themselves on video, or preferably both, individuals try to make gradual improvements in how they handle an encounter, practising as much as necessary.

Whereas in motor skills training the 'target behaviours' (the things people are trying to learn to do) might be operating a lathe or a press, driving a car or a bulldozer, using a loom or flying an aeroplane, in social skills training the list might include such items as:

holding conversations	job interviews	asking for dates
asking favours	asking for days off	cooling down arguments
meeting strangers	going to parties	refusing requests
giving condolences	DHSS interviews	appearances in court
conveying anger	giving compliments	showing sympathy
using the telephone	asserting oneself	resisting sales pressure

This list could be extended more or less indefinitely.

The overall point of this training, however, is not to produce a socialized 'automaton' equipped with set-piece conversational gambits for absolutely predictable situations. *Skilled* social behaviour is behaviour chosen to suit its purpose, which takes as many aspects of the situation as possible into account, and which above all is directed towards goals or the solution of problems of concern to individuals themselves.

Research on social skills training

On the basis of the foregoing account, social skills training certainly sounds as if it ought to be useful to offenders in many ways. By their actions, offenders have placed themselves at odds with society as a whole. Moreover, individual offenders, especially at the younger end of the age range, often present a pattern of social awkwardness, ineptness, or sheer inadequacy. Most important of all, large numbers of them commit their offences very much under the influence of others; a process which social skills training might be able to help them resist. Whether or not such training actually is useful for offender groups is however an empirical question; we turn now to look at some of the evidence that has been gathered on this point.

There is considerable evidence, first of all, to support the view that this training can be an effective means of helping people to get better at dealing with others. This has come from many sources and from work with very different kinds of people and problems. Not unnaturally, given its origins, skills training has been applied most extensively in the field of psychiatry, and has been shown to be valuable for helping patients of most types, from schizophrenics (Hersen, 1979; Gutride, Goldstein, and Hunter, 1973) to sufferers from a variety of neuroses or from 'social phobia' (Falloon, Lindley, McDonald and Marks, 1977; Ost, Jerremalm, and Johansson, 1981) and to the mentally handicapped (Stephan, Stephano, and Talkington, 1973; Wehman and Schleien, 1980). But social interaction difficulties are not confined within mental hospital walls; many 'normal' individuals too can find the interpersonal world an uncomfortable place to be. Social skills training has also been used to help socially isolated children get better at holding conversations and at making friends (Oden and Asher, 1977; Whitehill, Hersen, and Bellack, 1980); to assist shy males in interactions with women, and help members of both sexes overcome dating anxiety (Curran, 1975; Twentyman and McFall, 1975); and to enable women become more assertive – not only in their dealings with men but in the wider sense of standing up for their rights (Linehan and Egan, 1979). Finally, modified forms of social skills training have also proved effective for helping individuals acquire or improve skills they will need for working with others – for example as managers and supervisors (Rackman and Morgan, 1977), as nurses (Goldstein and Goedhart, 1973), as teachers (Brown, 1975), or as counsellors in various capacities (Ivey and Authier, 1978).

The social skills of offenders

As far as offenders are concerned, a first question that might be asked is whether they do in reality experience the kinds of problems or manifest the kinds of social-skill impairments which this training is designed to redress. The public image of the suave professional confidence trickster, which emerges from the pages of the tabloid press, certainly suggests someone who is a candidate for anything but social skills training. And some career offenders in their twenties or thirties, thoroughly acquainted with the criminal justice system, can be very impressive socially. But they are not very typical of the offender population as a whole; and the available evidence suggests that, at least in their teens when they probably embarked on their criminal lifestyles, they are unlikely to have been so socially competent (Spence, 1979).

No absolutely convincing generalizations can be made about the social skills of offender groups, but existing research does indicate that problems in this area are probably not uncommon. Freedman and her associates (1978) developed an *Adolescent Problems Inventory* with which to assess the social and decision-making skills of juvenile offenders. This instrument consists of 44 items, each of which is a description of a situation that might pose a problem for someone, such as 'Your mother forbids you to see a friend again'. Responses are classified according to the degree of competence shown (making use of a system of pre-arranged categories validated on the basis of research). When comparisons were made between boys in delinquent and non-delinquent groups on their responses to this inventory, it was found that the latter (dubbed as 'good citizens') were significantly more socially competent. This result was obtained again in a second comparison, between 40 boys in a correctional institution and 40 from a local high school, carefully matched in age, IQ, and background. In addition, it was discovered that when two groups of delinquent boys (from the same institution) – who showed different degress of 'disruptive behaviour' and had spent different amounts of time within the institution's secure unit – were compared, the less disruptive boys also apeared to be more socially competent than the members of the 'acting out' group. These findings led the researchers to suggest that lack of social skill was a factor which increased the risk that a young person might get into trouble.

A similar pattern emerged from work carried out by Spence (1981) with a group of young male offenders in a Community Home School in Britain. Spence asked a number of judges, working independently, to rate the social skills performance and the employability of 18 adolescent offenders, and compared these with ratings made by the same judges of a group of boys with no history of offending. She found that the quent group were rated as significantly less socially skilled and as significantly less oyable; on another scale, however, – for friendliness – there were no differences en the groups in the ratings they received.

Using a different approach, Priestley and others (1984) asked 250 prisoners from three British prisons to list what they thought would be the principal problems they would face following their release. More than a third (37.2%) of these adult male offenders cited 'people' or 'dealing with others' as a major problem, and many of the other difficulties they mentioned – such as family or marital problems, interacting with police, or negotiating with other officials – clearly contained a social-skill element within them. While no comparison group of non-offenders was available to act as a criterion, the self-reports of these men undoubtedly imply that greater social confidence or competence would help them gain greater satisfaction from their lives.

Indications that a lack of social skill or a tendency to react inappropriately in some circumstances can lead offenders into trouble comes from a study by Piliavin and Briar (1964) of the behaviour of juveniles in encounters with the police. These authors interviewed a number of juvenile bureau officers in an American city about their attitudes to young offenders, and directly observed a number of interactions between the officers and youths. It was found that apart from previous offence record (i.e. whether the youth was actually known to the officer concerned), the single factor which had the greatest influence on whether or not an individual was arrested was his *demeanour*; his behaviour in the situation and his apparent attitude towards the police. Youths judged by the authors as co-operative with police officers were very much less likely to be arrested than those who appeared unco-operative. This factor was especially important for first offenders; bureau officers estimated that '. . . the demeanour of apprehended juveniles was a major determinant of their decisions for 50-60 per cent of the juvenile cases they processed' (Piliavin and Briar, *op. cit.*, 210). Apparent nonchalance, silence, fractiousness or failure to display respect were among the kinds of behaviour which made arrest more likely. Impolitic or inept handling of the attentions of the police may in some cases then be decisive in bringing about an adolescent's first extended transaction with the law and acquisition of a criminal record.

Evidence from other quarters adds further weight to the view that many offenders lack social skills of certain kinds or exhibit social behaviour which may be markedly different from the norm. It has been frequently observed by those who work with sex offenders (e.g. Burgess et al., 1980; Timms and Noyes, 1982) that the latter are very lacking in social confidence, are anxious in the presence of others, have poor social skills, and are particularly at a loss when interacting with the opposite sex, which may contribute in part to their offence-proneness in this respect. Although the evidence is not absolutely consistent on this point, the bulk of it indicates that male sex offenders are very low in assertiveness (Marshall, Christie and Lanthier, 1977) and may be even less assertive than other groups of offenders (Williams, n.d.); have lower self-esteem and experience a greater degree of social anxiety than other offenders (Williams, n.d.); and are considerably handicapped with regard to the skills involved in interacting with women – what are known as heterosocial skills (Barlow, Abel, Blanchard, Bristow, and Young, 1977).

Working with another group of offenders – those sentenced to prison for crimes of personal violence – Kinzel (1970) found their social behaviour to be anomalous in another respect. When carrying on a conversation, most of us prefer to stand at a distance that is not too close to the person with whom we are talking. Social psychologists have dubbed this phenomenon 'personal space' and have found that its size varies according to the age, sex, and cultural origin of the participants (Argyle, 1975; Baxter, 1970). Kinzel studied the 'body-buffer zone' (another term for it) of two groups of offenders; those with previous histories of violence and those whose previous offence histories contained little or no personal violence. Measuring the size of this zone from eight different directions (front and back; both sides; and the four intermediate diagonals) by walking towards individuals until they instructed him to stop, Kinzel

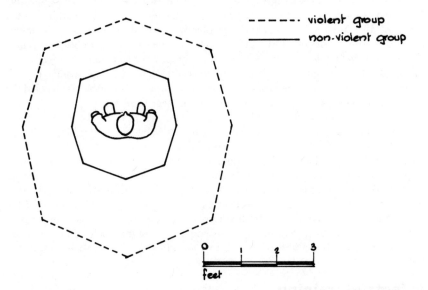

- - - - - - violent group
———————— non-violent group

0   1   2   3
feet

found that the violent offenders required a personal space that was on average 3.8 times the area found comfortable by the non-violent group, as illustrated in the figure above. The violent individuals, it was confirmed in interviews, tended '. . . to perceive nonthreatening intrusion as attack' (Kinzel, 1970, 102). They became extremely anxious when another person got too close; and for them this happened at distances which other individuals would have regarded as perfectly acceptable. But interestingly enough, as the procedure was repeated at weekly intervals over a period of twelve weeks, the violent offenders were able to become progressively more tolerant of others walking towards them.

Other investigations of the social skills of offenders suggest that they may in many cases be somewhat lacking in assertiveness, and tend to cope with conflict situations by resorting to aggression rather than dealing with them in a less destructive way (Keltner, Marshall, and Marshall, 1981; Kirchner, Kennedy, and Draguns, 1979). Kirchner and her colleagues compared the responses of a group of 32 prisoners (convicted of a variety of crimes) with those of a group of 29 non-offenders (participants in a vocational retraining programme, and similar in age, background, etc. to the offender group) on a series of self-report assertiveness scales and a number of role-play tasks. The scales were for individuals to say how they would react to a variety of interpersonal encounters; the role-play tasks invited their likely reactions to a series of prompts representing possible conflict situations (e.g. someone is accused of being slow and stupid at work; has to ask a friend to repay a loan; or has to resist sales pressure). The performances of all participants on the role-play prompts were videotaped and rated by a number of 'blind' observers (i.e. who did not know which individuals were offenders and which not).

Overall, the results showed that non-offenders tended to be more assertive and less aggressive in their dealings with others; while the offender group tended to be aggressive rather than assertive – many of them commenting afterwards that in a 'real' situation (outside the prison) they would have been likely to have been even more aggressive than their behaviour in the role-plays indicated. This finding clearly opens up the possibility that training in assertiveness might help some offenders cope with situations in a manner less likely to result in actual physical assaults or other aggressive behaviour. In a contrasting vein, Keltner and his associates (1981), working with a group of 48 prisoners in a Canadian penitentiary, found a trend towards under-assertiveness in a series of self-report and behavioural measures. Lack of assertiveness was more common than over-assertiveness or aggressiveness amongst the members of this group; though many exhibited both kinds of inappropriate behaviour at some stage. The fact that under-assertiveness was not associated with social anxiety led the authors to propose the use of skills training with prisoner groups.

Of course, what law-abiding adults call 'inappropriate', 'anti-social', or 'destructive' behaviour may not necessarily be perceived that way by those exhibiting it. To an adult, for example, verbal aggressiveness would be a relatively more approved form of behaviour than would a sudden, unexplained outburst of physical aggression. Lesser (1959) however found that amongst groups of lower-class ten- to thirteen-year-old boys, the reverse was the case, with verbal aggressiveness being seen as a relatively more unpopular trait than 'outburst' aggression. This finding serves to underline the importance, when using social-skills training or any other method of helping individuals to alter their behaviour, of tackling aspects of their behaviour which *they* think are problematic, otherwise the undertaking will almost certainly be destined to fail.

Effects of training

Offenders do, then – both on their own testimony and as appraised by others – seem to have gaps in their social skills or to act in an ineffective or inappropriate way in personal encounters, with outcomes that may be damaging to themselves as well as to others. Can social skills training help to improve their capacities in this area? The answer to this question is broadly 'yes', but can be given in more detail under a number of separate headings. First, there is some evidence that training can enhance the general social performance of individuals, and even at this level can increase their chances of staying out of trouble. Second, several other pieces of evidence show that training effects can be very specific, and can enable individuals to cope more satisfactorily with certain other groups of people – such as parents, policemen, or the opposite sex; or certain social situations – such as job interviews, social pressure, or potential conflicts. Finally, social skills training appears to have an impact not only on social *behaviour* as such, but also on people's attitudes and feelings about themselves and others.

General social skills

A wide range of skills for dealing with others are susceptible to training using social skills methods. They range from the most fundamental elements of social interaction, like the use of facial expressions or voice-tone and other aspects of 'non-verbal communications', to quite complex forms of social competence like the ability to negotiate with officials, perform well in job interviews, or resist social pressures. Some kinds of skill, like the ability to talk to others, to put your message across, or to co-ordinate different kinds of non-verbal 'signals' are common to all kinds of interaction and could be regarded as 'general' or 'basic' skills. Other kinds of training programmes

n a variety of settings that were
pproach have been used to good

of work in this area was carried
d Ganzer, 1973). Sarason used
k with juvenile delinquents in a
. Taking a series of scenes that he
ning sessions were run in which
role-played *first* an undesirable
situation. The same scenes were
Over a number of sessions, each
or situations were dealt with in
part in this work; a third of these
es of group discussions; and the
he other two cohorts could be
ity tests, self-ratings, behaviour
divism were used to measure the
image and social adjustment of

the 'modelling' and 'discussion'
group in terms of the way they
ey could exercise over their own
d the way they were allocated
favourableness of their 'case
al of three years (Sarason and
cussion' group members had re-
npared with anticipated rates of
tion and Diagnostic Centre in
e very striking and statistically
es were discernible between the
tter could remember the content
ch more able to cite instances in
oved useful in their lives. This is
bility to resist peer pressure to
ell us whether this situation was

carried out five years after the
m rate amongst members of the
f that amongst members of the
methods might best be used in
n just to rehabilitate established

An experiment similar to Sarason's was carried out by Scopetta (1972), again with institutionalized delinquent boys. This involved a kind of 'group modelling'; members of the institution's staff role-played problem situations encountered by the residents, who in turn role-played the same scenes. A significant decrease in anti-social behaviour was observed amongst these boys as compared with members of a group who had discussed the same issues; however no long-term follow-up was reported in this research. A point worth emphasizing however is that the people who ran the sessions here were paraprofessionals – residential workers who did not have to have a great deal of prior training.

It should be noted that both sets of results just described were obtained using just one of the methods of social skills training, that of modelling. When other kinds of exercise, such as instructions, behavioural rehearsal, the giving of feedback and the setting of social skills 'homework' assignments are used, the advantages of training appear more clear-cut. Ollendick and Hersen (1979) used just such a strategy with a group of adolescent offenders, comparing their subsequent behaviour with that of other groups, carefully matched, who took part in discussions or acted as 'controls'. Moreover, the offenders who took part in this work had on average four or five arrests behind them, whereas Sarason and Ganzer's groups had been first offenders. Using a similar batch of measures – psychological tests; self-ratings; ratings of recorded role-plays by external observers; and indices of actual day-to-day behaviour – Ollendick and Hersen found that the social skills group proved significantly better than either the discussion or control groups, which did not differ from each other on 'post-test'. Members of the training group were more socially skilled, less anxious, more in control of themselves and generally better adjusted following the training sessions. Unfortunately, no evidence as to the longer-term effects of this work has yet been made available.

A number of other pieces of work have been reported which demonstrate the value of training in general social skills for offender groups. Lindsay, Symons and Sweet (1979) worked with groups of psychiatrically disturbed adolescents amongst whom were numbered several young offenders. They ran a series of sessions which began with training in basic skills of verbal and non-verbal communication, and subsequently moved on to apply these skills in such areas as holding conversations, assertiveness, resisting group pressure, dealing with authority, job interviews, and interacting with the opposite sex. Evidence from written tests and interviews, from a self-report questionnaire, and from ratings made by independent observers attested to the value of the skills exercises for these adolescent groups. Also working with adolescents, Thelen, Fry, Dollinger and Paul (1979) used a modelling procedure similar to Sarason's, but with the 'model' role-plays recorded on videotape. Again beneficial results in terms of the social adjustment of the participants were evidenced in the short term. Unfortunately, perhaps because of the brevity of the sessions or the fairly limited scope of the training undertaken, these benefits were no longer visible at a 'post-test' phase two weeks later.

This kind of finding – that social skills training can have immediate results but that these do not necessarily persist over a longer period – has also emerged from the work of Spence and Marzillier (1979, 1981; Spence, 1980, 1983) with adolescent offenders in a Community Home School in Britain. Training which focused on the rudiments of social interaction – for example the use of eye contact; making appropriate head movements; or giving verbal feedback (i.e. simple acknowledgements which show you are listening to someone, such as 'mm', 'eh', etc.) – was found to alter the social behaviour of some of these adolescents in a way which could still be detected two weeks later. Spence and Marzillier tried similar exercises with other groups, and supplemented them with role-plays of more complex situations identified by the boys themselves. The training had an immediate impact, producing improvements which were maintained over an interval of three months. After a six-month period, however, the effects of the training were no longer discernible; and over the same period, the social skills group members were no less likely to get into trouble with the police than members of 'placebo' and 'control' groups. The conclusion may once again be that while the training is effective for those segments of behaviour actually dealt with in training sessions, other aspects of behaviour, and particularly those to do with offending as such, will not be influenced unless they are dealt with directly.

Specific skills

Evidence in support of this view comes from a number of research studies with offenders in which specific social skills have been tackled; some of them with aspects of behaviour very closely related to the committing of offences itself. They include:

1. Conversation skills

The ability to hold an ordinary conversation, and to communicate on a simple, everyday level with another person is perhaps one of the most fundamental, and certainly one of the most valuable skills anyone can possess. Yet some individuals cannot cope even with this relatively uncomplicated form of social interaction. Two separate pieces of work with delinquent girls, however, show that it is possible to train individuals in the components of conversation skill. Maloney et al. (1976) and Minkin et al. (1976) worked with small groups of adolescent girl offenders whose abilities in this area were noticeably lacking. Using a combination of instructions on some of the main features of conversation (e.g., asking questions, or giving feedback), with modelled demonstrations, followed by practice in which the girls were able to see their own performances recorded on video, it was shown that the girls could dramatically improve their ability to talk to others. This conclusion was drawn on the basis of changes in various measurable aspects of conversation skill, together with sets of ratings made by 'blind' observers who did not know any of the girls. In fact, following training, the girls' conversational skills were rated as better than those of a comparison group of girls from the local junior high school (Minkin et al., 1976).

2. Job interview skills

Methods similar to the above have also been used to help offenders manage better in specific kinds of conversations – job interviews for example. Spence (1981) noted with at least one group of adolescent offenders that they were rated as less employable by interviewers than a group of boys with no criminal convictions. Braukmann et al. (1974) ran three brief experiments in which delinquent boys were given training (instructions, modelling, feedback, etc.) in posture, eye contact, and other elements of interview skills. In all cases, the boys showed considerable improvement as, notably, they did also in one experiment in which 'naïve' trainers – individuals themselves given only brief instructions as to how to apply the training methods – were used.

3. Talking to the opposite sex

Another kind of conversation which is a source of anxiety for many people, but especially so for those convicted of sex offences, is one in which members of the opposite sex are taking part. Many of the pieces of work already considered included coverage of this kind of interaction within more broad-based training programmes; a number of projects have however concentrated attention on meetings with the opposite sex or have been aimed at offenders for whom this is an area of special difficulty. Most of the work in this field has also been with adult offenders or psychiatric patients. By and large it has followed the instruction–modelling–role-play–feedback sequence, usually conducted over a series of sessions spread out over a number of weeks. For example, Crawford and Allen (1979) used such a programme in 16 sessions over a three-month period with groups of male patients at Broadmoor hospital. Beginning with relaxation exercises, they moved in turn from elements of non-verbal communication (facial expression, smiling, eye contact, posture and gesture), to vocal skills, to conversational skills, to role-plays of slightly more complex everyday scenes, paying particular attention to interactions with members of the opposite sex. Both in their own views and in those of others, the patients' skills improved substantially over the training period. Part of the evaluation on which this result is based consisted of ratings made by observers of the individuals' behaviour when role-playing a party situation with a female stooge. Similar findings, though documented in less detail, were obtained by Burgess and others (1980) and by Gordon and Williams (1977), working with sex offenders in a British prison and in a Canadian prison respectively. Again, in the work done with these male offenders, interaction with a female was a focus of the social skills sessions which were run.

4. Family interactions and conflict with parents

Much has been written about relationships between young people and 'authority figures', and dealings between the two have long been considered a sensitive and conflict-ridden area in which, according to some theories at least, the roots of juvenile delinquency may lie. Social skills training has also been applied to aspects of this relationship: looking, for example, at interactions between young offenders and their parents. There seems little doubt that arguments at home can be a contributory factor towards the commission of some acts of delinquency. Kifer et al. (1974), extrapolating from this assumption, set about training pairs of adolescents and parents (mother-daughter or father-son) to negotiate their way through a series of simulated conflicts. The situations chosen were all however ones which had sparked off real disagreements between the parent-child pairs involved; whether to spend money on clothes or a bike, for example, or whether to take up a part-time job. In an initial session the duo role-played the scene as they imagined it might happen at home. In ensuing sessions, they were given training in *negotiation* skills (e.g. identifying a point of conflict; stating a number of options; communicating an argument clearly) and put these into practice in further role-plays which included some instances of *role-reversal* between adult and child. Finally the conflict was role-played again as in the first session. Videotapes of all the sessions were analysed for the frequency of various kinds of negotiation skill. The results showed that instances of negotiated agreement between the two adversaries became much more common as the training progressed. Follow-up of the parent-child pairs at home revealed a substantial increase in the use of negotiation to solve conflicts (with actual conflicts which emerged) and a higher rate of agreement than the partners to the conflict had experienced before.

Another 'experiment' in the same field is interesting in that it yielded as one of its outcomes a reduced rate of recidivism amongst the offenders taking part. Parsons and Alexander (1973) examined patterns of interaction amongst families of delinquents, and identified a number of areas in which they thought communication between family members was 'maladaptive'. On the basis of what they had learnt they devised a training programme, consisting of discussion, instruction, modelling, and reinforcement, with the aim of making communication more rewarding and effective between family members, and addressed particularly to areas of conflict which appeared to have precipitated delinquent acts. Forty-six families given this kind of training were subsequently compared in their communication patterns and in the recidivism of their delinquent members (after a six- to eighteen-month follow-up) with other groups of families using client-centred therapy or psychodynamic therapy, or given no 'treatment' at all. The recidivism rate amongst 'training' family members was significantly less than for the other groups, and was *half* the rate then prevailing in the county where the work took place.

A yet more remarkable finding of this research, however, concerned the effects of the training on the *brothers and sisters* of the young offenders who had taken part in the training sessions. The researchers' interests were not confined to the subsequent behaviour of the participants; their wider aim was to examine the possible impact of the exercise on the family as a whole. To measure this, Klein, Alexander, and Parsons (1977) assessed delinquency rates amongst the siblings of those who had been involved in the sessions. The families were followed up for periods totalling between two-and-a-half and three-and-a-half years. The recidivism rate amongst the original 'target' group of children remained at a level significantly below that of the controls, and was still considerably superior to the rate amongst the other 'treatment' groups. Moreover, rates of re-offending amongst their siblings were also significantly reduced, again being half that observed in the control group (20% as against 40%) and much lower than that obtained in the other comparison groups (59% to 63%).

5. Encounters with the police

A second kind of 'authority figure' with whom offenders have to contend, but who unlike most parents may hold a menacing significance for them lasting well beyond their teens, is the police officer. We have already seen how the end-products of interactions between juveniles and the police may be crucially different depending on the conduct of a youth at the moment of confrontation itself. Werner and his colleagues (1975) undertook some research with the aim of identifying the key factors at work in this type of situation; and on the basis of what they discovered, used social skills training to prepare a number of young offenders for face-to-face interactions with police. From a range of attributes of behaviour nominated by police officers and by juveniles as likely to influence whether someone was arrested or not, Werner et al. selected 'facial orientation', 'politeness in short answers', 'expression of reform', and 'expression of understanding and co-operation' as aspects that could be trained using social skills methods. A number of youths took part in a series of role-plays designed to develop these aspects of skill. Their behaviour in a 'post-test' phase, as appraised by objective measures (i.e. frequency counts of various features of their performance), and as judged 'blind' by police officers and by a number of independent observers, showed that they were much better prepared for this kind of situation than they had been beforehand, and were much less likely to be apprehended as a result. The before-and-after difference in their behaviour was especially marked as compared with that of the members of a 'control' group not given any training. An individual's reactions in this critical encounter, then, may also be altered in a way that could influence his or her chances of committing subsequent offences.

6. 'Perspective taking'

To many people, there is an unquestioned, taken-for-granted link between crime, or other forms of anti-social behaviour, and selfishness or self-centredness amongst those who are its authors. While few attempts have been made to test this proposition empirically (as compared with the considerable efforts expended in the search for other personality differences between offenders and non-offenders), one experiment carried out by Chandler (1973) is of interest in that not only were differences in egocentrism between delinquents and non-delinquents obtained, but they were also shown to be modifiable using social skills training. Chandler first of all compared two groups of 11-to-13-year-old boys, one of 'chronic' delinquents and the other of non-delinquents, on a specially prepared test designed to measure their ability to see situations from a point of view other than their own. There were measurable differences between the two groups on this criterion, delinquents being significantly more 'egocentric' than their non-offender peers. Next, the offender group was split into three; one sub-group was given a set of training exercises in 'perspective-taking' skills; another (the 'placebo' group) was involved in making films; and a third acted as a 'control' group. The skills training comprised a number of sessions in which the young offenders role-played a series of incidents that might happen to people their own age; each was run several times so that all the participants got to play each part in turn; and every scene was recorded and played back using video. The 'placebo' group made films about people other than their own age, spent the same amount of time on the project, and had no opportunity for video feedback on themselves. Chandler found that, following the training, the role-playing group members were significantly *less* egocentric than members of the other two groups (there had been no differences at the outset). But he also found that, after an 18-month follow-up period, the training group members were significantly less likely to re-offend than members of the other two groups. Members of the training group also committed significantly fewer offences during this period than they had in the 18 months prior to training – a fact which was not true of the other groups. Although as Chandler points out these results do not demonstrate that ego-centrism is the *cause* of anti-social behaviour, they certainly indicate the potential of exploring the 'perspective-taking' dimension through role-play in social skills training groups.

7. Resisting pressure to drink

Although hardly an offence in itself, drinking is certainly a facilitating factor in the commission of many offences. Apart, obviously, from drunken driving and large numbers of other motoring offences, evidence shows that not a few thefts, burglaries, and acts of violence are committed when their instigators are under the influence of alcohol. For some offenders who become dependent on alcohol, a pattern of breaking the law while drunk becomes an integral part of their way of life. Any form of assistance which helps an individual control his or her drinking might also therefore help him or her to avoid breaking the law. Social skills methods may have something to offer here in that they can be used to help people assert themselves in contexts in which they are under pressure to drink. Foy and others (1976) used instructions, modelling, role-play and feedback to train two alcoholics – one with a 15 year and the other with a 25 year history of dependence on alcohol – to refuse offers of drink or requests to drink. Post-training evaluation showed that the individuals had improved their ability to cope with this kind of pressure. One of the trainees was still successfully abstaining from drink after a three-month follow-up; the other had relapsed. Though not conclusive, this study shows that with concerted effort skills training might be valuable for helping those who would like to overcome drinking problems which are an ingredient of their offence behaviour in general.

8. Aggression and violence

The application of skills training techniques to offending behaviour can be made absolutely directly in another area: that of anger, aggression and violence. With the exception of a few cases of extreme psychiatric disturbance, when individuals act completely randomly and spontaneously, most violent crimes are a result of some interpersonal encounter in which aggression has gradually built up between two or more people. Some of this violence may be very much a product of uncontrolled feelings or irrational beliefs harboured by one person; while for other individuals violence could be said to be the continuation of conversation by other means. In chapter six we will examine an approach to the reduction of violent feelings and behaviour through the acquisition of strategies of self-control; in social skills training, a violent act is dealt with by helping an individual to discover *alternative ways to behave* which will enable him or her to deal with a situation without resorting to physical violence or a torrent of verbal abuse.

This tactic for helping to defuse violent situations is known as *assertiveness training*; a form of social skills training normally associated with the attempt to help shy and diffident people become more outgoing, or more able to stand up for themselves if taken advantage of by more self-assured and perhaps manipulative individuals. But it can also be used to help people cope with a potentially violent situation without becoming aggressive *and* without any loss of face. Several cases of successful anger management have been reported which hinged on the use of assertiveness training. Foy, Eisler and Pinkston (1975) worked with a man whose second wife had left him following a series of beatings, who had assaulted his foreman at work, and who was subject to what the authors called 'explosive rages'. Seven scenes which provoked him considerably were pinpointed, and a series of assertive rather than aggressive responses which he could make in these situations were modelled. He then tried these out for himself. Monitoring of his behaviour over the training sessions showed that he gradually managed to use more of the assertive methods of response; on a six-month follow-up, he still succeeded in approaching the situations non-agressively – and further to the point had improved his relationships at work and at home. Rahaim, Lefebvre and Jenkins (1980) worked with a police officer who experienced uncontrollable aggressive outbursts, and who had broken the arm of a man he apprehended for reckless driving. Again, training in the use of assertive replies to a number of flashpoint situations gradually helped him to overcome his agressiveness, though we cannot be certain how durable this result was since no follow-up was undertaken. Frederiksen and others (1976) used instructions, modelling, behaviour rehearsal and feedback to train two psychiatric patients who were both prone to 'abusive verbal outbursts'; and found the training to be effective in that it generalized to the patients' behaviour in situations other than those used in role-plays, and to aspects of their behaviour not incorporated in the training programme. A longer-term follow-up of these and other patients with similar problems was reported by Frederiksen and Rainwater (1981), who had used a mixed package of assertiveness training, 'cognitive restructuring' (learning to see a situation from different viewpoints), relaxation training, and training in controlled drinking (both of which will be described in chapter six). Although there was a 50 per cent drop-out during the training, follow-up of those who stayed on proved very positive (over periods varying from six months to two years). None had been re-hospitalized; all had improved their social skills and had fewer conflicts with their families; and for most there were significant decreases in the frequency and severity of 'explosive' behaviour. Finally, Rimm and others (1974) worked with a group of men who expressed anger in an inappropriate and anti-social way (one was on probation for breaking 3,000 dollars-worth of windows). These men were allocated either to an assertiveness training group or to an 'attention placebo' group which was in essence a discussion group about individuals' feelings of anger. Both in terms of 'objective' ratings and self-report, the training group emerged as significantly more assertive, less anxious, more confident, more comfortable in social situations, and less liable to feelings of anger.

Using a slightly different approach, Goldstein and his colleagues (Goldstein et al., 1978; Goldstein, 1981) have worked with aggressive children and adolescents employing a variant form of social skills training known as *Structured Learning Therapy* (Goldstein et al., 1976). The aim of this work has been to help violence-prone individuals learn *pro-social* alternatives to their typical abusive or destructive reactions. The methods used revolve around the use of modelling tapes or ready-made examples of appropriate ways of handling different kinds of encounter, though extra effort is also expended in trying to ensure that the training 'transfers' to other, real-life interactions. Though much of this work is still in progress, early results indicate that it is possible to teach individuals '. . . negotiation, self-control, relaxation, responding to anger, and other skill alternatives' (Goldstein et al., 1978, 75-6) as well as assertiveness and perspective-taking, with which they can replace their conventional aggressive impulses.

9. Attitudes to self and others

One final area in which social skills training can be quite specific in its effects is on the attitudes, beliefs and feelings of individuals. Though normally conceived of as a tool for helping people to alter their behaviour, the things they actually *do*, training inevitably has side-effects in terms of what people feel and how they think, and the methods can be addressed directly to these areas themselves. Some research carried out in this vein may be relevant to work with offenders. Many of the projects that have already been cited affected (either as a main effect or as a by-product of their work) individuals' feelings of confidence, their attitudes to themselves and other people, their levels of anxiety, or sense of self-control (see for example the writings of Crawford and Allen, 1979; Gordon and Williams, 1977; Lindsay, Symons and Sweet, 1979; Ollendick and Hersen, 1979; Rahaim, Lefebvre, and Jenkins, 1980; Rimm, Hill, Brown and Stuart, 1974; Sarason and Ganzer, 1973). A few workers have also set out with the aim of influencing attitudes or self-perceptions through the use of role-play and related techniques. Culbertson (1957) for example tested the hypothesis that participation in role-play would bring about related changes in attitudes; specifically, she explored whether white Americans who expressed strong racial prejudice on an attitude scale would be affected by taking part in role-plays in which they had to argue *against* their usual point of view. The theme of the role-plays – conducted before the days of the Civil rights movement in the United States – was a discussion about integrated black-and-white housing, which the participants would by inclination have been against but had to be in favour of for the purposes of the enacted scene. On other measures used after the role-playing session, a significant shift in attitudes was found towards a less anti-black point of view. This shift was more marked for those who had participated in role-plays than for those who had acted as observers. In so far as vehemently held attitudes may influence some individuals' propensity to offend, this result may suggest a strategy for tackling jaundiced, irrational or self-damaging viewpoints.

Working with groups of young offenders, Spence and Spence (1980) found that social skills training also had an impact on self-esteem and sense of self-control. As we saw in chapter four, and as we will see in chapter six, many offenders have a very low opinion of themselves, and are rather fatalistic in their beliefs about the extent to which they can influence themselves and the world around them. Spence and Spence found that training increased individuals' 'internal' control, i.e. their belief that they themselves were responsible for what happened to them, and also boosted their self-esteem, though the results here were less clear-cut. Unfortunately, both these changes had been eroded at a six-month follow-up, possibly because the participants were during that interval resident in an institution. The results nevertheless indicate a potential role for skills training in helping individuals to adopt more positive attitudes towards themselves and a more active approach towards the solution of their own problems, one of which may be their offence behaviour.

Overall then, social skills methods appear to have something to offer the search for means of approaching criminal behaviour directly. They can affect the general social performance of offender groups; can help them cope better in a number of respects with different degrees of proximity to actual offending; and can influence attitudes in a similar way. Lest it be thought that these methods can only be used in the context of research, on which this review has necessarily concentrated, the remainder of this chapter presents exercises for direct use with offender groups. The methods have been used in a less formal manner with numbers of offenders, in intermediate treatment (Howe, 1979), in local prisons (Fawcett et al., 1979), in training prisons and in probation settings (Priestley et al., 1984), in women's prisons (Lowe and Stewart, 1983), and in high-security hospitals (Howells, 1976).

Social skills training methods

Three themes relevant to offenders and offending behaviour will be pursued in the account of social skills training methods that follows:

1. the assessment and development of general social competence
2. resisting pressure from other people to commit offences; and
3. applications to violent offences.

Assessing social skills deficits

Social skills training methods are not designed to be used 'across the board' with groups of offenders; they should be tailored to the specific difficulties and needs of particular individuals. Failure to comply with this simple precaution will lead, if not to disaster, then at least to problems that could have been avoided. The best place to begin therefore, with any programme of social skills training, is with some simple methods for assessing deficits.

A social skills checklist

The simplest way of starting to assess social skills deficits is to present someone with a checklist to which he or she responds by acknowledging each item as problematic or not. This can be done as a YES : NO response; or it can be *scaled* by providing various degrees of competence, as in the example on p. 96.

In this checklist, the items have been divided into three blocks: A, B and C. The first block is devoted to aspects of 'non-verbal communication'; the second to 'assertion'; and the third to 'pressure' in various forms. The items presented here are simply illustrative; there are innumerable social skills checklists in existence, and our advice would be to adapt one or other of these or to invent a brand new one of your own. The results in any case should be regarded as provisional, a starting point for further exploration by other means.

An exploratory interview

A checklist can be used privately by the individual concerned, or it can form the basis of an interview in which the items and the responses are given and received verbally. Or the written responses can be further explored by the interviewer, or the whole topic can be started from scratch. In the latter case, the person conducting the interview might begin by saying something like:

'I'd like you to think about some of the things you sometimes find difficult when you're with other people, or to do with what other people are doing. Things that maybe make you feel awkward or embarrassed or where you do something to make other

Social skills checklist

Here is a list of things that people have to do nearly every day when they meet other people. Which of them are you good at? and which of them are you not so good at? Look at each item in turn and decide how good you are at doing it; then put a tick in the space opposite which is nearest to how good or bad you think you are.

	I am good at this	I am not bad at this	I am not very good at this	I am bad at this
A				
1. Looking people in the face				
2. Being watched by lots of people				
3. Staring people out				
4. Smiling at people I fancy				
5. Keeping a straight face				
6. Not blushing when I am caught out				
7. Looking angry when I feel it				
8. Hiding my disappointment				
9. Knowing what other people are feeling				
10. Standing close to other people				
B				
1. Joining a group of people already talking				
2. Having to tell people who I am				
3. Going into a room full of people				
4. Being interviewed				
5. Starting a conversation with a stranger				
6. Giving people directions in the street				
7. Carrying messages				
8. Saying what I want to say				
9. Understanding what other people say				
10. Answering questions/asking questions				
C				
1. Having an argument				
2. Being told off				
3. Being ordered about				
4. Making a complaint				
5. Refusing to do something				
6. Apologizing, making excuses				
7. Giving someone bad news				
8. Praising someone				
9. Responding to praise				
10. Asking for help				

people feel like that when you don't mean to. Some of them might be quite simple, like getting on a bus that's quite full and asking for your destination in front of everyone; and some of them might be quite complicated, like having a serious disagreement with someone at home. Can you think of something very simple to start off with?'

The conversation that ensues should follow what the interviewee is saying as far as possible, but the interviewer may wish to keep in mind some broad categories like those used in the checklist; e.g. non-verbal skills, verbal encounters, and conflicts; plus some more specific topics such as problems at school or at work, friends, the opposite sex, family relationships, leisure, arguments; and to have handy some examples and illustrations with which to prompt the person being interviewed. At the end of the interview a summary – either spoken or written – should be offered to the person on the receiving end.

An open-ended questionnaire

For the more verbally able, an open-ended questionnaire is a useful way of eliciting areas of social skills deficits. It can be based on items such as:

---

1. What are some of the problems you will have to overcome in the next few years of your life? List as many as you can up to ten.
    1 ....
    2 ....
    3 ....
    4 ....
    5 ....
    6 ....
    7 ....
    8 ....
    9 ....
    10 ....

2. Now re-write the list you have just written so that the most difficult problem is at the top, and the least difficult at the bottom, and the rest are placed between them in a rough order of difficulty.

3. Is there anything about the way you act towards other people which you would like to change in any way; and if so, how?

4. Are there any situations involving other people that you try to avoid? What are they? Why do you try to avoid them?

5. Do you ever feel nervous about meeting someone or speaking to someone? If so, who – and why?

6. Are there any people you admire because of the way they get along with other people? What is it that makes them so successful?

These are, of course, suggestions; for use in your own work you should devise different and more appropriate items.

Situation tests

Verbal report is a useful way of gathering information about perceived levels of social skill, but it is no substitute for looking at actual behaviour in concrete situations.

'Situations', either presented verbally or written on individual cards, can be used both for self-report and for starting role-plays in which actual behaviour can be observed and assessed as in the examples shown on p. 98.

Role-played responses to situations like these (and others which you have invented) can be used in a number of ways to spot skill deficits.

Observation

Observation of role-play can be *more* or *less* structured; can focus on any of the many

YOU ARE ON A TRAIN COMING BACK FROM A CAMPING HOLIDAY. YOU ARE VERY TIRED AND TRY TO GET SOME SLEEP. SOMEONE IN THE SEATS OPPOSITE STARTS TO PLAY A TRANSISTOR RADIO VERY LOUDLY. WHAT DO YOU DO?

SOMEONE YOU KNOW QUITE WELL – BUT NOT YOUR BEST FRIEND – ASKS YOU TO LEND HIM / HER £5 TO PAY OFF A DEBT TO SOMEONE ELSE WHO IS BEGINNING TO GET A BIT NASTY. YOU WOULDN'T MIND HELPING BUT IT WOULD MEAN NOT GOING OUT YOURSELF THIS WEEKEND. WHAT WOULD YOU SAY?

YOUR GIRO HAS NOT ARRIVED FROM THE SOCIAL SECURITY FOR THE SECOND WEEK RUNNING. YOU GO INTO THE OFFICE TO COMPLAIN.

YOU HAVE TO GIVE A VOTE OF THANKS TO A VISITING SPEAKER AT YOUR CLUB.

A NEIGHBOUR COMES TO THE DOOR TO COMPLAIN ABOUT YOUR SON'S BAND PRACTICE BEING SO LOUD. HE IS VERY ANGRY AND SWEARS A LOT.

component parts of skilled interaction; and can be done by others or by oneself. At its most basic, observation consists of having one (the worker) or more persons (the group) watch a role-play and report afterwards their impression(s) of the subject's performance. WHAT did he/she do? HOW well was it done? What else could have been said or done? Provided these commentaries are honest and lacking in malice, they can provide valuable evidence about the skills of the person concerned, which can be used in turn to begin the business of improving them. More structure can be given to this whole process by devising and then using simple observational schedules which record the presence or absence of certain bits of behaviour; the frequencies with which they occur; and their degree of skilfulness in appropriate cases. An even more vivid way of providing feed-back on behaviour is to film it on videotape and replay it to the person involved. This has the added advantage of allowing him/her to observe and assess the behaviour in question. (See below p. 101.)

Changing behaviour: social skills methods
Resisting pressure to commit offences

The proposition that offending behaviour is *social* behaviour is nowhere more evident than amongst young offenders. Four out of five juveniles in a study conducted in Bristol

and Wiltshire committed their offences in the company of at least one other off
(Priestley, Fears, Fuller, 1977), and in a quarter of these cases the groups of offe
contained brothers or sisters. West and Farrington followed a birth cohort of L
offenders into adult life; of the offences they committed as juveniles 'five sixths oi u.,
burglaries (46 out 56), and three quarters of the thefts from shops (18 out of 24) were
recorded by the police as having been committed with (typically, two) others' (West
and Farrington, 1973). They also found that boys who reported delinquency amongst
their friends were highly likely to be delinquent themselves, a finding that duplicates
the experience of Sheldon and Eleanor Glueck in the United States, who reported that
90 per cent of their delinquents 'chummed' with other delinquents, compared with only
ten per cent of non-delinquents who did so (S. and E. Glueck, 1950).

It is not necessary to cast these groupings in the mould of delinquent gangs, nor think
of their members as belonging to delinquent subcultures (Downes, 1966), to
acknowledge their essential reality at the time the offences were committed. There is in
fact evidence as to the impermanence of such groups, at least so far as the commission of
offences is concerned:

Offenders in Sheffield: % committing offences

Age	solo	pairs	groups	no.
10-14	36.5	36.1	25.4	208
15-16	41.0	29.5	29.5	122
17-20	62.8	24.4	12.8	172
45+	91.0	9.0	0.0	67

(Baldwin, Bottoms, and Walker, 1976)

As offenders grow older, in other words, they commit fewer and fewer offences in the
company of others and become solo operators instead. These facts raise a number of
possibilities when working with younger offenders; the most important of them being
that groups often decide to do things which none of their members would set out to do
alone. Group decisions are demonstrably more 'risky' than individual ones. (See
chapter seven, p. 155.)

For some young offenders therefore, refraining from offence behaviour is both more
straightforward – avoid the company of *those* other young people – *and* more
problematic – those other young people constitute the social world; they are precisely
the friends and companions who provide a sense of identity and self-worth. To
renounce their company may be to pronounce a sentence of death on one's social
existence.

The answer then, is not so simple, but neither is it so impossible that it should not be
attempted at all. It is to help individual young persons to find both the inner resources
and the overt activities which will permit them to resist the headlong flight down the
slippery slope that can characterize decisions (by groups of contemporaries) to commit
offences. In the interrogative the issue becomes 'How can a young person stand out
against a group drift towards an offence *without* sacrificing the continuing esteem and
companionship of his/her peers?' 'With difficulty,' is the answer that springs most
readily to the lips of the realist. But the answer, if one is to be found, must come not from
the worker but from the young people themselves, and in terms that make sense to *them*.

The topic can be broached with further examples of SITUATION CARDS as shown
on p. 100, and they can be used to set up roleplays for *modelling* purposes.

Distribute cards like these, together with others of your own devising. Invite
participants to make initial statements about what *they* would do in these
circumstances, and then discuss more generally alternative ways of responding. The
more promising of these strategies may be role-played and recorded on video. Group

You are on the way home from the pub with two friends. As you pass an empty house with a 'FOR SALE' notice on the gate, one of your friends picks up a stone from the side of the road and suggests you have a competition to break a window each with only one shot. There are cars passing by and the houses each side are lived in and have lights on. You are half-way through a one year suspended sentence for criminal damage and might be sent down for a fresh offence. What would you do?

An old friend calls at your house late one night. He has some electric razors which have just 'fallen off the back of a lorry'. He asks you to look after them till tomorrow. You owe him a favour but if your father found the goods he would probably hand them over to the police. Do you agree to take them? How can you turn him down without losing his friendship?

Three mates have a grudge against someone else you know. He let one of them down in an incident you know nothing about. They have decided to attack him one night on his way home from a part-time job he does, to teach him a lesson. They ask you to keep watch at the end of the alley whilst they do him over. You have no quarrel with the person they plan to attack and wish to keep out of it, but are afraid they will think you are soft. What can you say?

It is late at night, after the last bus has gone, and you have a five-mile walk back home. It is raining cats and dogs. Your friend suggests taking a car to drive home in comfort, and dumping it at the side of the road. He says he has done it several times before and never been caught; and even if you don't want to join him he is going to do it; and even if you were caught you could always say that you thought it was your friend's car anyway; that he had offered you a lift and you accepted. What do you do?

members should also be encouraged to identify situations from their own experience in which pressure to commit offences either is, or is likely to be exerted. One or more of these can be re-created using the ACTION REPLAY format (p. 28) above.

Coaching

Watching someone else cope satisfactorily with a tricky situation is one thing; doing it for yourself is another. With people who have difficulty imitating models effectively, a different technique may be tried; that of 'coaching'. The idea of a 'coach' is easily understood as a way of acquiring or improving a sporting skill – the 'coach' watches the would-be world-champion in swimming or athletics or gymnastics and gives advice about technique based on long experience and expertise, and on the things an observer sees but to which the person performing an action is sometimes blind.

A social skills coach performs precisely the same function with respect to some aspect of social behaviour which the actor wishes to improve in some way: watching and appraising a performance, and making suggestions for improving it.

Identify a situation of pressure to commit an offence: e.g.

You meet two friends who are on their way to set fire to the school you all once went to. They have a can of petrol, some newspapers and a box of matches. You hated the school yourself, and especially some of the teachers who made your life there miserable. They begin to persuade you to go with them because you would all get your own back on the school, and the chances of being caught – it is a dark night, and there is no-one about – are quite small, they say. You would half like to join in, and they are very pressing in their invitation, but if you are caught doing any more offences your 'father' has threatened to 'knock your head off' – something you believe him capable of.

Reproduce the scene that ensues with an 'actor' who is not very resistant to two persuasive and persistent friends and who eventually 'gives in' and goes along to help burn down a place haunted by so many memories of humiliation. Stop the action at this point, and turn the clock back to the beginning of the encounter. Appoint two people to be 'coaches' to the actor who has just been persuaded to take part in the fire-bombing of the school. The coaches sit or stand on either side of the actor during the replayed incident, and as the action unfolds they whisper words of advice and make suggestions in his/her ear about how better to cope with the pressure to take part in the proposed incendiarism. The actor is free to accept or reject their help but should make every effort during the second performance to resist the pressure to join in. If needs be the coaches can call for the action to be suspended, particularly at critical junctures, so that they can take their student off for private tuition in a corner of the room prior to resuming the struggle. If the help and advice of the coaches is so good that the balance of the contest is tipped too strongly in favour of the resister, the case of the arsonists can be bolstered by supplying them in turn with their own coaches. The proceedings are apt to become hilarious, but none the less useful for providing the individual with insights, strategies and concrete actions that can be used in similar real-life occasions in the future.

Self-modelling

Having watched others perform actions thought difficult, and having performed them oneself with the aid of coaches, a further step in the preparation of the student is to record video scenes in which he or she acts as a 'self-model'. Self-modelling means performing in role-play the behaviour that the person wishes to reproduce outside the training context. Watching such a self-modelling tape can give an individual greater confidence to do whatever it is he/she wants to do.

Rehearsal and practice

Role-play has its critics on both sides of the footlights. Some of them claim that its artificiality militates against proper application in the real world. If role-play went no further than a single, slightly silly run-through of a situation, then there would be some merit in the accusation, but properly conducted role-play goes far beyond that simple beginnning. The key to skilful behaviour lies in rehearsal, repetition, and practice under conditions which are increasingly akin to those that prevail in reality.

The difficulties in the way of doing this at all effectively should not be underestimated; it demands persistence and patience over quite long periods – rather as it would if someone were in training to become a long-distance runner.

Video playback

Several references have been made to the uses of video in social skills training. A growing number of agencies and organizations have access to video equipment, but either do not know how best to use it, or have had disappointing results with it in the past. (One of the disappointments can be the frequency with which 'users' break into premises out of normal hours and abstract the equipment.) Our experience is that it is worth mastering the simple mechanics of the machine and moving on to use it in a flexible and continuous way with individuals and groups of offenders (McGuire et al., 1984).

One of the issues it is usually necessary to clear with offenders is their concern about leaving permanent likenesses on tapes which *might*, in their view, fall into the wrong hands, i.e. those of the police. Assurances can be given about this and if necessary tapes can be ritually wiped at the end of every session in which the video is used. Once past this obstacle, and the natural diffidence felt by some people about seeing themselves on the small screen, the most obvious use of video is to tape simple role-plays so that the

---

Video Rating Sheet
'Resisting pressure'   Name ....

● How confident did he/she   Very   Not at all
  seem to be   confident   confident

  |_____|_____|_____|_____|

● How effective was his/her   Very   Not at all
  use of   effective   effective

      -eye-contact |_____|_____|_____|_____|
      -posture |_____|_____|_____|_____|
      -gesture |_____|_____|_____|_____|
      -voice-tone? |_____|_____|_____|_____|

● How convincing were his/her statements?

      Very convincing   Not very convincing   Not at all convincing

● What else could he/she have said?

      _____

      _____

      _____

● What else could he/she have done? _____

      _____

      _____

● How would you rate his/her chances of getting out of this situation?
    10%   20%   30%   40%   50%   60%   70%   80%   90%   100%
Ring the figure nearest to your personal estimate.

participants can observe in replay – and depending on the sophistication of the hardware, in slow-motion too – how they actually *looked* and *sounded* during the episode in question. Simply seeing yourself on TV can be an education in itself; but in social skills training the magical effects of a single exposure to replayed role-play performance is not enough. Something more systematic by way of feed-back must be added to the untutored impressions of the participant. Structure of this sort can be provided in a guided commentary, given by a group leader, or elicited in discussion from group members. Or, in the direction of even greater precision, participants can be supplied with ready-made rating sheets on which to mark their judgments of particular performances. Rating sheets can range from the simple to the sophisticated; a simple version for looking at attempts to resist pressure to commit an offence might look like the sheet shown on p. 102.

Besides feedback, which is one of its most immediate uses, video can be used to store pre-recorded role-plays from many sources for use in social skills sessions. These can be specially reconstructed episodes of behaviour which you wish to discuss and do something with in a group; or they can be examples drawn from the recordings made by previous groups with which you have worked, and retained with their consent for future use.

An extension of this simple principle is to pre-record a sequence of alternative behaviours with which someone might respond to a situation he/she finds hard to handle. In the following extracts young offenders are modelling a skill some young men find difficult to master, that of purchasing contraceptives over the counter of the local chemist's shop (YM = Young man; SA = Shop assistant):

YM	Can I have one of those there. Oh yeah, and can I have a packet of Durex?
SA	How many did you want?
YM	Five please.
SA	Five packets?
YM	Yes five packets please.

YM	Do you sell Durex?
SA	Yes.
YM	Well, what sort do you sell?
SA	We have a range here . . .
YM	Do you sell the multi-coloured Durex?
SA	Yes, we do.
YM	Could I have one of those then?
SA	Just the one packet?
YM	Yeh, just the one.
SA	That'll be 50p.
YM	Ta, magic, ta.

YM	Do you sell Durexes?
SA	Yes we do, we have a range here if you'd like to have a look.
YM	Have you got any Fetherlite ones?
SA	Yes, they're there, look.
YM	How much are those?
SA	50p. One packet?
YM	Yes please.

Keeping track

Just as printed or written forms can be filled in and filed serially to provide a running record of attitudes or behaviour, so video images can be stored in sequence to show demonstrable changes in ways of behaving. An ideal, although expensive expedient is to have a short video-tape reserved for each participant of a series of sessions so that a video record can be kept and perhaps presented to the person concerned to keep at the end. The value of such a record is that progress can literally be *seen* as it happens.

Video letters

Groups of offenders working on their problems in one place can communicate with similar groups a hundred miles or more away through the medium of 'video letters'. This novel form of correspondence is conducted by making and exchanging films which respond to each other much as written communications might. The topics depend on the memberships and concerns and current activities of the groups involved, and the correspondence might be short or long-lived. It would be possible, given compatible video machines, to contrive a correspondence with groups of offenders in other countries such as the USA or Australia.

'Sealed predictions'

At the termination of a period of working with offenders, it is interesting to ask them to predict how successful they think their efforts will be, over the succeeding six months or a year, at keeping out of trouble. A time and place is arranged for group members to re-assemble; then each person makes a private video prediction, and the complete tape bearing several such recordings is sealed into a package, signed across the closures, and fixed with sealing wax or security tape. When the group re-convenes at the appointed time the tape is removed from its secure package and replayed to the satisfaction or consternation of those present, and in the absence of those 'unavoidably' detained elsewhere.

Assertion

The idea of *assertion* is one that acts as a bridge between the passivity of the unwilling group offender and the unwarranted aggression of some violent offenders. A properly assertive person is someone who can steer a middle course between these two extremes; saying what he/she wishes to, without causing offence to others; standing firm when necessary and giving way with dignity as the occasion demands. The methods have been widely used to help women to stand up for themselves in a 'man's' world; and to help many individuals to overcome their shyness and diffidence in social situations.

Like other social skills methods, assertiveness training offers no instant miracles; when it works it is a reward for hard work. Nor is it simply a matter of learning parrot fashion some tricks to be trotted out without discrimination. At its most minimal that may be all that some people can realistically aspire to, but the true aim is to equip them with repertoires of response that can be deployed flexibly and appropriately in changing circumstances. Stereotyped behaviour, even if it is more assertive, is no more than a pale reflection of real social skill.

As with social skills, the first step is to ascertain the nature of the problem; using, for example, an ASSERTION SKILL SURVEY (see opposite).

Assertion in groups

A more active test of assertion can be made by dividing a group into smaller groups of no more than four members each. Each member in each group is supplied with a list of six items. These can be subjects for inclusion in a programme of evening classes; leisure activities; items required for survival on the moon or in the jungle; policies from party

Assertion skill survey

How confident do you feel about doing the following things well? Put a ring round the number which shows how confident you feel – 1 means not very confident and 5 means very confident – 2, 3 and 4, are somewhere in between.

	1	2	3	4	5
1. Going into a room full of people					
2. Walking past a crowd looking in your direction					
3. Carrying a large parcel through the street					
4. Walking along with someone whose appearance is remarkable/odd.					
5. Leaving a meeting early.					
6. Stopping someone in the street to ask the way.					
7. Knocking at a neighbour's door to deliver a message.					
8. Ringing up a firm to ask about a job.					
9. Asking someone to do you a favour.					
10. Asking someone to lend you some money.					
11. Giving someone a compliment.					
12. Being praised by someone.					
13. Telling someone you are mad with him/her.					
14. Being told off by someone.					
15. Complaining about the service in a cafe.					
16. Asking someone to go out with you.					
17. Telling someone you don't want to go out with him/her.					
18. Starting a conversation with a stranger.					
19. Asking a question at a meeting.					
20. Arguing with someone about a joint decision.					

manifestos; footballers; swimmers; tennis players; entertainers; politicians; food; anything else of interest to the participants.

Each group has to produce an agreed short list incorporating approximately half the numbers of items they start off with; a syllabus, a football team, a cabinet, a menu, a manifesto, or whatever. Each member of the group is urged to fight for the inclusion of his/her items on the final list, and to make an estimate in advance of how many of their own will feature in it. Allow sufficient time for decisions to be reached, then look at the end products, and compare the composition of the lists with each member's predictions. If the lists are randomly assembled in the first place the outcome will reflect degrees of assertion and persuasiveness amongst participants.

Complaining

Another test of assertion can be conducted by observing the relative performances of individuals when matched with each other as complainer and complainee in situations such as 'returning a faulty pair of shoes to the shop where they were bought', 'complaining about bad service in a cafe or restaurant', 'complaining about a car service that has not been carried out properly'. An observer watches each complaint and adjudicates on who is the winner between the two protagonists. The situations should be repeated a number of times, and those who turn out to be consistent losers in these confrontations present themselves as obvious candidates for some simple assertion training.

Coping with queue jumpers

The world can be divided into two great camps; those who *always* say something if someone pushes in front of them in a queue, and those who *hardly ever* do so, in the same circumstances. Set up situations in which the members of a trio play the parts of a bar-person, someone waiting to be served, and someone who pushes in and gets served first. As in the complaining situation, the person who makes little or ineffective response to the intrusion could benefit from assertion training.

Assertion training

Like social skills training, of which it is a growing sub-branch, assertion training has to deal with two distinct aspects of behaviour – the non-verbal and the verbal.

'Non-verbal communication'

Various aspects of non-verbal communication skill can be simply assessed in small groups. Each member thinks of a number of emotional states that can be conveyed without words i.e. by facial expression, gesture, posture, voice-tone; and writes each of them on a separate piece of paper which is then folded and placed on the floor in the centre of the group. Examples of such states might be 'hate', 'fear', 'love', 'happiness', 'surprise', 'curiosity', 'jealousy', etc.

Each person picks up one of the pieces of paper in turn, reads the inscription without showing it to the other members of the group, and then portrays the emotional state by any channel of non-verbal communication he or she chooses. Facial features can be re-arranged to convey the emotion or feeling, limbs disposed, gestures made, voices inflected around random numbers or nonsense syllables. The other members must guess what is being 'said'. If they cannot guess they can be told; the next person repeats the process . . . and so on until everyone has had a go at one or more expressions. The exercise tests for two kinds of skill: that of portraying feelings independently of the verbal contents of any interaction; and that of perceiving and accurately identifying these signals in the unspoken discourse of others. Individuals may be good at either or neither.

Specific training

Posture – an alert and erect posture is more likely to convey to others a sense of purpose and determination than is a submissive or defeatist one. The subject should practise standing up, with shoulders back, *not* in an aggressive or defiant way, but simply as an expression of inner confidence – even if, to begin with, it is not all that heart-felt.

Gaze – meet the eyes of the people with whom you are arguing; again not defiantly or aggressively but with a steadiness which matches inner purposes; direct statements of refusal or questioning should be accompanied by a direct look at the person/people being addressed. This tactic should be practised until it is automatic; catching the eye of the other person whilst making a statement of opinion or decision.

Voice-tone – the same strictures apply to voice tone. In a properly assertive performance the voice should be strong enough, but not aggressive, firm without sounding inflexible, and spoken with a conviction which conveys inner unshakeability and determination.

Gesture – another area where a balance has to be struck between the assertive and the aggressive. Well conceived gestures that accompany determined statements will give them more force and emphasis in an argument.

Verbal skills

This is a more difficult area to tackle, requiring as it does a grasp of syntactical rules and specific vocabularies, and the capacity to combine and recombine these elements in useful and effective patterns of responses to the speech of others.

Developing verbal skills: situational phrasebooks

Diffidence and inability in social situations are often linked to a lack of words; the person literally does not know what to say. When such deficits are identified – by self-report, in interviews or group discussion, as a result of running role-plays – one way in which the worker can help the tongue-tied is to develop rudimentary phrasebooks for use in specific situations (Johnson and Morrow, 1979).

Some examples of broad categories of 'talk', in the use of which the socially skilled feel easy, are illustrated overleaf, and broken down into forms that are adapted to three arenas of discourse in people's lives: a formal or 'polite' one for use with officials and strangers; a less formal one that might be used at home or with less imposing public figures; and an informal or vernacular mode for use with friends and peers.

Items for inclusion in each compartment can be generated by conducting a brainstorm, or in small group discussions, or by leaving a list on the wall for individuals to add contributions as suitable words and phrases occur to them.

Violence and social skills: working with violent offenders

So far in this book, we have attempted to treat separately the different elements that appear relevant to offending behaviour: values, self-esteem and self-perception, self-control, decision-making and, in this chapter, social skills. We now give an illustration of how to combine methods from these separate topics into a unified programme of work, in relation to offences of violence against the person.

We have argued elsewhere for the adoption of a general problem-solving framework for use in social work, whether with offenders or otherwise, and it is one that can be pressed into service when using social skills methods applied directly and specifically to offence behaviour (Priestley et al., 1978). It consists of four simple stages, which together constitute a précis of the 'scientific method':

> *Assessment* – gathering information about the problem and the principal actors involved in it; following its natural history up to the present time; appraising strengths and weaknesses.
> *Setting objectives* – deciding on one or more concrete courses of action that will bring about some change in the situation and move the individual closer to the overall solution of the problem.
> *Learning procedures* – any method whatsoever which helps achieve these objectives, and in doing so, provides an opportunity for learning how to repeat this process again in the future.
> *Evaluation* – checking up on the results of the *learning* stage to highlight successes so far achieved and to determine what remains to be done.

At each of these four stages, attention can be paid, both separately and together, to three linked aspects of problems; the *information* that is required for their solution; *attitudes* which help or hinder in their achievement; and the *skills* which people need to go on solving their own problems for the foreseeable future.

This framework also permits workers to put together packages of materials in the form of *programmes* which tackle particular problems. In this context they might be

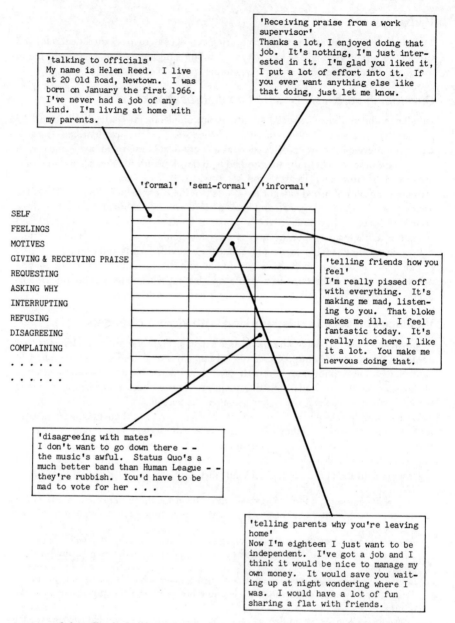

'talking to officials'
My name is Helen Reed. I live at 20 Old Road, Newtown. I was born on January the first 1966. I've never had a job of any kind. I'm living at home with my parents.

'Receiving praise from a work supervisor'
Thanks a lot, I enjoyed doing that job. It's nothing, I'm just interested in it. I'm glad you liked it, I put a lot of effort into it. If you ever want anything else like that doing, just let me know.

'formal' 'semi-formal' 'informal'

SELF
FEELINGS
MOTIVES
GIVING & RECEIVING PRAISE
REQUESTING
ASKING WHY
INTERRUPTING
REFUSING
DISAGREEING
COMPLAINING
. . . . . .
. . . . . .

'telling friends how you feel'
I'm really pissed off with everything. It's making me mad, listening to you. That bloke makes me ill. I feel fantastic today. It's really nice here I like it a lot. You make me nervous doing that.

'disagreeing with mates'
I don't want to go down there − − the music's awful. Status Quo's a much better band than Human League − − they're rubbish. You'd have to be mad to vote for her . . .

'telling parents why you're leaving home'
Now I'm eighteen I just want to be independent. I've got a job and I think it would be nice to manage my own money. It would save you waiting up at night wondering where I was. I would have a lot of fun sharing a flat with friends.

aspects of the offender's life such as values or self-esteem; or they might be specific offence patterns, such as take-and-drive, burglary, violence, or sex.

A violence programme

The first step in the formulation of a programme is to decide what its aims are, so that these can act as guides to the selection of methods and materials. They can also be used to explain to potential programme participants what they might hope to gain from taking part. For example, the declared aims of a programme might be:

1. To help individuals explore their own aggressive feelings and behaviour.
2. To give individuals an understanding of the effects of violence on them and others.
3. To find and practise strategies for the control of violence.

The proceedings proper can begin with an exposition of the programme by the organizer(s), followed by the showing of a relevant film or role-play recorded on video, or the description of some violent offences by their perpetrators, all for the purpose of introducing the topic and focusing the minds of group members on it.

Stage 1 – Assessment

The aim during an assessment phase is to provide programme members with opportunities for looking at themselves and their violent behaviour and at the feelings and attitudes which accompany it.

Any of the methods described in previous or subsequent chapters can be adapted where necessary and pressed into service for this purpose: 5-WH (p. 24), diaries and diary forms (p. 26), 'Action Replays' (p. 28), force-field analysis (p. 32), personal interviews or written statements (p. 95), an assertion checklist (p. 105), anger inventory (p. 134), or feelings thermometer (p. 135).

Further exercises might consist of 'sentence completion' or 'story completion', using items such as those shown below.

COMPLETE THE FOLLOWING SENTENCES
I lose my temper when . . .
I get mad when . . .
I can't stand people who . . .
I would hit anybody who . . .
Anybody who messes with me is going to get . . .
If people push me around they . . .
The things that most wind me up are . . .
Anyone who stares at me is . . .
If someone calls me names I . . .
I think skinheads are . . .
I think mods are . . .
I think rockers are . . .
I think punks are . . .
I think hippies are . . .
I think blacks are . . .
I think NF members are . . .
People who tell me what to do make me . . .
People who poke their nose into my business are looking for . . .
I am going to hit the next person who . . .
If people try to make me look small in front of my mates, I . . .
When I disagree with people I usually . . .
I would only back down from a fight if . . .
Kicking people in the face is . . .
I would use a weapon if . . .
My pet hate is . . .
The worst thing anyone could do to me is . . .
The worst thing I could do to someone else is . . .
The worst thing I have ever done to someone else is . . .

STORY COMPLETION . . .
Complete the following stories in your own words:

Terry is standing at the bar in a disco by himself. As another man walks by with his girl Terry steps back and his arm is jogged by someone else so that some of his rum and black spills on the girl's white cotton skirt and makes a big red stain. The boy friend says to Terry, 'You stupid bastard, look what you've just done. You're going to give me the money for cleaning that.' Terry says, . . .

Tony is drinking in a bar by himself. A man next to him is talking to someone in a loud voice, boasting about the jobs he has pulled and the people he has conned and beaten up and pulled strokes over. He goes on and on in a very loud and boastful way. Tony turns to him and says, . . .

Jenny goes with Bill to his flat. They eat some food and drink some wine he has bought; they listen to some music. When the wine is finished, Jenny says she has to go because she has to be up early the next day. Bill says, 'Where does that leave me?' Jenny says, . . .

The end product of doing any or all of these exercises should be a considerable quantity of self-generated data about personal violence and its meanings for the individuals involved. All of them will have been accompanied by conversation or group discussion, and by not a little thought and reflection.

Stage 2 – Setting objectives

The precise objectives to be set by someone in respect of his or her violence will clearly be highly individual. They are best arrived at in interview sessions conducted by the worker, or in group discussions. Given an overall goal of reducing the incidence of violent behaviour, the objectives may be about avoiding certain situations where violence is likely to occur, for example by putting a particular public house 'out of bounds' to yourself or keeping out of the company of certain people known to be partial to a punch-up. They may include the practising of self-control techniques, or the development of verbal tactics to deflect or defuse approaching violence. The emphasis in all cases should be on specifying realistic and attainable goals, breaking down larger and more complex ones into smaller and more manageable parts. Thus a violent husband or father might list the following objectives:-

1. To find out more about violence in families.
2. To persuade my partner to play a part in my self-control programme.
3. To do relaxation exercises every day.
4. To resolve conflicts by verbal rather than physical means.

If at all possible, behavioural measures should be attached to some of the goals. The actual incidence of violence is the most obvious measure to use; its absence signifies total success, its reduction a partial one. Outbursts of verbal abuse could also be used as indices, or self-reported feelings of lost self-control, or uncontrollable rage. Lesser measures might include rates of swearing or feelings of tension. Whatever they turn out to be, the worker and the offender should collaborate in producing a written version of them which both will keep for future reference.

Stage 3 – 'Learning' methods

Information on violence

Helping violent individuals to achieve their goals of self-improvement can entail using any of the social skills methods which have been outlined earlier (or some of the self-control methods to be described in the next chapter), but the worker may also wish, at this juncture, to help the people with whom he/she is working to relate their own

experience to the wider picture of which it is a part. One way of doing this is to p
some material about violent offending generally, about its forms and variation
about some of the theories that have been proposed for its origins. Precisely how
done will depend on the nature and complexion of the offender group and d
interests and knowledge of the worker. Background information about ethological,
psychoanalytic, behaviourist or other approaches to violence may prove useful in this
respect, if for no other reason than the kind of debate such ideas are likely to spark off
about 'nature' versus 'nurture' in explanations of human aggression. Another avenue
to explore, which might be more meaningful for violent individuals as it may be closer
to their own experience, would be amongst typologies of violent offenders put forward
by sociologists. For example:

Two typologies of violence

Hans Toch interviewed more than ninety violent American men and grouped their
violent acts into two main categories; those which were concerned with increasing the
status and self-esteem of the individual in his own eyes or the eyes of others; and those
where the violence served purely private purposes, i.e. was self-gratifying, without
reference to others (Toch, 1969).

Status-enhancing

Some of the specific forms of *status-enhancing* behaviour listed by Toch are:

reputation defending – living up to the expectations of others.
norm-enforcing – a self-justifying use of violence to enforce rules of conduct.
self-image defending – attacking people who cast aspersions on the violent individual.
self-image promoting – trying to impress violent or criminal peers.
self-defending – acting first before other violent people do.
pressure-removing – explosive outbursts to solve situations not otherwise manageable by the individual.

Self-gratifying

Under this heading Toch lists:

bullying – violence as a sadistic and pleasurable activity.
exploitation – instrumental violence to secure the compliance of weaker people, e.g. as victims of sexual assaults.
self-indulging – treating others as objects without feelings or rights.
catharting – blowing off steam.

The most commonly occurring type of violence, accounting for 19 out of 69 cases, was
that of *self-image promoting*, followed by *reputation defending* (10 cases), and *self-image
defending* (9 cases). These are all kinds of violence which have clear roots in the
interaction between a person's idea of himself and what goes on in the real world to
confirm or disconfirm this image. These kinds of violence fall firmly therefore within the
province of social skills training. An attempt to understand violent acts in similar terms
has been made by Lonnie Athens (1980), writing from a symbolic interactionist
viewpoint. Athens characterizes violent acts as falling into three main classes:

physically defensive – where violence is offered by someone else and responded to with even
more violence.
frustrative – where others do not co-operate with the actor in things
including having sex.
malefic – construing someone else as an evil person who is casting aspersi<

Life for punk rocker on murder charge

A P U N K rocker . . . .
. . . . killed a man
because he smiled at him, a
court was told yesterday. He
was imprisoned for life for
murder.

Mr . . . . . . G . . . . . , QC, prose-
cuting, told . . . . Crown
Court, that Mr M . . . . (18)
was walking home with some
friends after a night's drinking.
Another group were across the
road and one of them, N . . .
C . . . . . . aged 23, called out to
him something like : " Are you
a punk rocker or vandal, or a
mixture of both ? "

Mr M . . . . ran across
the road and struck Mr C . . .
. . . . . one blow with a knife
which penetrated his heart. Mr
C . . . . said with some amaze-
ment : " He has knifed me,"
said Mr G . . . . . . Mr M . . . . .
. . . . . replied : " It is his own
fault. He has brought it on himself." A passing motorist picked
up Mr C . . . . and took him
to hospital, but he died an hour
later.

When interviewed by detectives, Mr M . . . . told them
: " I always carry a knife for
protection. Some people don't
like punk rockers." He said that
Mr C . . . . " stood in front of
me, smiling, and I thought he
was trying to take me down in
front of my mates. I came over
all hot just as though I was
blushing."

Mr M . . . .

. . . . denied murdering Mr C . . . . on September 11 last year.

He also identifies a composite type – *frustrative malefic*, which starts out as frustration but only results in violence because the actor construes the other person as evil and deserving of chastisement.

According to Athens, the likelihood of individuals engaging in these different forms of violence depends to some extent on their self-images, of which he distinguishes three:

> *violent* – someone who sees himself as having a violent disposition and likely therefore to respond with violence in a whole range of situations.
>
> *incipient-violent* – someone who is verbally aggressive and thinks in terms of violence, but does not always follow up words with action.
>
> *non-violent* – someone who does not think of him or herself as a violent person, and who does not have a reputation for it.

Work with violent offenders therefore needs to engage with a number of elements: the self-image and self-esteem of the actor; the ways in which individuals interpret specific kinds of situations in which violence is likely to occur; and the psychology of self-control for impulsive and self-gratifying offenders.

Training methods

Actual training methods may concentrate on non-verbal aspects of communication in potentially violent encounters; or on the words that pass between people; or on what is going on in the mind of the person concerned.

'Eye contact'

Some of the implications of personal space for violent conduct were touched upon earlier in this chapter. An equally important facet of non-verbal communication that sometimes leads directly to physical confrontation is 'eye-contact'. Murders have been committed because 'he looked at me', as in the news item opposite.

The menacing quality of gaze can be demonstrated quite simply by inviting members of a group to turn to the person next to them and look him/her straight in the eyes for as long as they can endure it. The duration of contact varies from a few seconds to several minutes, and in these latter cases the hostile nature of the activity is almost palpable. Non-assertive individuals may need help in maintaining eye-contact for longer periods whilst saying what they want to say; aggressive people may need help in moderating the amount of eyeball they give out, and in refraining from interpreting the stares of others as a sufficient invitation to a brawl.

Threats: a picture dictionary of gestures and expressions

For this exercise you will require a still camera: either a 35 mm one, if you have access to developing and printing facilities (which is the cheapest way of doing it, but more long-winded); or, if you can afford more expensive but immediate prints, a Polaroid or Kodak instant camera. Whichever is used, the aim is the same, namely to create a set of pictures showing as many gestures and expressions as possible which unmistakably convey unspoken messages of threat, insult, challenge, hostility, aggression or violence.

The range of expression and gesture which can be used to transmit hostility is quite large; its exact parameters depend only on the imagination and inventiveness of the participants. The results can be grouped and classified and presented in a variety of ways: alphabetically; in terms of intensity; or offensiveness; by the part of the body or face that is most prominently used; by the intended object/recipient of the gesture or expression; by situation in which they are most likely to be used.

Some of the results can be used as assessment methods with other groups of offenders. How do they construe the gestures and expressions? How would they respond to them? Which are acceptable in *these* circumstances but not in *those?* Which of them would they use themselves? In what circumstances?

The key thing in the whole exercise is to make manifest, and to think and talk about, an aspect of 'taken-for-granted' behaviour that relates intimately to the expression of violence in our society.

'Three degrees'

An exercise to widen someone's range of responses. Videotape the same person three times; in *take one* he/she responds to someone asking for a loan with outright rejection, stemming from deep dislike; in *take two* he/she takes a neutral stance, neither rejecting out of hand nor gladly agreeing to the loan; and in *take three* he/she is so pleased to lend the money that it is practically thrust down the throat of the applicant. The activity can be varied to match the needs of the actor.

Feelings on film

A videotaped series of modelled emotions and their expression can be used to help someone with a restricted emotional range. The models may be workers or their colleagues, or other offenders; possibly members of previous groups.

Violent incidents

At the heart of a 'violence programme' must lie a series of efforts to re-create realistic 'violent' incidents in which one or more of the participants can act differently so as to reduce the likelihood of actual violence occurring. This rules out of the reckoning absolutely unprovoked attacks by hitherto unknown assailants, in the absence of all preliminary interaction between them and their victims. The only defence against such events is the possession of extremely quick reflexes.

However the situations are created – using an Action Replay format, or starting with situation cards, or free-hand essays by participants – the main purpose is to identify those points in the interaction when the 'actor' could have said or done something differently. Different tactics can be modelled by the worker, or on tape, or by other group members; and the person with the problem then makes some effort, with or without 'coaches', to do likewise. These efforts may be arduous to begin with, and are hardly ever blessed with anything resembling instant success. But as with any skill, practice is the key to eventual success, and scenes should be rehearsed in role-play as often as time and perseverance permit.

Contingencies in violent situations: writing an algorithm

Naïve accounts of violence may imply that it 'just happened', without malice or forethought; but closer scrutiny of violent incidents suggests that many of them are the end-product of sometimes quite prolonged interaction between the parties concerned, whether they be individuals or groups. This exercise is aimed at providing some insights into the contingent nature of violence by inviting two groups of offenders, working independently in separate rooms, to construct an algorithmic representation of the speech exchanges that precede violent incidents. No need, of course, to mention the word 'algorithm'. Simply start by asking each group to consider some possible responses to a stranger who calls out to one of them standing alone in a crowded bar:

HEY YOU!   Write this on a card and put it up on a wall, with plenty of space above and below and to the right of it.

Ask the group to discuss and agree three possible responses to this opening shot. One reply should be conciliatory or neutral, i.e. not intended to lead to violence. One should be such as to lead almost certainly to violence; and the third should be problematical, not necessarily provocative, but not conciliatory either. These should be written on separate cards and displayed in a column just to the right of HEY YOU! e.g:

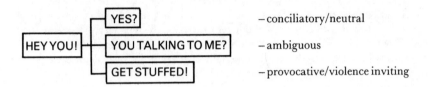

'GET STUFFED' leads to violence – fix a red star to that card; or another card marked 'POW' in red ink.

The groups then consider the likely next move of the aggressor for each of the other two replies, and write a likely response from someone who is clearly bent on provoking a violent retaliation; e.g.

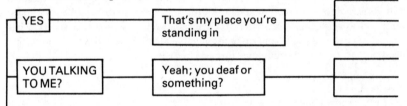

For each of the replies 'That's my place', and 'You deaf?', the groups devise three further ripostes in the categories used for the first, i.e.

    conciliatory
    ambiguous
    provocative

In both cases the 'provocative' reply is assumed to lead to instant violence and is marked with a POW! card. For each of the other two responses, further replies from the adversary are invited, both in a provocative vein; to each of which three further responses are invented, to each of which . . . . The process can go on indefinitely, but the wall-space will almost certainly give out after three or four rounds.

The completed algorithms can be used in several ways. The first is simply the learning that takes place in doing the exercise, about the possibilities of alternative responses to provocation from third parties/strangers.

Another use is to copy all the items onto fresh cards, numbered or lettered so that the series can be reconstructed, and to apply them as a test to the other group. The first card is presented, together with the first three possible replies, and the other group is asked to choose one. (To make this less obvious, the order in which the three replies are put up should be randomized.) If they choose the *violence* response, they lose points, (say five penalty points) and then move on to choose one of the other remaining statements. Whichever they choose, the appropriate riposte is put up and the process repeated until the series is exhausted. (All the cards can be put up at the end.) Roles are then reversed and the second group administers its own *algorithm* to the first group.

Discuss with the two groups the nature of contingent replies and how they affect what happens next. Point out the rapidly diverging number of possible routes; and the fact that after not many such interchanges you would begin to need a wall about the size of Wembley Stadium on which to display them.

Teaching negotiation skills

Conflicts arise in all social relationships. Unresolved, they can sour otherwise fruitful friendships. Resolved badly they can lead to violent argument, and to violence itself. The ability to settle differences without resort to fisticuffs is a clearly desirable social skill. There is also evidence that training offenders and members of their families in these skills can not only reduce the amount of friction between them but also the incidence of criminal activity on the part of the minors.

The following version of that training is designed for use with members of the same group of offenders, but the same procedures can be applied with any pair of potential protagonists who are willing to take part.

Work with two people at a time. Invite them to identify and then role-play a realistic conflict between them. It might be a disagreement about how to spend a windfall, or an evening; where to go on holiday; or a dispute about someone they both fancy. The list of possibilities is endless – but they should decide on one. Ask them to dispute the point for some minutes as acidly and obstinately as they can. Stop the action and discuss what happened, pointing out the taking up of immovable attitudes and the use of invective and insult as substitutes for argument. Propose five rules for a re-play:

1. *No personal abuse.*
2. Make clear statements of own position.
3. Clearly identify points of disagreement.
4. Propose alternative solutions.
5. Reach agreements; either *compliant* ones where one party moves to the position of the other, or *negotiated* ones where both move to a third position.

Examples may need to be given of how to state positions, and identify differences, and propose alternatives. The worker could also model appropriate negotiation behaviour with a colleague, or show a prepared video tape to the same effect. Run the conflict situation again and observe the behaviour of both participants for evidence of the five rules in operation. At the conclusion discuss the replay; commend participants for statements of type 2, 3 and 4, and for the absence of 1. Point out unhelpful comments where they occurred and suggest additional statements that could have been made.

Re-run the conflict and give feedback afterwards. Video taping the three (or more) episodes will allow the two parties to the conflict to view the complete series at the end of the session and to see to what extent they have been able to adopt negotiating procedures and reach agreements.

Stage 4 – Evaluation

The last step in running a violence programme is to find out how successful it has been. This serves three principal purposes: to discover whether the whole enterprise has been worth the time and effort invested in it; whether it has worked for all the participants or – more likely – for just some of them, and to identify who they are; and if possible, to isolate which parts of the programme have worked and which have not.

These questions can be asked and answered at different stages of the proceedings. A more or less constant evaluation of the acceptability of the materials, of their plausibility and surface validity, can be carried on by asking participants to rate activities at the end of each session or group of sessions, e.g.

Was this session useful?
What do you think you have gained from it?
Could it have been improved? If so, how?
How confident do you feel about controlling your violent behaviour in the
   future?

Very confident   Not at all confident

L_____I_____I_____I_____I

The results of these simple questionnaires, together with more *extempore* comment and discussion, can be used to make running adjustments to a programme whilst it is in progress. A collection of ratings also permits some measure of confidence to be taken over a period of time.

A second stage of evaluation is provided in the reports brought back to meetings by individuals who have been attempting to put the methods into practice when confronted with potentially violent situations in their everyday lives. They may or may not report success; successes are encouraging for everyone concerned – failures point to the need for more or different exercises.

The third, and decisive stage of evaluation has to await the passage of time – at least two years for reasonably reliable results, to see how many of the graduates of a programme have been reconvicted of violent offences. And thereby hangs more than one difficulty. The most accurate long-term follow-up of violent offenders can only properly be undertaken with the assistance of the Criminal Records Office, which is simply not forthcoming for all ordinary purposes.

Probation officers may be in a position to check systematically for local reconvictions, and people who work in prisons will know when discharged prisoners are in trouble again because their records will be requested by any new prison of reception. But that will not necessarily indicate the nature of any fresh offence, nor the outcome of any court cases. Offenders themselves can be asked to co-operate with follow-up procedures by reporting what happens to them subsequently, but the attrition rate for such attempts is almost certain to be high. In the end the worker may have to settle for the most imperfect record of the results of his/her work with violent offenders; sad but not altogether surprising, perhaps, in a society which uses the threat of violence to justify an enormously costly apparatus of policing and custody, but shows not the slightest interest in its effectiveness.

If, by one means or another, it proves possible to assemble a reasonably complete series of reconviction statistics, these can be assessed in one of three ways:

1. The subsequent records of the individuals can be assembled with their own previous criminal form. If the pattern of their reconvictions as a group is *away* from the commission of further violent offences it may be not unreasonable to infer that your programme has had some effect.
2. If numbers permit, a control group of offenders can be compared for comparative purposes. They should be matched with the experimental group on key features such as sex, age and type of offence, and also in terms of the nature and extent of their previous

records. Beyond that, the complexities of the task become self-defeating; much less than that makes it meaningless.

3. Fairly homogeneous groups of violent offenders, e.g. in terms of age and type of offence, can be compared with the British Offender Survey data held by the Home Office Research and Development Unit (Phillpotts and Lancucki, 1979.)

6 Training for self-control

On the face of it, an alcoholic fined for drunkenness, a persistent shoplifter, an indecent exposer, a person with 15 convictions for car theft, a heroin addict, and an individual who attacks someone else in a rage, do not appear to have a great deal in common. The offences are all different, both in kind and degree of severity. The motivations and causes may be different, as are presumably any problems which underlie them. The people themselves may be as assorted a collection as any you might find amongst the characters of a Restoration play or in a random sample taken from the market-place on a Saturday morning.

Yet despite the undoubted heterogeneity, these offences could all be typified as having one similar ingredient: they all derive, at least in part, from a *lack* or *loss* of control by the individuals who committed them. Though this may not constitute a complete account of an individual's offence behaviour, in that it may have a lengthy history or quite complex psychological roots, the issue of control may be crucial in maintaining the behaviour – and could be pivotal in altering it or stopping it completely.

In previous chapters we have looked at offences or offence patterns which (a) are the result of values and beliefs which individuals hold, (b) are a by-product of the way some offenders see themselves, and (c) are brought about largely because of a person's inability to resist pressure or deal with some other social encounter in a skilled and satisfactory way. In this chapter, we want to look at types or habits of offence which – though to different degrees and with different sorts of feelings or behaviour – are a consequence of the fact that individuals have lost control of themselves.

What range of offences might be worth approaching in this light? 'I didn't know what I was doing'; 'I couldn't stop myself'; 'I lost my head'; 'Something just came over me'; 'I'm hooked on this stuff' – the notion of being taken over by events or external circumstances is a factor in people's explanations of many of the things they do, quite apart from the behaviour we describe as 'offending'. For practical purposes it is useful however to consider two main categories of offence as being partly due to a loss of self-control:

    a. habitual, addictive, or compulsive behaviour – which might include alcohol-related offences, drug-taking, compulsive theft, offences which are the result of obsessional thoughts, mood changes, or addictive gambling;

    b. impulsive acts, especially some kinds of personal violence, criminal damage, or sexual offences, where people are overcome with excitement, anger, or other strong emotions.

The distinction between these two groups cannot be made absolutely clear-cut, but is primarily a question of time: the first has to do with patterns of behaviour which are established, built up and repeated over long periods; the second consists of relatively sudden, volatile, 'outburst' pieces of behaviour.

Many strategies have been devised over the years for the treatment of people who manifest some of the problems included in this list. Medication of various kinds; aversion therapy; group psychotherapy; psychoanalysis; behaviour therapy; or just straight incarceration, have all been tried with varying degrees of success. In recent years, however, a newer approach to some of these problems has been developed, which has amongst its principal features the fact that it puts the individual him- or herself in charge of the process of self-repair; and that it uses techniques which have much more affinity with the idea of training than with the traditional concept of treatment, with its medical and professional overtones.

This innovation is called *self-control training* and our purpose in this chapter is to describe it briefly, examine some of its existing uses, and see to what extent it can be applied to the Gordian knot of offence behaviour.

Origins of self-control training

Self-control training has developed within clinical psychology and psychiatry over the last 10 to 15 years, although some of the ideas it employs were put forward in the nineteenth century and others have their roots in a longer-standing tradition of 'folk psychology'. The last two decades have witnessed a growing rapprochement between three previously discrete schools of thought:

1. *Behaviourism and behavioural training.* Early behaviourism emphasized the governing of behaviour by external punishments and rewards, and made a valuable contribution to the field of training by advocating the breakdown of complex pieces of behaviour into simpler, and more easily learned, elements. Behaviour therapy, a clinical outgrowth of behaviourism, was founded on the possibility of modifying behaviour gradually, in small easily-achieved steps; and a considerable number of techniques were devised for helping to accomplish this. Behaviourism, however, tended to ignore, or at least give little credence to, individuals' own statements about their feelings or perceptions of themselves.

2. *Cognitive theory* on the other hand was concerned first and foremost with individuals' thought processes; with the way they gathered and used information from the environment; and with their beliefs, concepts, ideas, and the constructions they used to understand and shape their own perceptions of the world and of those around them. This approach tried to comprehend what was going on inside people's heads; the way thinking is structured; the development of complex mental processes; and how the way people see things influences their subsequent actions.

3. *Humanistic psychology*, emerging from yet another set of philosophical roots, sought to deal with the person as a whole, and attempted to understand face-on the complexities of the individual personality. Its paramount concern was with individuals' feelings towards themselves and their relations with others, with their emotions, attitudes, and identities. As such, it asserted the individual's right to resist the attempts of 'scientific' psychology to break him or her down in a mechanistic fashion.

Self-control training is a product of the cross-fertilization that has taken place between these three approaches, and it combines aspects of each of them. It employs the notion of changing feelings or behaviour in a step-by-step sequence, and deploys the associated battery of techniques. But it focuses, as a means of achieving this, pre-eminently upon internal thought processes. It places both of these in the context of individuals' conceptions of themselves and their own assessments of ways in which they would like to change. Its overriding aim is to help people secure control over areas of their feelings or behaviour which are creating difficulties for themselves and others.

Self-control methods

Only those who acknowledge a particular kind of problem and who are motivated to do something about it can be candidates for self-control training. The training itself consists of a number of methods which can be used separately or in combination. They include:

Self-observation – an essential preliminary to altering anything about yourself is to gather general information about it – the frequency of occurrence of problem behaviour; its severity; its consequences; factors which affect its onset. Training often begins, therefore, with individuals being asked to make some simple recording of their own behaviour and experiences over a pre-selected period.

Relaxation training – many of the problems to which self-control methods have been applied are reactions to stress which themselves have caused difficulties for an individual (e.g. smoking, drinking, overeating, depression). Learning to govern your emotions by being able to relax autonomously, indpendently of external 'props', is a major stepping-stone towards self-control.

Desensitization – the systematic use of relaxation to help individuals overcome specific fears or other unwanted emotions, by associating pleasant or relaxing thoughts with (normally) stress-inducing experiences and repeatedly linking the two until the unwelcome feelings can be controlled.

Imagination training – to become better at coping with certain kinds of feelings, or to prepare for stressful events, individuals may be asked to conjure them up in their minds, and to use relaxation or to direct their thoughts in such a way that they can mentally 'rehearse' what they will feel, say and do next time a situation recurs. Thus people can train themselves in the use of:

imaginal rehearsal: running through a future event in your mind in order to be better prepared for it;

covert modelling: imagining yourself coping with a difficult situation in a specific way which you have worked out in advance;

covert sensitization: stopping yourself from doing something by building up unpleasant and off-putting associations with it.

Self-instructions – many people regulate their own feelings and behaviour through a process of self-talk, a kind of 'interior monologue'; and this method of acquiring greater self-control is based on the premiss that 'the things people say to themselves determine the rest of the things they do' (Farber, 1963, 196). Self-instruction training is an attempt to help people regain control over feelings or behaviour by changing the nature of the things they say to themselves. This can take several forms, e.g.

thought stopping: training yourself to interrupt a damaging or self-defeating chain of thoughts;

self-prompts: developing a list of statements to make to yourself which you can use to guide your own feelings or actions;

stress inoculation: a variant form of training in which individuals learn to use self-prompts for the purpose of making themselves relax under pressure, and then apply what they have learnt in actual stressful situations.

Self-monitoring, practice, and *self-reward* – all of the methods described here are designed for use in real-life settings; for them to be effective, therefore, individuals have to put them into service in their lives and follow their own progress as they do so; evaluating their own performance and giving themselves rewards as seems appropriate.

This is a brief sketch of the main techniques used in training for self-control. The object of this chapter is to delineate these methods more fully, by illustrating ways they have been used or suggesting ways they might be used with particular reference to offending behaviour. There is one other crucial component of this training which in operative terms is prior to any of the methods listed above. This is that the general idea of self-control, the aims and practicalities of every method and exercise must be *explained* to individuals before they begin to use them. Individuals must *choose* to try this kind of training before they embark on it; and the processes on which it is based are fully self-conscious – the intention is to place the issue of control at the centre of the person's awareness. For these reasons, individuals must understand the procedures involved. Fortunately, most of the methods can be described in pragmatic, common-sense terms.

Research on self-control training

In the comparatively short time that has elapsed since its inception, self-control training has given rise to a literally enormous amount of research; the proportion of this concerned with offending behaviour has however been disappointingly small. Nevertheless the areas in which its methods have been applied cover almost the entire gamut of human psychological problems: from emotional difficulties like depression or anxiety (Beck et al., 1979; Goldfried, 1979); to 'excesses of habit' such as over-eating or smoking (le Bow, 1981; Pechacek and Danaher, 1979); to behavioural problems like impulsivity in children, or the uncontrolled and disorganised speech of schizophrenics (Meichenbaum and Goodman, 1971; Meichenbaum and Cameron, 1973; Meyers et al., 1976); and even to the cognitive control of pain (Turk, 1978). (Readers who would like to pursue this field further could consult the volumes edited by Goldfried and Merbaum (1973), Mahoney and Thoresen (1974) or Kendall and Hollon (1979)). But more impressive than its range of application is the encouraging nature of the results which have emerged from the bulk of this work; which suggest very strongly that the methods can be effective where other approaches have foundered. This is not to claim that self-control training is a panacea for all human misery – it has notched up some notable failures as well as successes – but it is certainly worth inspecting as a possible tool in work on offence behaviour. No attempt will be made here to survey the wider field of self-control research. Instead, we would like to look in a little more depth at two areas which have the closest bearing on the subject-matter of this book: problem drinking and the controlled alternative to abstinence; and work on the self-control of anger, aggression, and violence.

Controlled drinking

Intoxication with alcohol is without doubt a major contributory factor in the commission of many offences. First there is the offence of drunkenness itself, of which nearly 120,000 people were convicted in the United Kingdom in 1979 (Davies, 1982). Then there is drunken driving, which led to a further 68,000 convictions in the same year, while one-third of the fatal road accidents involved drivers who were legally drunk (Davies, *op. cit.*). Many burglaries, car thefts, assaults and other crimes are committed 'under the influence'. Hensman (1969), interviewing 188 inmates of Wandsworth prison, ranging in age from 21 to over 60 and convicted of a variety of offences, found that 68 per cent had been drinking immediately before their last offence, 55 per cent were drunk at the time of the offence, and 12 per cent could not remember the offence due to an alcoholic 'black-out'. Amongst younger offenders too there seems to be a strong relationship between drunkenness and offence behaviour (Heather, 1981). Almost half the murders recorded in the United Kingdom each year are similarly connected with alcohol (Shaw, 1982). Although the precise role of the drug in the commission of more serious crime remains unclear, and alcohol cannot properly be labelled a 'cause' of offending as such (Greenberg, 1981), it must certainly be included in any list of variables that may lead to it. For a proportion of those who become completely addicted to alcohol, drinking and offending may form a closely interwoven pattern which persistently dominates their lives.

Apart from straightforward drunkenness, it is impossible to prove that most of these offences would not have occurred if their protagonists had not been drinking beforehand, but it is a fair guess to say that many of them would not have done. In so far as it is a 'social lubricant' – 'the great exciter of the *Yes* function in man', said William James – alcohol also aids and abets the commission of large numbers of anti-social acts.

In its extreme form, abuse of or addiction to alcohol has traditionally been regarded as a disease. The advent of Alcoholics Anonymous in the United States in the 1930s gave wide credence to the view that alcoholics suffered from some sort of allergy which meant that even a single drink would lead to prolonged, uncontrolled drinking. The concept of alcoholism as a disease propounded by Jellinek (1960) in the 1940s gave substantial medical authority to this idea. For the greater part of this century, and in the minds of many people even at the present day, the only possible cure for alcoholism is total abstinence. The proliferation of AA groups throughout the world since the foundation of the fellowship has attested to the appeal and value, for many thousands of ex-drinkers, of this approach to their problems. But it has also meant that all drinking problems have been interpreted in terms of the 'disease-abstinence' model; and the entire weight of medical technology has pulled in this direction, with aversion therapy, drug treatments, and small group psychotherapy all designed to reinforce tendencies to abstain.

In more recent years, however, this framework for understanding alcoholism and problem drinking has come to be questioned by many people. Some research by Davies (1962) had shown that a small number of patients under treatment for alcoholism at the Maudsley Hospital in London had subsequently returned to normal, social drinking. The possibility that controlled drinking rather than total abstinence might be an attainable goal for some problem drinkers came to be seriously entertained. In parallel with this, drinking patterns slowly came to be seen as examples of socially learned behaviour which, like other behaviour of that type, was modifiable and amenable to change (Heather and Robertson, 1981).

The evidence that problem drinking is a product of social learning rather than of moral weakness or physical allergy is now overwhelming. There is also powerful evidence that alcoholics and heavy drinkers can, through the use of procedures similar to those we have been discussing in this chapter, learn to control their own drinking behaviour.

The physiological effects of the substance we call alcohol are the subject of much popular misconception. Alcohol is essentially a depressant drug which acts on the nervous system in such a way as to slow our reactions, disrupt co-ordinated movement (so affecting speech, balance, driving etc.), and eventually put us to sleep just as would an anaesthetic. If consumed in sufficiently large quantities its effects can even be fatal. Yet alcohol is commonly assumed to make us more garrulous, less inhibited, more likely to laugh, less guarded and more willing to reveal the truth about ourselves. None of these latter outcomes are however due to alcohol *per se*. They are the learned pattern of behaviour which is accepted in our society as the expected way to act when tipsy or partially drunk. In other societies, while the bodily effects of alcohol obviously remain the same, the way these effects are construed may be radically different. MacAndrew and Edgerton (1969) have adduced anthropological evidence on how drunkenness is experienced by members of different cultures. While for us drinking alcohol is associated very largely with excitement, sociability and so on, in some other cultures the expected reaction is for people to become withdrawn, contemplative and uncommunicative. We learn to enjoy alcohol and to 'be drunk' in much the same way as the marijuana users studied by Becker (1953) learned to use that drug – by watching, copying, or being explicitly guided by others.

Given the accumulation of these kinds of evidence and the development of the social-learning view point on alcoholism, increasing attention has been paid in recent years to the possibility of *controlled* or *social* drinking as a goal in the treatment of alcohol problems. Two other batches of results have lent support to this idea. The first shows that over long periods a proportion of those who are diagnosed as alcoholics do become social drinkers rather than complete abstainers. The second shows that help given to problem drinkers along the 'self-control' lines being described here can be effective in enabling them to regulate their own intake of alcohol.

Evidence relevant to the first of these points has been reviewed by Pattison, Sobell, and Sobell (1977) and more recently by Heather and Robertson (1981). The former surveyed no fewer than 74 pieces of research in which a return to controlled drinking by previous alcoholics was reported. The latter, taking these and other newer results into account, reached the conclusion that '. . . total and lifelong abstinence is not always necessary as a solution to the alcoholic's problems . . . some alcoholics, either spontaneously or in actual defiance of the professional advice they have probably received, have been able to achieve stable patterns of normal, harmfree drinking' (Heather and Robertson, 1981, 130). Perhaps most significant amongst the findings assembled by these authors, both in terms of the scale of the work involved and their impact on the alcoholism field, are the documents known as the Rand Reports which were prepared on behalf of the National Institute on Alcoholism and Alcohol Abuse in the United States. These writings (Armor, Polich, and Stambul, 1976; Polich, Armor, and Braiker, 1980) describe the follow-up of a large sample of problem drinkers who had passed through Alcoholic Treatment Centres established by the United States government in the early 1970s. The initial (1976) report showed that, 18 months after treatment, a total of 22 per cent of the alcoholic group had returned to normal drinking. The second report, of a four-year follow-up of the same population, which adopted stricter criteria for defining the 'controlled drinker', found 18 per cent of the sample drinking normally. Twenty-eight per cent were then abstaining but only 7 per cent had been abstainers continuously over the four years. For those who showed slightly less severe symptoms of dependence, the proportion of normal drinkers rose as high as 45 per cent, and even amongst those with pronounced dependence symptoms, 12 per cent had resumed normal drinking. The findings of this research show clearly that many alcoholics and problem drinkers, far from being victims of a disease that it is utterly beyond their ability to overcome, can in fact learn to drink without doing so to excess – can, in other words, learn to take charge of themselves in the face of what is undoubtedly a very serious problem of loss of control.

No one who works in this field assumes that the goal of controlled drinking would be possible or appropriate for *all* problem drinkers. Successful abstainers are by no means encouraged to attempt social drinking simply because others have managed to achieve it. Heather and Robertson (1981) have discussed possible guidelines for deciding whether this goal might be a suitable one for any given individual. Nor of course is it suggested that all controlled drinkers have secured this position by virtue of self-control training methods. That such methods can however be successfully used for this purpose has been demonstrated in several research reports.

For example, Marlatt and his co-workers (Chaney, O'Leary, and Marlatt, 1978; Marlatt, 1979) used a 'skill training' package with a group of patients in an alcohol treatment programme based in a psychiatric hospital. The training leaned heavily on role-play and other social skills methods, but also involved the use of self-statements and imaginal rehearsal (with reference to how patients would cope with a series of stressful situations known to spark off drinking bouts). The trained group were compared at a one-year follow-up with a parallel discussion group and 'no treatment' control. Results showed that the trained group consumed fewer drinks, spent fewer days drunk, and fewer days drinking at all, than either of the other two groups – all of these differences being statistically significant (the discussion and no-treatment groups did not differ from each other on any of these measures).

A different mixture of training methods was used by Sobell and Sobell (1978) with patients classed as 'gamma alcoholics' (i.e., physically addicted to alcohol). Over a series of training sessions, one group of patients was given a number of 'treatments' which included the traditional behavioural method of avoidance conditioning (electric shock therapy), but also incorporated training in problem-solving skills; 'stimulus control training', i.e., learning to regulate drinking to specific times and places and to avoid situations which triggered it; and training in the self-regulation of alcohol intake. Members of a comparison group were given medication, took part in group therapy and had access to treatment along the lines of Alcoholics Anonymous. Whereas the goal of the first of these groups was controlled drinking, the latter aimed at the more familiar target of abstinence. Follow-up of the patients' progress was undertaken after one-, two-, and three-year intervals. In terms of numbers of days spent drunk, numbers of days functioning well, and numbers of days of controlled drinking, the 'training' group proved significantly better than the comparison group; similar findings emerged from a wider appraisal of the patients' general social adjustment (including whether or not they were at work). There was some evidence that the differences between the two groups narrowed in the third year but the results still favoured the trained group.

Both of these research studies were concerned with diagnosed alcoholics, people severely dependent on alcohol whose lives had been considerably disrupted as a consequence. Reviewing a collection of 14 research reports on self-control training with such individuals, Heather and Robertson (1981) calculate that on average 41 per cent of the participants in these studies returned to normal drinking, suggesting that self-control exercises of one form or another may have a substantial and effective role for helping people with even quite serious alcohol problems.

But the methods have also been used with 'problem drinkers', individuals not actually hospitalized for alcohol treatment but experiencing serious difficulties in their lives as a result of their drinking habits. Numerous offenders would almost certainly fit such a description. Here too Heather and Robertson (1981) have drawn the evidence together, scrutinizing the outcomes of 13 research reports on the use of self-control methods with such groups. Amongst the methods used in these studies have been self-monitoring of drinking patterns; 'BAC discrimination training' – teaching individuals how to estimate the level of alcohol in their own blood (see p. 148); practice in drinking more slowly or in a self-regulated fashion; 'stimulus control' – identifying situations associated with drinking (times, places, people) and reorganizing them as necessary to reduce their influence; setting agreed limits of alcohol consumption in advance; and relaxation training. Again, the general picture which emerges is that 'problem drinkers' can learn to control their own drinking and can reduce it to less damaging levels. In 5 of the 13 reports cited, self-control and allied training methods proved more effective than other forms of intervention as routes to the controlled drinking goal. Of particular interest is the finding that many excessive drinkers could moderate their drinking using a self-help manual and a variety of self-monitoring exercises and self-control techniques. This opens up the possibility of helping such individuals, amongst whom many offenders would be numbered, to regulate their drinking without recourse to elaborate, punishing, or highly medicalised forms of treatment. This is not to say that these methods can be used willy-nilly with anyone who gets into trouble partly as a result of heavy drinking; great care must be exercised when dealing with alcohol problems and there is also evidence that the worker's approach has an influence on the eventual outcome. Nonetheless self-control methods have been shown to work and some of the exercises set out later in this chapter are based on the assumption that, on the strength of this, they may be used to help individuals alter their own drinking and related offence behaviour.

Violence and self-control

Though offences of violence constitute only a comparatively small proportion of all recorded crime, they receive a disproportionate amount of attention in public reporting and discussion of the subject. There are obvious reasons for this. But it is also partly caused by an uneasy ambivalence in social attitudes to violence: while it is 'officially' disapproved of, under some circumstances the opposite is the case – the values of toughness are openly admired in our culture, and violent behaviour is paraded nightly before large audiences in the cinema and on television. There is also no doubt that the frequency and manner of reporting of serious crime in the press serves to reinforce widely held attitudes towards deviance, with the underlying aim of consolidating and perpetuating a particular view of the world (Cohen and Young, 1973).

As with drinking problems (with which many violent offences are indisputably linked) popularly held views of the origin of violence see it as an inescapable fact of life, a feature of human nature which we can do little to change and can only do our best to suppress. The latter we achieve by external manipulations, by imprisoning or otherwise constraining the offender; sometimes by methods scarcely more justifiable than the things the offender did in the first place.

The parallel with alcohol problems can be taken even further, in that there have also been vigorous attempts to explain aggressiveness in terms of biology (the aggressive 'instinct'; the extra Y chromosome; levels of various hormones), often based on extrapolation from observations made on animals. But similarly, more recent explanations have tended to view aggression pre-eminently as a product of individuals' past experiences and of situational influences. This *social learning* view of aggression (Bandura, 1973) now has considerable empirical support. Long-term studies of the development of aggression suggest that family, school and other environmental factors play a crucial part in the aetiology of violence-proneness (Farrington, 1978; Lefkowitz, Eron, Walder, and Huesmann, 1977; Rutter, 1978). If individuals live in overcrowded homes; are neglected by their parents; are subject to harsh and inconsistent discipline; are exposed to violent 'models' in the form of parents or older children, they may be more likely to become violent than others who do not endure these hazards. Such background experiences may also instil habits of thought which increase the likelihood that the actions of others will be perceived as hostile or threatening (Dyck and Rule, 1978; Nasby, Hayden and De Paulo, 1980; Nickel, 1974). Though a tendency towards aggressiveness, once established, may be a fairly stable component of an individual's make-up, the fact that such tendencies are learned in the first place indicates that there is a potential for altering them through training, particularly training which builds upon individuals' own efforts to control their predispositions to violence.

Self-control training has, therefore, been used to help individuals try to secure a tighter hold on their own violent impulses. The principal piece of research in this area was conducted by Novaco (1975) whose work focused on the idea of *anger control*. Loss of temper is a key precipitating element in the commission of many violent acts, and Novaco was interested in whether individuals who had pronounced difficulty in subduing their angry feelings and behaviour could manage to do so through training.

In his research, Novaco applied and extended some of the methods developed by

Meichenbaum (1977), which had been applied to the process of self-control training work with impulsive children and with schizophrenics. But he also tested a number of other methods both separately and in combination with them. The participants in this research were 34 students and staff members from the University of Indiana together with residents of the local community. All had real problems with anger management; during the course of the training, several of them committed assaults, criminal damage, and other violent acts. Each person was given an 'Anger Inventory' (see p. 134), an in-depth interview on his or her anger problems, was asked to keep a diary of anger experiences, and to construct a hierarchy of seven situations which provoked increasing degrees of anger. A number of other measures, including blood pressure and GSR (Galvanic Skin Response, an index of emotional arousal) were also taken. For research purposes the participants were divided into four groups.

Over a series of five 45-minute sessions, one of these groups took part in training consisting of (a) the use of self-instructions or 'coping self-statements' designed to help individuals handle anger-producing situations in a more controlled way (individuals practise applying these statements using *imaginal rehearsal*, see p. 144 below); and (b) relaxation training using the Jacobson (1938) technique in which successive sets of muscles are systematically tensed and relaxed. The other three groups respectively received self-instruction training alone; relaxation training alone; or acted as a 'control' group.

The effects of training were evaluated using self-reported ratings of anger, the anger inventory, measures of blood pressure and GSR, responses to a number of imagined and role-played provocations, and reactions to a direct provocation specially set up (without forewarning to the participants) in the laboratory. On all the measures except the GSR, the 'combined treatment' group (self-instructions plus relaxation training) proved substantially superior to the control group, manifesting '. . . a very significant improvement in subjects' ability to regulate and manage anger' (Novaco, 1975, 43). The combined treatment also proved better than either self-instructions or relaxation training alone; these groups emerged as more successful than the control group only on some of the measures used. All in all then, self-statements and relaxation exercises, when practised by very anger-prone people over even just a few training sessions, resulted in dramatic reductions in their propensity to act violently – accomplished through dramatic increases in their capacity for self-control.

In his later work, Novaco (1977, 1978, 1979) re-cast his approach to the problem of anger control in terms of the *stress inoculation* model as articulated by Meichenbaum (1977). In essence, the idea of inoculation as used here means the same thing as in preventive medicine; people are given a small amount of an unpleasant or noxious experience, in a quantity they can deal with, in the hope that this will help them learn to cope with bigger doses of the problem later on. Applied to aggression, anxiety, and other unmanageable feelings, stress inoculation has three phases, *cognitive preparation, skill acquisition*, and *application training*. The exact meaning of these terms will be spelled out later in this chapter. Novaco (1977) has reported using this package with a hospitalized psychiatric patient who had severe problems in the control of anger. Over a period of three-and-a-half weeks while the training was being implemented, the patient showed gradual increases in his ability to manage his own feelings and behaviour, as judged both by himself and by ward staff. Over a follow-up period totalling two years after discharge from hospital, the patient continued to show a marked diminution in his proclivities to anger and violence.

Elsewhere, the stress-inoculation model has been applied with positive results to problems of aggression control manifested by two quite dissimilar groups of offenders.

Schrader, Long, Panzer, Gillet, and Kornblath (1977) worked with six adolescents, who although in trouble for drug abuse had substantial histories of verbal and physical aggressiveness. These workers used anger control methods drawn from Novaco's work. Five of the six participants made significant improvements in self-control during the 'treatment' phase; and for four of these individuals, the gains were maintained at a follow-up three months later – this depite the fact that the initial training time had totalled only five hours. In contrast Atrops (1978) worked with a rather different population, mentally abnormal adult offenders held in a special hospital, and compared stress-inoculation training with self-instructions, social skills training, and two 'control group' conditions. The offenders ranged in age from 19 to 56. The results were judged in terms of individuals' performance in a number of provocative role-plays recorded on video tape; their self-reports; and ratings of their behaviour in the hospital. As in the Novaco (1975) research, the combination of methods as 'stress inoculation' proved most effective and had a significant impact on these offenders' ability to manage their own aggression in the short term. The gains were not maintained at a follow-up, but given the modest level of input as contrasted with the relative refractoriness of the problem, the short term improvements nevertheless remain impressive. More recently, the methods have proven to be successful when applied to yet another anger-related difficulty, that of marital violence (Deschner, 1984).

A final point of considerable importance about Novaco's methods is that their use itself does not require lengthy training or a background in psychotherapy. This issue was explored by Novaco (1980) in an experiment in which he trained a group of probation officers to use the methods in a series of seven 90-minute sessions spread out over seven weeks. An evaluation of the officers' ability to assess and handle anger problems, carried out by a group of 'blind' judges at the end of the training and again two months later, showed that they performed much better than members of a matched control group with equivalent experience who had not been given the training.

Other research projects employing self-control methods, though not based on the stress-inoculation approach, have reported similarly encouraging results. Camp, 1980; Camp, Blom, Hebert and van Doorninck, 1977 worked with aggressive boys aged between six and eight years old. The boys were identified by means of teachers' ratings on a School Behaviour Checklist; 23 boys from a total sample of 832 so rated eventually took part in the research. As is customary, the boys were divided into an 'experimental' and a 'control' group. The former was trained by means of a programme entitled 'Think Aloud'. For half an hour per day over a total of six weeks, two specially trained teachers worked with these children, using techniques akin to the 'self-instruction' training devised by Meichenbaum and Goodman (1971). When compared at the end of the six weeks with the control group of aggressive boys (not given any training) and with a group of 'normal' boys, the trained group showed a significant improvement on many psychological tests, including several measures of impulsivity. Whereas at the outset of the training the boys had performed like their aggressive peers, at the end they were much more like the normal group: the control group of aggressive boys showed little change. Teachers' ratings of their aggressiveness showed no significant change, however; though the boys were seen as more 'pro-social' in a number of other respects. Thus, although not successful in all its aims this research illustrated the considerable potential of self-control methods with an age-group far removed from the participants in Atrops's (1978) study, and one ordinarily thought to be just as difficult to work with, though for entirely different reasons.

Self-instruction or 'cognitive self-guidance' methods were also used by Williams and Akamatsu (1978) with groups of juvenile delinquents in a medium-security institution.

As with much of the research already discussed, the 'target' behaviour for training was performance on psychological tests of impulsivity; once again, the training proved successful in helping individuals to be more self-controlled in their approach. In this instance, although the 'self-instruction' group did better than a comparison group not given any training, they did *not* do better than another group given practice without self-instructions on similar test materials. However, the self-instruction group was the only one to show improved performance on a different kind of test not used in the training, i.e., it was only amongst members of this group that the training appeared to *generalize* to other kinds of task where impulsiveness hampers successful execution.

That the effects of self-control training are not restricted to enhancement of psychological test scores is illustrated in a case study reported by McCullough, Hontsinger, and Nay (1977). They worked with a 16-year-old boy who had a history of severe temper tantrums stretching back to the day he started school. He frequently went into rages, got into fights (in one of which he had broken a team-mate's wrist), was extremely verbally abusive, and on several occasions had been suspended from school. He agreed to try self-control methods as a possible means of diminishing his violent outbursts. In a preliminary training session, the boy analysed what happened when he lost his temper; practised role-play of behaviour incompatible with violence; and learned thought stopping and relaxation as ways of calming himself down when he became tense and potentially volatile. Subsequently, he was seen once a week by a therapist, and his teachers completed weekly records of the number of times he had lost his temper or managed to control it. Over the ensuing four months, the boy was reported as losing control on three occasions; but on 11 other occasions (which previously would have gone the same way) he succeeded in controlling himself. Information was obtained about the boy for a total of 22 months after the end of his weekly sessions, altogether 26 months since the start of his training. Only two further aggressive outbursts were reported, and although the boy continued to have difficulties in concentrating on his school work, he was evidently much more capable of controlling himself. This was in spite of the fact that his teachers, who had initially agreed to help as much as possible, continually failed to praise his success on occasions when he controlled his temper.

Impulsive, angry, aggressive tendencies can thus be handled by individuals using self-control training methods. This applies both to cognitive performance, i.e., to tasks or psychological tests requiring concentration, and to social behaviour itself. Though the evidence on this cannot perhaps as yet be regarded as definitive, it is certainly positive enough to justify its experimental use by those working with offending behaviour. In the remainder of this chapter we set out a number of suggestions for applying what has been learnt from research to this problem. Such an endeavour must necessarily commence with the gathering by individuals of information relevant to the difficulties they are trying to solve. It is assumed that, on the basis of your knowledge of a given offender – assembled perhaps by means of interviews or other methods outlined in chapter two – you decide that self-control training might be a suitable course of action to pursue. Before training itself can proceed, individuals need to undertake additional exploration of their problems from this perspective. It is with self-assessment exercises geared to such a purpose that we therefore begin.

Assessment of self-control problems

The paramount emphasis in the methods we have been describing in this chapter is that they demand that *individuals themselves* be placed in charge of the attempt to control their behaviour. This accent on intrinsic or inner-directed processes distinguishes self-control training absolutely from drug therapies, incarceration, behaviour modification and other approaches in the tradition of treatment or of punishment, which depend on the action of external agents for the alteration of uncontrolled behaviour. For the alcoholics who achieved social drinking did so as a result of their own efforts; the aggressive people who succeeded in controlling themselves did so without institutionally imposed sanctions. Fundamental to their success, however, was the belief that they *could* learn to control themselves if they wished to do so. Problem drinkers who accept the disease model of alcoholism and endorse the views of AA are not usually considered suitable for controlled drinking treatment. An important early step, then, in applying self-control methods, is to explore the extent to which people believe that they can influence their own lives, and solve their own problems, by their own actions.

Locus of control

While it is unquestionably true that there are *real* areas of freedom, and *real* limitations, within all of our lives, there are other spheres of freedom and control which are determined by our own beliefs. Some restrictions can be classed as 'objective' – a 6' 6", 15-stone man is unlikely to become a champion jockey – but others, particularly in the more fluid areas of interpersonal action, are just as likely to stem from individuals' own perceptions of what they can and cannot do. Differences between people in the degree to which they think they command their own destinies have been conceptualized by psychologists in terms of *locus of control* (Lefcourt, 1976; Rotter, 1966). Some individuals attribute the causes of most of the things that happen to them to their own decisions and actions; they see themselves as authors of most of the events in their lives, or at least of the general conditions in which they are living. Others, while not perhaps seeing themselves entirely as pawns of fate, nevertheless tend to ascribe most of the things that happen to them or around them to luck, or to forces which are beyond the sway of individuals. The former could be characterized as having an *internal* locus of control, the latter an *external* bias in the way they interpret the causes of events.

The beliefs which individuals hold about this can be ascertained by a variety of methods. Straightforward discussion with them of their own feelings and behaviour and the causes of their actions may in itself reveal some of their underlying asumptions; and certainly if they have pronounced fatalistic views this will emerge in many of the things that they say. 'Locus of control' can also be gauged by means of questionnaire methods. The Rotter (1966) Internal-External Scale for example consists of 29 pairs of statements; individuals are asked to take each pair in turn and tick whichever of the two statements they agree with more (or disagree with less). The scale includes items like the following:

7. ☐ A. No matter how hard you try some people just don't like you.
    ☐ B. People who can't get others to like them don't understand how to get along with others.

17. ☐ A. As far as world affairs are concerned, most of us are the victims of forces we can neither understand, nor control.
    ☐ B. By taking an active part in political and social affairs the people can control world events.

25. ☐ A. Many times I feel that I have little influence over the things that happen to me.
    ☐ B. It is impossible for me to believe that chance or luck plays an important part in my life.

In each of the examples shown here, choice A is an external score and B is an internal one (in other items the reverse is the case). When individuals have completed all items they can be told how the scale is scored and arrive at an overall total of their internal and external choices.

This scale was intended for use with adults. However, many other similar scales exist, and some are designed for use with younger groups. Nowicki and Strickland (1973) for example developed a scale for use with those aged between eight and 17 years of age. Some of the items it contains are:

8.   Do you feel that if things start out well in the morning it's going to be a good day no matter what you do?

16. Do you feel that when you do something wrong there's very little you can do to make it right?

31. Most of the time do you find it useless to try to get your own way at home?

A 'yes' answer to each of these questions would indicate greater external locus of control; a 'no' answer the reverse. For other statements the oposite would be the case. There are 40 items in all which at the end yield an 'external' score or measure of someone's overall orientation towards a belief in an external determination of events. On both this and the Rotter (1966) scale the items tend to be American in style and content, but they can be 'translated' fairly easily into more familiar phraseology.

We are not suggesting that scores on these scales should be taken away, written into reports, or otherwise used as indices of anything immutable about the people with whom you are working. On the contrary they should be a starting-point for discussion and exploration. If you are working with one individual talk at length with him or her about the views which emerge, and why for example he/she sees one sphere of life as susceptible to personal influence and another totally beyond it. If you are working with a group record all members' scores on a large sheet on the wall, and discuss differences between very 'internal' and 'external' scorers, replies to individual items, and the basic underlying concepts of personal freedom and control.

The limits of control

Both the above scales are founded on an assumption that individuals entertain a *general* belief about the relative influence of internal and external factors in ordering their lives. But it may be objected that the amount of control we feel we exert varies greatly from one situation to another (and there is some evidence that juvenile offenders differ from their law-abiding peers in this respect; see Kendall, Finch, Chirico and Ollendick (1978)). For example, prisoners at different stages of their sentences perceive differing levels of control and power residing in their own hands (Levenson, 1981). An alternative approach to assessing self-control is therefore to ask individuals to plot its limits within different regions of their lives. To do this, a rating scale like the one shown on p. 132 can be used. This is a list of diverse aspects of life over which individuals might feel they can exercise different amounts of power. Most of us can decide, for example, how to wear our hair, whom we will mix with socially, or how we will vote in an election. But we would expect to have less of a say about our general state of health (though there are obviously *some* steps we can take to safeguard it), or about the choice of people we have to work alongside. We might be virtually powerless to influence our job or promotion prospects; the kinds of houses we live in; or our level of emotional tension. Looking at the list in another way however, some areas of apparent freedom could be illusory in that we are really very much influenced (for instance) by what other people think, or by what we read in the newspapers. Equally, in other areas we may have much more freedom than we customarily suppose, because we have just got into a habit of accepting certain restrictions placed upon us. The general point is, that for almost all the items in the list, the level of control we wield is a subjective rather than an objective phenomenon. The aim of this list is to bring out people's perceptions of their ability to decide what happens in various segments of their lives.

Rating scale	Completely under my control			Completely out of my control		
1. When I get up in the morning	1	2	3	4	5	6
2. The kind of food I eat	1	2	3	4	5	6
3. The sort of clothes I wear	1	2	3	4	5	6
4. My choice of a job	1	2	3	4	5	6
5. What I do with my spare time	1	2	3	4	5	6
6. The kind of house I live in	1	2	3	4	5	6
7. Whom I mix with socially	1	2	3	4	5	6
8. My general state of health	1	2	3	4	5	6
9. What other people think of me	1	2	3	4	5	6
10. The amount of alcohol I drink	1	2	3	4	5	6
11. My moods in general	1	2	3	4	5	6
12. Whether or not I get into trouble	1	2	3	4	5	6
13. How I vote in elections	1	2	3	4	5	6
14. Whether I will be a success or a failure	1	2	3	4	5	6
15. My temper	1	2	3	4	5	6
16. Whether or not I get into fights	1	2	3	4	5	6
17. What I will be doing this time next year	1	2	3	4	5	6
18. How much money I spend	1	2	3	4	5	6
19. Whether I'll get what I want out of life	1	2	3	4	5	6
20. Whether I feel tense or relaxed	1	2	3	4	5	6

All individuals are asked to do is to put a ring round the number which corresponds with the degree of control they think they have as far as each item on the left is concerned. A score of 1 would indicate complete control, a score of 6 complete lack of it; other scores intermediate amounts. An overall score could be obtained by summing over all 20 items, giving a broad index of 'internal–external' locus in the sense described above. But responses to individual items would be more interesting; if you are working with a group comparisons could be made between members' replies; and the factors which *do* influence the kinds of things included in the list could be mapped out. Other items could of course be added and the content in general could be angled towards selected topics of concern to individuals or groups. It is best however if a spread of items is included; it might then be possible to help people define an actual boundary which divides 'internally' and 'externally' controlled spaces of their lives; and once again, comparisons could be made between individuals as to precisely where such a boundary falls.

Self-observation

The methods just outlined are designed to help individuals take an overall look at the idea of control in their lives; to appraise in rough terms whether they believe they can be in charge of themselves; or to help them at the very least discover what are some of the other forces which make them think, feel and act the way they do. As a prelude to self-control training, however, much more thorough exploration needs to be undertaken of the problems with which individuals are faced. In the remainder of this section we examine some methods of undertaking this. We begin with the general idea of self-observation and the self-monitoring by individuals of the occurrence of losses of control.

'Self-observation' does not mean gazing ardently at yourself in the mirror, or systematically trying to catch glimpses of yourself reflected in shop windows as you pass them by (however rewarding these experiences may be for some people). In chapter two we came across the idea of asking individuals to compile a diary of an offence; to analyse an offence in terms of the '5-WH' mnemonic; or to take a single incident and look at it in fine detail by means of role-play and video playback. With self-control problems, like habitual drinking, compulsive theft, or frequent loss of temper, such incidents recur over and over, and it is their very repetitiveness which constitutes and at the same time magnifies the problem. Extended logs or diaries of the recurrence of the problem can therefore be kept. In fact, charting out the patterns which the unwanted feelings or behaviours take is an essential piece of groundwork before self-control training itself can begin.

Time when drinking began	Circumstances: where drinking took place, who was there	Antecedents: what was happening, how did you feel	Amount and type of drink consumed	Consequences: what happened, how you felt

If the problem is excessive drinking, for example, individuals can be asked to try to keep a daily *drinking diary* like the one shown here, which is based on the format suggested by Marlatt (1979). This provides two important types of information for those trying to regain self-control. First, it is a record of the frequency, severity, and other dimensions of the offending behaviour itself; and second, it may help someone identify some of the causes of his or her drinking, or at least some of the factors which facilitate its onset or continuation. If such a diary is kept even part of the time over several days or weeks, patterns might emerge which will prove very useful in the application of training exercises later on. Diaries akin to this have also been used by Novaco (1975) in his work on anger, and in the treatment of depression (Hollon and Beck, 1979).

Diaries like these focus mainly on the occurrence of the events (e.g., drinking) or pieces of behaviour which are causing difficulty for someone, although individuals should also record their feelings as fully as possible. But given that self-control training often relies on changing individuals' *thoughts* in order to help them effect changes in their behaviour, it is also important to help them record the kinds of things that go through their minds when a problem appears. In some cases, for example very sudden and unexplained violence, it may seem that there was no time for any intervening thoughts; action just 'took over' and the offender lashed out, apparently without any forethought whatever. In most situations however, even with what appear to be thoughtless, impulsive, spur-of-the-moment acts, there has been some (albeit rudimentary) thinking beforehand, and it is more common to find that there has been a build-up, an inner struggle, a period of cogitation prior to the commission of the offence.

Individuals can also therefore be asked to make some attempt to record the thoughts that precede their uncontrolled behaviour. They can do this either retrospectively, for example in an interview in which you ask someone to cast his or her mind back to a particular incident, or *in vivo*, by keeping a log of self-statements as they happen or very soon afterwards when they are still fresh in the mind. Exercises like this have been used to good effect in self-control training (Hollon and Kendall, 1981) and are known as *dysfunctional thoughts records*. This means that a person records three basic types of information, as shown in the table below. People can be asked to do this in relation to

SITUATION Where I was, what I was doing	THOUGHTS What I was thinking or saying to myself	FEELINGS How I felt at the time

particular circumstances (e.g., 'every time you go shopping'; 'whenever you walk along a quiet street where there are lots of parked cars'; 'whenever people come round whom you've had arguments with before'); or alternatively at intervals selected and agreed upon in advance (e.g., hourly, at four o'clock each afternoon, on Thursday evenings, etc.). Since the aim of the exercise is to pinpoint 'dysfunctional' thoughts which contribute to losses of self-control, and which might provide a lever for personal change (as in the use of self-instructions), the choice of when to try to record these thoughts depends on the kind of problem being dealt with, its frequency, and other relevant facts.

Anger inventory

A different approach to the assessment of self-control problems is to invite individuals to identify situations in which they occur by means of a checklist or questionnaire. A method like this was used by Novaco (1975) in his work on anger control. It is called the *Anger Inventory* and it consists of a list of 90 brief descriptions of situations which might make someone feel angry. Beside each is a rating scale on which individuals are asked to say how angry they would feel in that situation, from 1 (= this would not make me at all angry) to 5 (= this would make me very, very angry). Here are some sample items:

4.	Being singled out for correction, when the actions of others go unnoticed.	1 2 3 4 5
17.	Watching someone bully another person who is physically smaller than he is.	1 2 3 4 5
31.	Being pushed or shoved by someone in an argument.	1 2 3 4 5
50.	You are sitting next to someone who is smoking and he is letting the smoke drift right into your face.	1 2 3 4 5
75.	Being mocked by a small group of people as you pass them.	1 2 3 4 5
86.	Getting punched in the mouth.	1 2 3 4 5

For most people who commit acts of violence, their behaviour is situation-specific, in other words it is set in motion by certain people, circumstances or events. While for some individuals who are tense and highly-strung there may be many such situations, in other situations, though feeling stressed, they are unlikely to actually become violent. The purpose of the anger inventory is to help violence-prone people narrow down the settings in which their feelings erupt. The more accurately they can pinpoint these, the greater are the chances that they will be able to make effective use of self-control training. The completed inventory can also be used as a 'baseline' against which individuals could check any progress they are making later on.

Feelings thermometer

Apart from helping people to identify and list those circumstances which provoke feelings of anger, the inventory just described also contains a crude rating scale on which individuals mark the degree of anger they feel in any given context. For some self-control training exercises, however, it is necessary to have a more finely differentiated measure of how individuals' feelings respond to various things that happen to them. One way of obtaining this is to use an imaginary 'feelings thermometer' like the one depicted below.

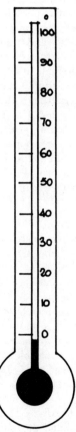

This idea can be used to help individuals take their 'emotional temperature' and its use need not be confined to work on anger or anger management – any emotion, such as anxiety, depression, excitement, or sexual arousal can be analysed in the same way. The basic purpose of the exercise is to help individuals construct a gradient of what are for them successively more anger-producing or anxiety-producing states of affairs. The degree scale on the thermometer represents gradual increments in the strength of an emotion just as the centigrade scale on a real thermometer denotes steady increases in heat. To use the thermometer, individuals first imagine some situation which for them is completely relaxing: in which they feel tranquil and untroubled, free from any upsetting thoughts or emotions. This can be taken as a kind of 'resting state' and can be described in a few words opposite the zero at the bottom of the scale. Next, addressing themselves to the kinds of feelings that are a problem for them, they make a list of a number of different events or situations which make them feel varying amounts of the emotion in question. Finally, they try to place these in order on the thermometer, writing brief details about them adjacent to the relative 'temperature' they think each would produce. They can do this by taking the extremes first – the item which overwhelms them with panic, or makes them erupt into physical violence, can be written at the top; items which evoke only mild apprehension or slight annoyance, just above the bottom; and intermediate items inserted at appropriate points in between.

If you are working with one person, compilation of a feelings thermometer can provide a starting-point for a very thorough and penetrating discussion of his or her feelings: at what stage they become unmanageable, why some people, places or events are more irritating or worrying than others; and so on. The thermometer also supplies the foundation for some of the relaxation and stress-inoculation exercises to be outlined later on, and this is the primary reason for its inclusion here. But it can in addition be used in a group context. For example, individuals may make comparisons between the items on each other's scales, again a fruitful starter for discussion. Alternatively, in residential settings or other places where there is an ongoing group, a large thermometer could be displayed on the wall, and members invited to record on it any incidents which they have feelings about, at corresponding places on the scale, so providing a continuous monitor of the group's atmosphere. The items entered by individuals at particular times might help to bring into the open resentments, aggravations or fears which previously had been harboured privately or had simmered threateningly within sub-sections of the group as a whole.

Plotting mood swings

Some offences are committed when people are feeling excited, energized, 'on a high'; others when they are in the depths of depression, desperately seeking something to do. Whether emotional instability is a feature of the 'criminal personality', as some have claimed, or whether mood changes are more often the product of circumstances, temporary fluctuations in the way people feel can certainly predispose them to some kinds of offence. At least they may be more 'at risk' when in certain frames of mind; more likely to shoplift when depressed; to go thieving as a relief from boredom; to act impulsively when already in a fairly animated state. The key to altering offence patterns for some people, then, may lie in helping them secure control of their moods. A necessary preamble to this, as with other forms of self-control training, is for individuals to observe their own mood swings, and if possible to detect the factors which precipitate their various 'ups' and 'downs'.

A way of doing this is to ask individuals to plot oscillations of mood on an undulating chart like the one shown below, a bit like the track of a roller-coaster in a fairground. The peaks represent times of elation, over-activity, or restlessness; when people feel agitated in a positive but perhaps slightly menacing way. The troughs are the low points in people's lives, when perhaps they feel bored, or dejected, even despairing. The shape of the line drawn here is quite arbitrary and it will obviously be necessary for individuals to draft something which corresponds with the 'shape' of their own moods. For example, they may never experience periods of elation, only bouts of depression; and the length of time for which different moods persist is bound to be uneven. If they feel they cannot graph their feelings in this way, they could instead give themselves a daily 'mood rating' on say a ten-point scale, and see what pattern emerges after a week, a month, or longer.

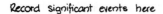

Record significant events here

'NORMAL' STATE OF MIND

Record accompanying feelings here   TIME ⟶

The important thing, however, is that people link the way they are feeling to things that are happening in their lives at the time. As suggested here for instance, they might record details of situations or events above the line, and the accompanying feelings below it. In this way, after they have maintained the 'mood chart' for what seems like a worthwhile period, they may be able on inspecting it to isolate some of the events which are associated with the onset of the feelings they are trying to control. It is on these occurrences, as the possible catalysts of changes in mood, that self-control training exercises would concentrate.

The exercises that have been described in this section should enable workers and offenders to answer a number of questions about self-control or the lack of it. First, do individuals hold a general belief in the external determination of events and think there is little they can do to alter themselves? Second, which areas of someone's life are presenting self-control problems, and are there other areas that are under control? Third, how frequent and severe is the occurrence of the uncontrolled behaviour? What goes through the individual's mind before, during and after it occurs? Fourth, do different kinds of things that happen to people produce or make more likely the unwanted feelings or behaviour? Fifth, are individuals more prone to do the things they are trying to stop themselves doing when they are in certain moods? And are these moods themselves very much influenced by external events? If people have answered some of these questions they will be in a better position to do something to manage their own feelings and behaviour more effectively. The crucial element of self-control training is that it concentrates directly on this issue of management and control; it is not intended to restructure the individual's personality, as are other more 'therapeutic' approaches to problem behaviour. The material generated by the self-assessment process is the substance with which individuals then work, using some of the methods described in the next section.

Training exercises

A basic outline of self-control training methods was given earlier in this chapter. In what follows, we will elaborate on this and set out specific exercises in greater detail. We start with the comparatively simpler exercises and move on to other, more complex methods of which the former are the building-blocks.

Relaxation training

Given that many self-control problems derive from various forms of tension and stress (or from maladaptive attempts to cope with them), one of the most valuable skills an individual can acquire is the ability to *relax*. If you are working with violent or violence-prone offenders, or with those whose offences are in part related to anxiety or excitability, then training in relaxation may be helpful for them. There are many different versions of relaxation training, but a number of more or less ubiquitous ingredients are found in a majority of them. One is that participants should be seated in a fairly comfortable, reclining chair in conditions of relative quiet, which may preclude this sort of exercise if you are working in a room next to a prison gym or your office overlooks a building site. Another is that individuals are asked to become conscious of their respiration and to take deep, regular breaths. Beyond that, most relaxation procedures tend to be variations on two principal themes:

Progressive physical relaxation

The first, developed by Jacobson (1938), operates primarily at the bodily level, through helping individuals to lower their muscular tension. At the outset, people may have to be given some simple instructions on how to go about this, but the longer-term aim is that they should learn to use the method themselves. The technique involves taking different sets of muscles one at a time, tensing them for a short period of say ten to fifteen seconds, and then allowing them to relax for a similar interval. The exercise might commence say with the right hand. The person first clenches his or her fist as tightly as possible, then releases it, each for the prescribed amount of time. He or she then moves on to the right forearm or upper arm. The sequence of muscle groups suggested by Rimm and Masters (1979) is: hands, biceps, triceps, shoulders, neck, mouth, tongue, eyes and forehead; exhalation of air from the lungs; back muscles, abdomen, thighs, stomach, calves and feet, toes. Most people report feeling much more physically relaxed after performing this exercise, which altogether might take about twenty minutes or so.

Visualization

A second technique, sometimes used in conjunction with physical exercises, sometimes separately, relies on individuals' ability to exploit the 'mind's eye' as a means of inducing relaxation. People try, in other words, to use *mental imagery* to help themselves feel more calm and composed, by conjuring up pleasant, soothing scenes in their minds. The content of the scenes will of course vary from one person to another, and be entirely dependent on people's experiences, their preferences, and their imaginative capacities. They have to picture the scenes as vividly as possible, perhaps for several minutes at a time, and see if they can use them to lessen their feelings of unease, irritation, resentment, or whatever. In a way this is like engaging in a kind of guided or deliberately manufactured daydream, and some people may find it difficult or distasteful for this reason. Others however will find the idea feasible and even appealing. The net effect, again, if people can successfully summon up images of tranquillity using this method, should be a greater degree of mental and physical relaxation.

It may be that some combination of these two exercises will be best for certain people; whatever appears most suitable and actually workable for any given person is the method that ought to be used, at least initially. For relaxation methods to have their desired effects in the long run, they have to be conceived of as *training* by the individual: he or she must practise the techniques as regularly and as frequently as possible. This in itself may help people become less anxious or wound up; there is a sizeable accumulation of evidence as to the efficacy of relaxation exercises for a variety of emotional problems (Rimm and Masters, 1979). But in addition, relaxation is a vital component of the method of 'stress inoculation', to be discussed later in this chapter, and of systematic desensitization, which we consider next.

Systematic desensitization

The technique known as desensitization was originally developed by Wolpe (1958) and is a direct product of the deployment of behavioural methods in psychotherapy. Put at its simplest, desensitization means the removal of the troublesome feelings that are attached to some object or event in someone's mind, by associating the object or event with feelings of relaxation instead. It is thus an application of the relaxation methods we have just encountered: but rather than being used to help people cope with general feelings of anxiety or anger, here they are used to deal with emotions which are aroused on specific occasions, by specific circumstances in people's experience.

To use the methods, individuals have to start with a hierarchy of situations which elicit different levels of a particular feeling. This might be obtained from a *feelings thermometer* or other exercise like the one we met with earlier in this chapter. So desensitization combines and extends two of the methods we have already described: the feelings thermometer and relaxation training. To do it properly, individuals must first construct an ascending list of people, places, objects, events, situations which arouse varying degrees of their anxiety or anger. Next they must learn to use relaxation methods; and must also be at least moderately able to imagine and mentally recreate some of the worrying or annoying scenes which concern them. All of this is essential groundwork before systematic desensitization can even begin.

The exercise is intended, by the way, for use with *irrational* feelings to which individuals are prone. It should not, and in any case probably cannot, be used to subdue the quite understandable emotional reactions which are produced by some circumstances. Numerous fears, of situations which contain real danger for example, are wholly rational. Many moments of anger, when we are treated unjustly or unfairly for example, are entirely legitimate. Certain kinds of emotion are an intrinsic part of our psychological make-up and we may be dependent on them for our survival. But on other occasions our feelings may be inappropriate, disproportionate, with a variety of results ranging from subjective discomfort to the inflicting of damage on ourselves or other people. It is for these sorts of feelings that methods such as desensitization are designed.

The actual procedure for desensitization involves asking people to think of some of the items in the hierarchy they have constructed, while simultaneously attempting to relax and to rob the items of their potency as emotionally disturbing or provocative events. In practice it is best if a hierarchy or thermometer with roughly ten or twelve items can be used. A session begins with relaxation so that before undertaking desensitization itself, people are in a reasonably placid frame of mind. (They could also be asked to rate their feelings verbally, or on a written scale.) When this has been achieved, individuals are invited to think about the item nearest the bottom of the hierarchy, which makes them feel the mildest degree of anxiety or annoyance (or whichever feeling they are concentrating on). They have to imagine this as realistically as they can, but to try to remain calm and relaxed while doing so. In practice, individuals are usually asked to signal when they have a clear image of the scene in mind (by raising a finger for instance) and to signal again if they experience any of the feelings they are trying to conquer. If they succeed in picturing the scene for ten seconds or so without any upsetting effects, they are asked to stop thinking about it briefly, and then to imagine it again, this time for up to half a minute (Rimm and Masters, 1979). If people signal that they are feeling anxious (or whatever) at any stage, they are asked to put the scene from their minds and relax; if this continues to happen, they may have to describe other scenes – even less unsettling – for inclusion in the hierarchy, and start work on these instead. If on the other hand they manage to contemplate the scene and to stay relaxed, they are invited to move on to the next item or scene in the hierarchy and the whole procedure is repeated with it. This process continues, over as many sessions as necessary, until individuals have reached the uppermost point on the thermometer scale. The overall purpose will then have been achieved: they will have succeeded in visualizing what are for them quite perturbing states of affairs, but will have done so without the undesirable consequences in terms of emotional upheaval and its likely effects on their behaviour.

Though systematic desensitization has for the most part been used with anxiety, and particularly with phobias, it has also been successfully applied to feelings closely connected with offences, and with actual offence behaviour. It has been used for example with alcoholism and problem drinking, where this was partly caused by people's anxiety or was an attempt to reduce tension (Hedberg and Campbell, 1974; Lanyon, Primo, Terrell and Wener, 1972). It has been shown to work effectively with sexual exhibitionists, using a hierarchy of items likely to lead them to expose themselves (Bond and Hutchison, 1960; Wickramasekera, 1968). It has been used to overcome chronic kleptomania, where this was known to be very much influenced by anxiety (Marzagao, 1972). It has helped individuals learn to control aggressive feelings in general (Evans and Hearn, 1973; Hearn and Evans, 1972), and those experienced while driving in particular (Rimm, deGroot, Boord, Heiman, and Dillow, 1971). And it has been shown to reduce racial hostility, to lessen the anger felt towards blacks by racially prejudiced whites (O'Donnell and Worell, 1973).

Self-instructions

Relaxation and desensitization represent one major strategy through which people can learn to gain control over feelings or behaviour which they find unacceptable and want to change. A quite different approach to the same problem is through altering *cognitions* – the internal thought processes by which we interpret the world around us, make decisions and guide our own actions as we set about trying to accomplish any particular goal.

There are some kinds of things which we do automatically, almost without having to think. Driving a car, operating a machine or cooking a familiar dish might be examples, in which the activity is so routine to us that we are not conscious of the numberless small-scale decisions involved. Most people can even do these things and think about something completely different at the same time. Conversely, there are other kinds of thinking which have no immediate impact on our feelings or behaviour (though of course they *may* do). Recalling something that happened last week; turning an issue over in the mind; considering a statement made by someone on television or in a book might be instances of this. Somewhere between these two extremes, of 'thought-less action' and 'action-less thought', are a large number of other ideas and reflections which have a very close connection with how we feel and what we do. They constitute a sort of conversation we have with ourselves; a series of statements addressed to ourselves which play a central part in self-regulation and self-control.

In fact, people spend a great deal of time talking to themselves in this way. This is not to say that we walk along the street muttering uninhibitedly to ourselves, a habit liable to make passers-by somewhat nervous. But we are forgiven if we occasionally speak aloud to ourselves; everyone recognizes that we have merely vocalized what is going on inside our heads anyway. We use this 'inner speech' amongst other things to remind ourselves of what we had planned to do; to give ourselves instructions when we are faced with a novel or difficult situation; to pilot ourselves through tricky interpersonal encounters; and to comment to ourselves on how well or badly we are doing.

But what if the instructions we give ourselves are wrong – if the things we say to ourselves are misleading, harmful, and just get us into trouble? As we saw previously, low self-esteem can be generated and reinforced by negative self-statements. The same is true of many other kinds of feelings and behaviour. Repeatedly thinking about something you'd like but can't afford may be a close forerunner of an attempt to steal it. Telling yourself that you can't manage without another pint, or that one more won't do any harm, will clear the way for further drinking. Promising yourself that if so-and-so looks at you that way again you will hit him can only lead to predictable, explosive results. Self-statements like these probably precede the commission of many offences; habits of thought like these may well be the fuel that helps to sustain *habitual* offending.

If individuals say such things to themselves and are perfectly happy with the consequences, there is little self-control methods can do to influence their behaviour. If on the other hand they would like to change, then *self-instructional training* may be worth pursuing. This consists of the attempt by individuals to alter their behaviour by altering the things they say to themselves. There are a number of exercises which can be used as part of this training and we will look at each in turn.

Thought stopping

By far the plainest instruction you can give yourself if you are trying to rid yourself of unwanted thoughts and behaviour is to say *'stop'*. Naive and simpleminded as this may appear to be, it has been shown to work with certain kinds of problems. It is especially suitable for helping people who have become preoccupied with thoughts they cannot control; with obsessional or near-obsessional states where the same ideas are reiterated or the same images recur continuously in someone's awareness. Thus if a person realizes that a particular line of thinking will ultimately lead him or her to commit an offence, he or she can learn to check the line of thought using this method.

As with most of the other techniques described here, people must first be given some instructions on the use of thought stopping but then must practise it themselves as often as possible in real-life situations. Working with an individual, the method requires that, first of all, you should explore some of the things that he or she thinks just before an offence takes place (assuming of course that the offence is agreed to be a result of loss of control). One route to doing this would be to use a self-observational exercise of the sort outlined earlier (a 'dysfunctional thoughts record'). During a self-control training session, people would then be asked to actually think *aloud* some of the things they say to themselves. At the point where the individual's thinking dwells on the possibility of the offence and seems to make it likely to happen, the worker shouts 'STOP!' in an attempt to scatter or block the individual's thoughts in their tracks. (If this is done as a complete surprise the first time, it almost always works.) Next, individuals are asked to repeat the process, but this time not to verbalize their thoughts; they are asked to give a signal when the unvited thoughts return. Again the worker calls 'stop'. Following this, individuals have to try interrupting *their own* thoughts in the same way; first with thoughts spoken aloud, then with covert thoughts. Obviously this may take some time and practice before it works, but in the long run it may enable people to overpower thoughts of temptation; of self-justification; of incitement; or of other kinds which carry them along towards the commission of an offence.

Horton and Johnson (1977) have reported using thought stopping with a man who was overwhelmed with thoughts of murdering his wife (who had left him). The procedure was used in a number of training sessions over a one-month period, in conjunction with other exercises designed to help him make himself think about other things. Over a seven-month follow-up period, the man became more able to banish homicidal thoughts from his mind, regained a more balanced view of himself, and seemed all round to be in a much better state of mental health. This result in a fairly extreme case certainly raises the possibility that the method could prove effective with other individuals whose offence behaviour occurs or persists partly because they are prey to uncontrolled thoughts.

Self prompts

Thought stopping can however only help to solve part of the problem of self-control. As in the case study just mentioned, individuals may need not only to curtail certain of their thoughts, but also to substitute other more positive and adaptive thoughts for them. Extra kinds of self-instructions may be called for. Self-instructional training has also therefore been used to help individuals develop sets of things they can say to themselves in order to secure firmer control not just over their thoughts, but over their feelings and behaviour too.

Several stages are involved in the implementation of this training. First, participants have to accept the validity of the notion that there is an intimate relationship between the kinds of things they say to themselves and their subsequent feelings or behaviour. The nature of this relationship may have to be expounded to them with examples. They need to be given a basic understanding of the ideas which underpin the methods they will be going to use.

Second, the individual who is experiencing self-control problems, and the person (presumably a paid worker of some kind) who is going to help him or her try to remove them must have a shared view of the situation. They must agree, in other words, on the basic definition of the problem; must perceive it in the same sort of way and be in general accord about what can be done to tackle it.

If both of these conditions have been satisfactorily established, more practical steps can then be taken. The focus of the training itself is on individuals' self-statements, and these must first be brought into the open. This can be done by drawing on one or more of the assessment methods already mentioned: for example an exploratory interview (of the sort suggested in chapter two); a diary of self-observations; or a record of 'dysfunctional thoughts' or of mood swings. As in thought stopping, individuals can be asked to imagine the moments prior to committing some offences and to speak aloud some of the things they remember saying to themselves. These might have included sentences like:

'It would be really easy to nick things in here . . .'
'Anybody could pinch a car from here. People sometimes even forget to lock them. Worth trying the doors just to see . . .'
'If he says that just once more I'm going to let him have it . . .'
'She deserves any trouble she gets, dressed like that . . .'

The focal point of individuals' efforts now becomes the *alteration* of these self-verbalizations, and their replacement with a new, more self-controlling, more adaptive set of statements or *self-prompts*. A range of statements for use in this context must be generated by individuals themselves; they must select from amongst them and decide which are most likely to work. Ideally they should end up with a list of between five and ten such statements, all carefully fashioned so as to result in different feelings or behaviour from that which inevitably flows from self-talk of the kind illustrated above.

The final phase of training then consists of individuals learning their self-prompts for use in real situations, and actually applying them as forcefully as they can whenever such situations arise. Such an unaccustomed activity may seem very odd at first, but individuals should find it gradually establishes itself as a habit. Two other elements must be added for the procedure to be effective. First, as with all forms of training, practice is required to enable individuals to improve their ability to control themselves, via self-prompts, in circumstances in which they had previously lost control. Second, individuals should be encouraged to self-monitor their successes and their failures, to judge for themselves from one possible offence 'opportunity' to the next whether they are managing to secure more governance over their own unruly emotions and behaviours. (Some suggestions for self-monitoring exercises are given below.) It is upon the combination of practice and self-monitoring that the outcome of virtually any training programme ultimately depends.

Although individuals' self-control problems, their typical thoughts, and the content of the self-prompts they may be likely to use are all liable to be extremely heterogeneous, there is no reason why these methods cannot still be used in a group setting. In fact people may be able to assist each other in developing self-prompts and in reinforcing each other's efforts. In Meichenbaum's (1980) estimation the group can be a useful vehicle for self-instructional training even though people are obviously in pursuit of highly individual goals within it. The flexibility of this method permits its usage, then, in both group and individual work.

Change matrix

Both thought stopping and self-prompts are ways of affecting feelings and behaviour through changing *cognitions*, the sorts of things people say to themselves which regulate (or *fail* to regulate) their own actions. But self-instructions can also be addressed as it were more directly to actions themselves. While in self-instructional training we give ourselves lists of things to *think* that will coach us through a difficult problem, it is equally feasible that we should also compile lists of things to *say to other people* and lists of things to *do* with the same overall purpose in mind. We might even take this a step further and give ourselves comparable lists of things to *avoid* thinking, saying, and doing. This represents a kind of sideways extension of the use of self-prompts, where individuals are asked to itemize as many things as they can think of that will help them eradicate a particular difficulty with which they are faced. People have to approach the problem more globally and marshal all their resources to overpower it. As a way of summarizing their ideas, they can be invited to fill in a *change matrix* like the one shown on p. 144 (or a larger version of it).

The first column of this table is intended for self-prompts in the sense just described – statements which people can make to themselves to help keep their feelings or behaviour within self-prescribed limits. The second column then contains possible things to say to others when individuals feel they are 'at risk' (i.e., when they are in a confluence of circumstances in which on prior occasions they have committed an offence) – with the aim for example of averting a conflict, deflecting group pressure, or

	THINK	SAY	DO
Things to:			
Things NOT to:			

otherwise retaining control of events. The third column is for actions themselves; for cataloguing activities which people can *give themselves to do* to skirt clear of rocks on which they have previously foundered. In the bottom row of the matrix, in contrast, individuals list thoughts, interlocutions, or behaviours which for the purpose of achieving their self-control targets are prohibited. These should not just be mirror images of items in the upper row. If people take stock of a problem with sufficient thoroughness they can almost always discern more aspects of situations on which their offence behaviour is contingent.

Should people have difficulty in finding things to insert in the boxes of the matrix, recourse can be made to the results of interviews, diaries, or other self-observational tools, a feelings thermometer, anger inventory, or any other assessment exercises as available. Alternatively, suggest they ask themselves a series of questions about their losses of control; for example:

> What kinds of thing do I think about when I'm well away from trouble?
> What kinds of conversations do I have (and with whom?) which sometimes lead to trouble?
> Are there things I could say, subjects to talk about, to manoeuvre a conversation in a different direction?
> What kinds of things am I often doing when (or just before) I break the law?
> What other ways do I have of spending my time?
> Are there things I can do to occupy my time which *don't* lead to trouble?

The answers to these and similar questions should supply an abundance of ideas for inclusion in the matrix, to become springboards for subsequent action.

If individuals wish to maximize their chances of being able to stop committing a particular kind of offence, a matrix like this presents them with the possibility of constructing a complete programme for personal change. By looking at their own inner speech, their verbal exchanges with others, and the things they are doing with their time, they should be able to develop a comprehensive strategy for steering themselves *away* from situations and events they know are offence-related and *towards* situations and events which they know are safer and more trouble-free. The change matrix thus represents a means of sharpening and consolidating individuals' plans for realizing greater self-control.

Imaginal rehearsal

To help individuals put into practice some of the tactics they have decided to use in self-control training, another kind of exercise which can be pressed into service is *imaginal rehearsal*. Just as in social skills training people 'limber up' for encounters using role-play and allied methods, so in self-control training they can prepare for awkward moments in advance by imagining them and thinking about what to do when they arrive. This could be called the self-control equivalent of role-play (though there is no reason of course why people should not use actual role-play if their problem revolves around an interpersonal situation). The exercise consists of running through an imagined scene, to try to be better able to handle it when it eventually occurs. There are two main ways in which this can be used. One is simply as a device for anticipating events; to estimate in general what might transpire, and especially to concentrate on what you yourself will say and do according to the circumstances, the reactions of others, and so on. Anyone who has ever been to a job interview will be familiar with this process which seems to set itself in motion almost involuntarily before experiences which we expect to be stressful. But we might also use it deliberately, say, before meeting someone with whom we have recently had an argument; and there is no reason why it should not be applied to any incident in which an individual's chances of suppressing inclinations to offend might be at stake.

A second use for imaginal rehearsal is in a form known as 'covert modelling'. Here, individuals picture a scene (which need not involve other people) which they are feeling uncertain about, and imagine themselves coping with it successfully. The idea of modelling in social interaction training was introduced in the last chapter; this procedure runs a close parallel to it except that the 'model' is the person him- or herself, and is visualized mentally rather than role-played 'live' or recorded on videotape. People have to consider what they would do and/or say to manage a particular event appropriately and effectively; and then play through the action in their minds, in such a way that they see themselves doing and saying the required things. This then acts as a kind of example to them of how they might deal with the real-life event. Such 'coping imagery' has been used to help people free themselves from phobias and to become more assertive (Meichenbaum, 1977; Rimm and Masters, 1979). It was also used by Hay, Hay and Nelson (1977) to help an alcoholic withstand pressure to resume drinking by imagining himself succeeding at this in a variety of situations in which he expected it would happen. A modified form of the technique was used by Hosford, Moss, and Morrell (1976) to help two prisoners: one who had a stuttering problem and whose criminal activity was principally aimed at obtaining the means to 'buy' friends; and another, highly anxious, life-sentence prisoner who used the method to bring about substantial changes in his own behaviour and considerably improved his chances of parole.

Stress inoculation

With very serious, well established, and apparently intractable problems such as habitual violence, no single technique from the selection described here may prove adequate to eradicate them or even reduce their frequency of occurrence. A form of training which combines different methods may be needed, as Novaco (1975) found in his work with aggressive adults. The more elaborate species of training devised by Meichenbaum (1977) and used by Novaco in this and later work is called *stress inoculation*. This draws together elements of relaxation training, the use of self-instructions, and imaginal rehearsal in a sequence of exercises which can be specially adapted for work on the self-control of violent feelings and behaviour.

As used by Novaco (1978, 1979) for this purpose, stress inoculation has the following three phases:

1. *cognitive preparation* – first, people are asked to think about aggression in general, and to find out as much as possible about their own feelings and behaviour in this regard. The anger inventory, an anger diary, feelings thermometer, analysis of violent incidents and other methods can be used at this stage. Most important of all, people must try to pinpoint situations in which their own violence occurs. In addition, the general ideas of self-control and stress inoculation, and the reasons behind specific exercises they will be asked to do, must be clearly explained to them.

2. *skill acquisition* – utilizing some of the exercises we have already discussed, offenders now try to develop the ability to relax, to use calming self-instructions, to find things to say which will enable them to solve problems verbally rather than physically. In general, they should try to identify *any* strategy which might help them increase their self-control, and make it ready for use.

3. *application training* – the skills individuals have acquired should now be practised in a series of progressively more provocative or stressful situations by means of role-play and/or imaginal rehearsal; coupled with self-monitoring of their own performance (using some of the methods to be suggested below).

In essence, the stress inoculation approach revolves around the idea of having individuals talk themselves out of or down from states of high arousal in which they might be likely to launch into violence. They do this by using relaxation methods (breathing, muscular control) which they modulate as necessary using self-prompts. Though stress inoculation involves what could be labelled an 'educational' component (making individuals more aware of the nature of aggression and how it can be overcome) and its application hinges on issues or situations defined by individuals during self-assessment, the principal feature of its use is the amalgam of relaxation and self-prompts applied to experiences of gradually increasing stressfulness.

At the core of the method is the idea of helping individuals to break down a stressful (potentially violent) encounter into a series of stages: (a) preparing for a provocation; (b) impact and confrontation; (c) coping with arousal; and (d) subsequent reflection. Novaco (1978, 1979) gives examples of the self-statements that might be used at each of these stages:

Preparing for a provocation
'This could be a rough situation, but I know how to deal with it.'
'Remember, stick to the issues and don't take it personally.'
Impact and confrontation
'As long as I keep my cool, *I'm* in control of the situation.'
'You don't need to prove yourself. Don't make more out of this than you have to'.
Coping with arousal
'My muscles are getting tight. Relax and slow things down.'
'He probably wants me to get angry, but I'm going to deal with it constructively.'
Subsequent reflection
a. conflict·unresolved:
    'Forget about the aggravation. Thinking about it only makes you upset.'
    'Don't take it personally. It's probably not so serious.'
b. conflict resolved:
    'I could have gotten more upset than it was worth.'
    'I actually got through that without getting angry.'

In the practice phase following the preparation of a battery of prompts like these, individuals attempt to use relaxation to keep themselves under control in imagined versions of potentially inflammatory situations. They must then repeat the exercise over a series of situations graduated in level of tension, much as in systematic desensitization. Whenever possible they should also try to do this in the actual situations (if they occur). Obviously, training in stress inoculation is a fairly time-consuming process, liable to extend over a number of sessions. To make it as useful as possible, it should be linked to some form of self-monitoring, to which we turn next.

Self-monitoring

Although the greater part of this chapter has been taken up with assessment and training exercises for the acquisition of self-control, in a sense the methods we have met with so far are just the beginning. For the proper execution of sought-after skills, all forms of training rely on *practice*. It is only after people have learnt to do some of the things described so far that the real work of developing self-control begins. They have to try over and over again to manage their feelings and behaviour in circumstances in which they had previously failed to do so. As with practice of any skill, this effort is meaningless unless its results are visible to trainees. In self-control training, information about their progress is gathered by individuals themselves in a process known as *self-monitoring* – a continuous appraisal and reappraisal of trainees' successes and failures in recapturing the control they have lost.

Self-monitoring can be carried out in a variety of ways. The different kinds of self-observation exercise, for example diaries, records of thoughts, or mood charts, can be maintained over a prolonged period and inspected at intervals for evidence of trends. Other self-assessment methods, like locus of control scales, the anger inventory, or feelings thermometer, can be completed, and results compared with those obtained first time round to see if any shifts have taken place. Individuals can rate their own feelings or behaviour on specially designed scales as in social skills training (for an illustration, see the video rating form on p. 102). All of these involve exercises we have already come across. Other kinds of self-monitoring methods include the following.

Event recording

To discover whether they are learning to control offence-related behaviour in the longer run, people can gauge their performance in terms of 'objective' criteria. For this purpose 'objective' means that the information so obtained could *in principle* (and if necessary, in practice) be verified by someone else. The easiest way of recording behaviour for this purpose is to count the frequency of some kind of event. Depending on the problem with which individuals are concerned, ask them to keep records of any of the following for themselves:

Offences committed	Arguments at home; at work; with friends
Arrests	Outbursts of swearing or verbal abuse
Convictions	Fights
Drinks consumed	Days when drugs are taken per week/month
Days drunk per week or month	Drug-free days per week/month
Days sober per week or month	Visits to shops *without* shoplifting
Alcoholic black-outs	Amounts of money spent on drink, drugs, or gambling
Numbers of car journeys made while over/under the legal alcohol limit	Successful (trouble-free) encounters with police
Numbers of car journeys made *without* breaking the speed limit	Numbers of 'normal' (offence-free) meetings with women

All of the above indices can be measured and kept track of without too much difficulty. It will be best if the figures are reckoned over pre-set periods (daily, weekly, or monthly) and entered on ready made sheets or graphs. The latter can then be reviewed from time to time for signs of any upward or downward movement in the chosen indicators. The point of making the recorded events verifiable is not so that checks can be made on their veracity; but rather to demonstrate to individuals that the changes they are making are not just in the mind: the fact that other people could attest to them helps to reinforce individuals' confidence, encouraging them to build on the successes they have achieved.

BAC discrimination training

The exercise just outlined is flexible enough to be used with a diversity of self-control problems; we look now at a type of self-monitoring with more strictly delimited aims. This is *blood alcohol concentration (BAC) discrimination training* and it has been used with some success with problem drinkers.

The effects of alcohol are closely correlated with the amount of it circulating in the bloodstream, which is expressed as milligrams of alcohol per 100 millilitres of blood (or *mg%*). The rate at which this rises when someone drinks is determined in the main by three factors: the amount of alcohol ingested; the speed of drinking; and the body-weight of the drinker. The idea behind this training is that if people become more aware of the amount of alcohol they are absorbing they will be more able to regulate it and to control their drinking in general.

Individuals can judge their BAC using two different sorts of cues: *internal* (their perceived state of intoxication based on how they feel, their movements etc.) and *external* (quantity of alcohol consumed over a given period). The latter are more reliable. Miller and Munoz (1976) provide a set of tables by means of which drinkers can calculate their BAC and plot changes in it over a timespan of up to four hours.

For this purpose, Miller and Munoz define *one drink* as '. . . the amount of beverage that contains a half-ounce of pure ethyl alcohol' (1976, 12). This amount of alcohol is contained in approximately a half-pint of beer, a large glass of wine, a small glass of sherry, or a standard measure of whisky. Knowing how much they weigh, individuals can then work out their BAC after one, two, three, and four hours of drinking following the consumption of various quantities of drink (up to a maximum quoted of 16 drinks). For example, the BAC of someone weighing roughly 160 pounds would increase as shown in the table below.

BACs (mg%) for a person weighing 160 lbs
Time spent drinking

Number of drinks	1 hour	2 hours	3 hours	4 hours
1	20	0	0	0
2	40	10	0	0
3	60	30	20	10
4	80	60	40	30
5	100	80	60	50
6	120	100	90	70
7	140	120	110	90
8	160	150	130	120
9	180	170	150	140
10	210	190	170	160

Using the data supplied by Miller and Munoz, individuals are invited to draw up their own BAC tables like the one shown here. They now know how their BAC will change according to various rates of drinking. This information in itself is very worthwhile for the purpose of self-monitoring. But in self-control training, individuals must take the further step of deciding what they would like their BAC ceiling to be. (Miller and Munoz suggest setting two upper limits: an absolute maximum, for special occasions, and a regular limit, for everyday use.) On this basis, individuals can then deduce the rates at which they must drink in order to remain within their own self-imposed limits on any given occasion. For example, if someone weighing 160 pounds wants never to exceed a BAC of 80 mg% (the legally permissible limit for driving), then he or she ought not to imbibe more than four drinks (two pints of beer or four whiskies) in one hour, five drinks over two hours, and so on. Comparative figures for other body weights can be found in Miller and Munoz (1976).

Tables like these, which individuals need to carry around with them if they are to use them properly, can be of benefit in two ways. They allow people to chart their blood alcohol levels if this is of interest in itself as part of general self-monitoring; and they can assist them in keeping their alcohol intake inside a preappointed range. In either case, a scan of the figures (if they are logged over time) will swiftly reveal people's degree of success in modifying their use of alcohol.

Self-reports

It is said that 'nothing succeeds like success'; and cliché though this may be, when it comes to training designed to help people solve their own problems, it becomes almost literally true. When trying to do something as difficult as cut down your drinking, stop yourself from acting so compulsively, or take command of your own feelings of hostility, any sign that you are going in the right direction makes you feel good in itself *and* gives a boost to renewed and more confident efforts. Individuals' perceptions of their own progress are thus all-important in self-control training; it is upon them more than anything else that their future progress depends. So people's reports on how they are doing from their own point of view, their thoughts and feelings about it, are a vital focus of self-monitoring.

Self-reports can be made informally, in interviews spaced out over a lengthy period, or in discussions in a group of which individuals are members. You should urge them to keep written or tape-recorded accounts of any incident that seems noteworthy to them. If they are resistant to this or fail to do it consistently, they can be asked in interviews to look back over a given period (e.g. the last week) and think of as many occasions as they can when they managed to control themselves in relation to the type of feelings or behaviour which they are attempting to change.

As an alternative, a more formal kind of self-reporting can be introduced, using for example a self-monitoring sheet like the one shown on p. 150; with its content (naturally) adjusted to suit the needs of the person using it. This is for recording instances in which individuals succeeded in using self-prompts; made themselves relax; delayed their normally impulsive reactions; or otherwise took command of their behaviour. The items on the left are dictated by the kinds of problem people are trying to solve, the methods they are using to do so, and the exact wording of the self-prompts or other devices with which they have armed themselves in the battle for self-control. The number of them can be varied according to the targets people have set themselves; and if the frequency of ten 'scores' on the right seems too formidable a sum to begin with, this also can be reduced (though a frequency of less than five might start to seem a bit pointless). When people have filled one sheet they should move on to another, and continue for as long as is necessary. The items on the sheet should themselves be altered if some are proving impracticable because they are unattainable, or too easy, or for any other reason which emerges in the light of experience. And as in the business of trying to increase self-esteem, people should give themselves specially designated 'rewards' at pre-selected points if they feel they have taken significant steps forward or are moving in general at a satisfactory pace.

SELF-MONITORING

When you're trying to achieve something that's difficult, it often helps to keep a record of your successes. This sheet is for recording the numbers of times you manage to control your own feelings or behaviour. All you have to do is tick or shade in one of the boxes on the right each time you achieve one of the goals on the left. When you have managed ten, start a new sheet.

Goal	Frequency
	1 2 3 4 5 6 7 8 9 10
Cooled down an argument.	☐☐☐☐☐☐☐☐☐☐
Looked away when someone stared at me.	☐☐☐☐☐☐☐☐☐☐
Stopped myself from saying something I would have regretted.	☐☐☐☐☐☐☐☐☐☐
Calmed myself down when I felt angry.	☐☐☐☐☐☐☐☐☐☐
Spotted when a situation could have got out of hand	☐☐☐☐☐☐☐☐☐☐
Spoke quietly instead of shouting	☐☐☐☐☐☐☐☐☐☐
Stopped myself from swearing at someone.	☐☐☐☐☐☐☐☐☐☐
Stopped myself from hitting someone.	☐☐☐☐☐☐☐☐☐☐
Said to myself 'there's no point in getting worked up about this'.	☐☐☐☐☐☐☐☐☐☐
Talked to someone I don't like without being hostile.	☐☐☐☐☐☐☐☐☐☐
I felt angry but told myself to do nothing until I'd cooled down.	☐☐☐☐☐☐☐☐☐☐
Kept control when someone was shouting at me.	☐☐☐☐☐☐☐☐☐☐

Biofeedback

A final, quite distinctive form of self-monitoring which we propose to mention is *biofeedback*. This refers to the process by which various physiological indicators, like heart rate, blood pressure, or alpha brain waves, which are normally outside our voluntary control, are brought into our awareness so that we can try to exercise conscious control over them. The means by which this is usually achieved is through the use of some sort of specialized equipment, for example, where electrodes are attached to the scalp, and connected to a machine which measures and records the gross electrical activity of the brain. Variations in this are then relayed to the individual in the form of an auditory signal or a moving dot on a screen. Although the early (sometimes quite exaggerated) claims made for biofeedback when it was first discovered have not been fulfilled by research, there is evidence that it can assist in the treatment of some illnesses (Melzack and Wall, 1982; Rimm and Masters, 1979). As far as offending behaviour is concerned, biofeedback may have potential applications for aiding those whose offences are partly linked to tension, excitement or aggression.

Such individuals may be able to monitor their own bodily state and use this as a method of making themselves relax. For this purpose, the elaborate technology of clinically-based biofeedback may not be needed. A number of much simpler devices are now marketed commercially; these are designed to monitor *galvanic skin responses* or *GSR*s. A GSR is a measurable change in the electrical conductivity of the skin, usually caused by changes in the level of moisture on the skin's surface, for example when we sweat. This in turn reflects underlying fluctuations in our level of emotional arousal. Instruments are currently available which can follow such changes in the palm of the hand or on the fingers. These emit a tone (or can be wired up to a visual display) which varies according to our overall level of excitation. By using a device of this kind, people can obtain feedback on their degree of success in making themselves more physically relaxed. This can be used both to help them relax on any given occasion by concentrating on the tone signal and attempting to alter it; and to monitor longer-term changes in their ability to relax, since most machines have a calibrated numerical scale, readings from which can be plotted over time. Though the signals and scale readings may not be absolutely accurate measures of emotional state, they are sufficiently sensitive to change to be worth exploring as a method of helping some offenders to observe, and influence, their own levels of tension.

A wide assortment of methods, then, can be used in self-monitoring. The choice from amongst them must be made by individuals themselves, which means that the aims of each method and the practicalities involved in using it must be carefully explained to them. Obviously you may have to help them make a choice; in this case the method *they are most likely to use* is the one that should be advised, provided of course that it is appropriate for the task they are undertaking. At reasonable intervals, you should help individuals evaluate the ground (if any) they have covered. Minor 'course corrections' can be suggested if this seems necessary; or completely novel methods tried if the whole thing seems like too much of an uphill struggle or they have more or less abandoned it themselves. In some cases what might be needed is a return to, and re-learning of, the initial methods. A person with a ten-year history of drinking, theft, violence or sexual exhibitionism is unlikely to be transformed in just a few sessions (though such things have happened). Professionals in many spheres go on 'refresher' courses to remind themselves of the purposes and methods with which they started out. There is clear evidence that a 'booster' or shot of the originally used exercises can have a similar positive effect in both social skills and self-control training.

7 Risk-taking and decision-making

If the way events are depicted in the media is anything to go by, most people's image of the behaviour we call 'crime' is that it is ugly, callous and threatening, rooted in greed, envy, hatred, or other equally base and malicious human motives. Some of it is the product of the inflamed passions or bestial longings of already aberrant individuals. Some of it derives from a loathing of, and a desire to get back at or to get rid of, authority. Some of it is painstakingly planned by small bands of cold, calculating professionals. It is as if, out there in the grim world of derelict housing estates, motorcycle gangs and badly-lit pedestrian subways, the forces of evil really were at work – to judge at least by the selection and presentation of crime news in most of our national and local dailies.

Offences of some very nasty kinds there certainly are. But any more than a casual inspection of the anatomy of most pieces of law-breaking reveals a pattern strikingly different from the one refracted through the distorting prism of the press. Some youths steal a car and are apprehended within an hour less than half a mile from where they took the vehicle. At one o'clock in the morning, a drunk man smashes a shop window and carries off a colour television set, staggering into two patrolling beat policemen a bit farther along the road. A burglar breaks into a probation office and steals a videotape recorder, leaving behind a typewritten message which instantly identifies him to the staff. A middle-aged woman is caught stealing a scarf costing less than £5: she may eventually be fined several times that amount. Juveniles break into empty warehouses, or steal items they can neither use nor sell, or do wanton damage to buildings within a few yards of their own homes. While some crime undoubtedly does pay, a vast proportion of it involves the taking of silly risks, the making of very bad decisions usually on the spur of the moment, the injuring of the offender's interests just as much as anybody else's – and all for very little financial or material gain anyway. Viewed detachedly, many offences, rather than appearing vicious and premeditated, look like little more than patently unintelligent behaviour.

Given the nature of much law-breaking, it is hard to escape the conclusion that for some people at least, the urge to commit offences must be very strong to warrant the potential costs involved. It is not perhaps surprising then that surveys of the explanations offered by offenders for their actions confirm that a search for excitement and the taking of risks is a main reason for the commission of some kinds of offence. West and Farrington (1977) carried out a longitudinal study of 389 boys in six London schools, following them from the ages of eight to eighteen. Just over a quarter of the group had been convicted of offences during this period. While the commonest motive for offending given by these boys was classed as 'rational', i.e., obtaining money or goods, the next largest category was 'enjoyment', cited as their usual motive for offending by 19.2 per cent of the sample. For damaging property and taking motor vehicles enjoyment was even more important, the corresponding proportions being 42.9 per cent and 60.4 per cent. Even for shoplifting, nearly a third of the group said pleasure was the chief motivation, and the figures for other offence types were by no means negligible. Approaching the matter slightly differently, Mayers (1980) asked a number of 'hard-core' delinquents in residential institutions for clusters of reasons why they committed offences. More than 80 per cent of this group mentioned economic reasons, but upwards of 62 per cent said that trying to overcome boredom was partly responsible as well. A wish for enjoyment then, and a willingness to run the inevitable risks, seems to be a significant ingredient of the tendency to fall foul of the law, especially perhaps amongst younger offenders or those who are described as 'petty recidivists'.

In this chapter we examine the possible role of this factor in offending behaviour: that the element of enjoyment may contribute to some people's proneness to offend and may even be a major attraction for some. Associated with this, the fact that many offences seem irrational, even self-defeating in character raises the further question of whether some offenders are simply very bad decision-makers, and whether anything can be done to help them make decisions which more effectively forward their own interests as well as those of others.

Risk-taking, excitement, and offence behaviour

A first question which presents itself, given the level of risk entailed in some crimes, and one which has certainly commended itself to traditional criminology, is whether there is some personality difference between offenders and non-offenders such that the former have more of a 'need' for excitement than the latter. One idea which has been pursued in this respect is that some sub-groups of offenders may be pronounced 'sensation seekers', i.e., may demand a high level of stimulation from the environment. Zuckerman (1971) developed a special questionnaire for measuring this variable, the *Sensation-Seeking Scale*, which assesses individuals' desires for 'thrill and adventure' through participation in dangerous sports or other activities; the strength of their wish for 'experience through the senses'; their lack of social inhibitions; and their susceptibility to boredom. On the basis of replies to this scale it has been tentatively suggested that drug abusers (Zuckerman, 1978a) and offenders diagnosed as 'psychopaths' (Blackburn, 1978; Emmons and Webb, 1974) have a higher-than-normal need for 'experiencing' – are 'pathological stimulation seekers'. In addition Farley and Farley (1972), working with institutionalized delinquent girls aged between 14 and 17, found an association between high scoring on the Sensation-Seeking Scale and more frequent escape attempts, disruptive behaviour, and aggressiveness. Other research reviewed by Zuckerman (1978b) has however shown more mixed results. It is difficult to draw firm conclusions from this research; for example, since Zuckerman's scale contains a number of items related to drug effects it may not be surprising that drug offenders should emerge as distinct on it. The 'psychopaths' studied by Blackburn and by Emmons and Webb represent only a small minority of very disturbed offenders; and in any case, both these pieces of research found them to score differently from comparison groups of other sorts of offenders. The findings thus tell us little about the considerable numbers of people who appear to be after thrills or new experiences and who get themselves into trouble as a result.

By and large, the quest for an understanding of offence behaviour in terms of systematic offender/non-offender personality differences has not been rewarded with many reliable results. As far as adult offenders are concerned, Eysenck (1964) has steadfastly promoted the view that such differences exist in the personality dimensions of 'extraversion-introversion' and 'neuroticism' on which he has done so much work; but his case is not regarded as proven by very many criminologists. For younger offenders, there is the suggestion that delinquents are '. . . overall, more likely to be extraverted and unstable, more impulsive, less sensitive to others' feelings and more liable to take risks' than non-offenders (Hoghughi, 1983, 64). However, '. . . personality patterns of delinquents are as widely diverse as are those of their ordinary peers and the differences between the two groups are neither always significant nor consistent' (*ibid.*, 65). The psychological heterogeneity even of persistent offenders seems to debar the possibility of detecting any facet (or collection of facets) which conclusively marks them out from their less criminally-inclined neighbours.

Nonetheless, concerning boredom, excitement, and the taking of risks – the areas in which we are interested here – there are some grounds for believing that differences between delinquents and non-delinquents could exist. West and Farrington (1977) found that offenders were more likely to be heavy gamblers than those who had no criminal records, in that if they did gamble they did so more frequently and with larger sums of money. In their use of leisure time, offenders were about three times more likely to 'hang about in the streets' than non-offenders; and they more often went to coffee bars, discotheques, and parties, and spent more time driving or riding around in motor vehicles. By contrast, they were noticeably less likely to attend evening classes. As we saw in chapter three, they appeared to drink more, and were more likely to become aggressive after drinking. (It should be remembered however that, the statistical significance of West and Farrington's results notwithstanding, the differences they found rarely accounted for more than half of their delinquent sample.) Some differences were also found by Farrington, Biron, and LeBlanc (1982) using one of the tests developed by Eysenck to measure 'extraversion-introversion' and 'neuroticism', the Eysenck Personality Inventory. Although overall there were no close relationships between these personality traits and delinquency, responses to two questions, 'Do you often long for excitement?' and 'Do you generally do things quickly without stopping to think?' were correlated with degree of delinquency, more entrenched delinquents being more likely to answer in the affirmative. The possibility remains then that a fondness for excitement and a tendency to be impulsive may predispose some young people to take more risks and to come into contact with the law (Stewart and Hemsley, 1979).

But the fact that research on character differences between offenders and non-offenders has not been very fruitful suggests that some individuals' hunger for excitement may be less a comment on the sorts of people they are than on the state of our towns and cities and the kind of environment that has been created for the young. Williamson (1978) has approached delinquency from this point of view. In areas where unemployment is high and people have little money to spend, where leisure facilities and other social amenities are few or are entirely lacking, delinquency may be a 'rational response' to the circumstances. In these conditions, '. . . For a large number, delinquency is considered a good risk' (Williamson, *op. cit.*, 333); burglary, theft, and taking motor vehicles may be advantageous in providing cash, goods or entertainment that cannot be otherwise obtained. In this respect offences may be 'utilitarian' but in other instances they simply provide 'something to do' to alleviate boredom. Where legitimate means of enjoying oneself are just not available – or those which are (such as Scouts) are unattractive – it is virtually certain that some young people will experiment with delinquent alternatives.

If offenders do relatively less well at school than their peers, and if they also tend to come from homes which are conflict-ridden, neglectful, or contain other members who are offenders – as substantial amounts of evidence indicate (Rutter and Madge, 1976;

Rutter, Maugham, Mortimore and Ouston, 1979) – then they may be more prone to end up in a position in which they are 'hanging about in the streets' with 'nothing to do'. And if, as seems not unlikely in this situation, they then associate with other delinquents – which according to some research is the single best predictor of future delinquency (Johnson, 1979) – the results seem almost inescapable. As we saw in chapter five, and as has been very well established in one research report after another, the bulk of juvenile crime is carried out in groups.

At this point, another vector may be operating which adds further to the chances that excitement may be sought, risks taken, and offences committed. When people are gathered together in groups and have to make decisions, in particular where they have a choice between 'safe' and 'risky' options in any given context, the decisions they make almost always tend to be riskier than would the decisions made by any of the individuals acting alone. This phenomenon is known as 'group movement to risk' or the 'risky shift'. Its occurrence has been demonstrated in a number of pieces of research in both 'laboratory' and 'naturalistic' settings. Wallach, Kogan, and Bem (1962) asked individuals, working first of all on their own, to make decisions about a series of hypothetical situations, in each of which there was a choice between a 'safe' course of action (little was ventured, but little guaranteed in return) and a 'risky' alternative (the outcome could be either very good or very bad). For example:

> 'A man with a severe heart ailment must seriously curtail his customary way of life if he does not undergo a delicate medical operation which might cure him completely or might prove fatal.'

The participants' task in each case was to state a minimal probability of success they would require before advising the 'risky' way out of the dilemma. Following their solo decisions, they were then formed into small groups (with five or six members) and asked to discuss the issues, present their own points of view, and come up with a unanimous decision for the group. In 26 out of the 28 groups taking part, there was a significant move towards the riskier choice across the set of decisions to be made. Further, when making decisions by themselves again afterwards, individuals tended to opt for the less conservative courses of action more often, and *still* did so when retested up to six weeks after the group sessions.

Comparable findings were obtained by Malamuth and Feshbach (1972) in an experiment in which individuals and groups had to make a 'real' choice, i.e., rather than dealing with imagined events, they had to decide between predictable and speculative alternatives in a situation in which the outcome affected the amount of money they made. Once again the groups were more likely to gamble than had been their constituent members beforehand. But strangely enough, when members were asked to make recommendations within the group before any discussion had taken place, their choices showed a movement towards risk even then; the 'risky shift' was not attributable to the group dynamics as such. Just being in a group seemed to make individuals more willing to take risks. As yet, no-one has satisfactorily accounted for the 'risky shift' effect, but it must certainly provide part of the explanation of what goes on in some delinquent groups. Individuals may propose offences that are more hazardous than anything they would contemplate on their own (perhaps as a way of preserving their self-esteem). Their reckonings of the chances of being caught may also differ in a group context. Pressures within a group may escalate to a point beyond which no-one can withdraw from the action without appearing a spoilsport, a 'chicken', or even a potential 'grass'.

There are three separate sorts of reasons then why some offences entailing (occasionally quite considerable) risks are committed. One is that offenders, some of them at least, may have a predilection for taking gambles even when the odds are known to them, or may just act impulsively without thinking about the likely results. Another is that, living in localities in which there is little or nothing to do, individuals – and particularly adolescents faced with problems at home or school or both – may become involved in offences purely as a relief from boredom. A third possibility is that membership of groups may increase the chances that risks will be taken once the possibility of an offence has presented itself. The strategies of social skills training or self-control training may have something to offer those who would like to break out of a pattern of offending of this kind (resisting group pressure, learning to control impulses), but some other methods may be useful too and suggestions concerning them will be made later in this chapter.

Decision-making and problem-solving skills

Whatever the explanation for the apparent recklessness of some offences, there can be no doubt that many of those who commit them look back with regret on what they see were 'bad decisions', though this may not stop them doing the same thing again when the next opportunity arises.

This should not perhaps come as any surprise, since at any one time there must be many people on whom offending does *not* recoil in any way. A sizeable quantity of crime for example, the so-called 'dark figure', is not even officially reported (Hood and Sparks, 1970). Detection rates vary a great deal from one type of offence to another; similarly, 'clear-up rates' of crimes known to the police vary from one part of the country to another (McClintock and Avison, 1968). It is a safe assumption then that for many members of the public who break the law, no great inconvenience is caused thereby in their lives. For many it must prove profitable. Even some known criminals must see the balance of rewards and punishments as broadly in their favour, and must regard scrapes with the law as a price that may sometimes have to be paid. But for the majority of offenders who have been convicted twice or more, the drawbacks must surely outweigh the gains. A conviction brings with it the problem of the sentence itself; a criminal record which may be a bar to future employment, considerable disruption within the family and other aspects of personal life, an assurance that one will be an object of police attention from then on, and numerous other unpleasant repercussions. But convictions attest to the fact that, all too often, the decisions individuals have made have been the wrong ones. Why should they go on and on placing themselves in this position? Put bluntly, is it for no other reason than that recidivists are just more stupid that everyone else?

In fact, it *is* a fairly consistent finding of research that habitual offenders perform less well on IQ and attainment tests than non-offenders; and are also generally less successful in school (Douglas, Ross, and Simpson, 1968; Prentice and Kelly, 1963; Rutter, Maughan, Mortimore, and Ouston, 1979; West and Farrington, 1973). There is also a suggestion that delinquents tend to do relatively less well in the parts of IQ tests calling for verbal skills than in the parts which tap 'spatial-mechanical' abilities (Camp, 1966; Prentice and Kelly, 1963), though support for this has been less uniform. A not surprising corollary of such results is that young offenders commonly take a negative view of school (Johnson, 1979; West and Farrington, 1977). On the basis of this evidence it has been contended (e.g. by Hirschi and Hindelang, 1977) that IQ is a causative factor in delinquency via its effects on school achievement. However, global differences between offenders and non-offenders in IQ (typically of the order of five IQ points) do not really tell us a great deal. Large numbers of people of below-average intelligence do not become delinquents; plenty who are above average do. Having a low IQ does not, in any case, mean someone must be mentally dull. Most intelligence tests sample only a highly selective slice of the gamut of human ability (one which happens to be closely associated with progress in school), and people with IQs well below average are still perfectly capable of, for example, drawing conclusions about the results of their own actions.

Could we obtain a clearer understanding of the unthinking and impetuous nature of some offences in other terms, by reference perhaps to more specific kinds of cognitive differences between individuals? Is it possible to isolate particular 'thinking', or 'decision-making', or 'problem-solving' abilities in which offenders might have deficits – and even perhaps to rectify those deficits in some way?

A long-term research project designed to answer some of these questions has been undertaken by Spivack and his colleagues (Spivack, Platt, and Shure, 1976). The foundation-stone of their research is the proposition that there are mental capacities which individuals use when coping with the routine difficulties of everyday life (especially where the latter revolve around, or must be solved through the agency of, other people) which are *distinct from* the types of ability measured by standard intelligence tests. Spivack and his group call these *interpersonal cognitive problem-solving skills*; and see their overall role as being to '. . . mediate the quality of our social adjustment' (Spivack et al., *op. cit.*, 4). Amongst the skills they have identified in this respect are the following:

1. *Problem awareness* – a general sensitivity to the fact that interpersonal problems exist, that people can both create and solve problems for each other; coupled with the ability to explore this when it happens to you.
2. *Alternative thinking* – being able to generate alternative possible solutions to problems; to think up a number of different things to do rather than always responding to situations in the same rigid way.
3. *Means-end thinking* – the ability to formulate the steps that are necessary to reach a given goal; to analyse what has to be done in order to make something you want to happen actually happen, and recognize obstacles in the way.
4. *Consequential thinking* – the possession and use of sufficient foresight to realize what the effects of your own actions are likely to be; similar to alternative thinking, but applied to outcomes rather than how to achieve them.
5. *Social cause-and-effect thinking* – appreciating that the things you do may have been influenced by the feelings and actions of others, and may in turn influence them; and an ability to see things from someone else's point of view (perspective taking).

Based on extensive research with normal and emotionally disturbed children, adolescents, and adults, with psychiatric patients, and other groups, Spivack and his co-workers have concluded that proficiency in the above kinds of skills, which collectively might be called 'social intelligence', develops with age. However, this development is dependent on children and adolescents having the opportunity to learn the skills, which they do by observing parents and/or others around them as they grow up, and absorbing their habits of thought and action. Such learning will obviously be impaired if children are never exposed to the use of one or more of the skills.

This is exactly what happens to some young people. In a series of comparisons between 'normal, well-adjusted' adolescents, and others (including delinquents) suffering from problems of various kinds, Spivack and associates (Platt, Scura, and Hannon, 1973; Platt, Spivack, Altman, Altman, and Peizer, 1974; Spivack and Levine, 1963) found the latter to be deficient in some of the thinking skills just described. The ones they most frequently appeared to lack were alternative thinking; means-end thinking; perspective taking; and for some individuals, the ability to foresee the consequences of their actions. These findings are in accordance with those of Chandler (1973) on egocentrism and perspective-taking, and of Freedman, Rosenthal, Donahoe, Schlundt, and McFall (1978) on social problem-solving, which we discussed in chapter five. For the Spivack group, many of the problems which may manifest themselves during adolescence, from psychiatric illness to delinquency, can be traced in part to a shortage of these sorts of skill.

The natural inference from all of this is that it should be possible to help maladjusted individuals by teaching them the necessary problem-solving skills. To this end, Spivack and his group have devised a set of training programmes for use with different populations, from kindergarten children (and their parents) to adult chronic psychiatric patients. The emphasis in much of this material is on prevention, i.e., the intention is that the programmes should be used with 'normal' groups to try to stop some of the difficulties developing. One of the programmes is for adolescents and young adults and it can be employed with offender groups. It consists of 19 sessions or units, designed to impart basic problem-solving skills (e.g., distinguishing facts from opinions), to assemble these into more complex skills (e.g., contrasting alternative solutions to problems), and to place these in an interpersonal context through the use of some additional exercises in social skills training (e.g., for recognizing and communicating feelings). Unfortunately, a full-scale evaluation of the use of this programme has not yet been reported. Preliminary evidence from the application of parts of it appears however to be positive; some of the techniques it embraces have been used by other workers in different settings with initially encouraging results (Bowman, 1978; Coche and Douglas, 1977; Coche and Flick, 1975; Copemann, 1973).

It should potentially be beneficial then to try to help offenders develop some of the components of problem-solving skill, if they habitually make wrong decisions (to their own eventual cost), and would like to get better at thinking situations through before acting, by considering alternatives, working out consequences, and so on.

The exercises to be described in the rest of this chapter are all variations on this unifying theme. If people take risks with unfavourable odds and all too often lose; if committing offences is part of an attempt to cope with the fact that there is nothing to do; or if they make choices which repeatedly seem to rebound on them, then it may be possible for them to reverse their fortunes by being more circumspect in situations where they know they have acted over-hastily or foolishly in the past.

Three different directions are explored within this theme. The first is concerned with risk-taking itself, and whether individuals *do* run risks because they are impulsive, need excitement, or are carried along by being in a group. The second is the issue of the use of time; whether (especially young) offenders end up in trouble because they are bored, and whether they can find more legitimate solutions to this. The third is the question of whether some offences are committed out of ignorance, imprudence, an absence of forethought, or an inability to solve personal problems by any other means.

Risk taking: habit or circumstances?

In attempting to account for the risk-taking involved in some offences, one of the primary notions put forward by psychologists, criminologists and others has been that of personal predisposition. In fact there are two different patterns this might take. In one, individuals could be said to be impulsive: they tend to act utterly, or almost utterly, without thinking, and plunge themselves into difficulties as a result. In the other, people take risks because they want to – or at least a part of them does. Though perfectly aware of the chances of 'coming unstuck', they are seduced by the uncertainty itself, and find any temptation to gamble more or less irresistible. If individuals want to change these aspects of their behaviour, but are finding it very difficult to do so, it may help them to think about the causes of their own risk-taking; the insights so gained may enable them to decide where to concentrate their efforts. To this end, a number of self-assessment exercises can be used.

Analysing offences

The most direct approach is for individuals to look quite closely at the offences they have committed. They can do this for example using the '5-WH' or 'Action Replay' exercises which were described in chapter two. Obviously, a whole constellation of factors may be operating at the moment someone commits an offence: motives, attitudes, values, feelings, and previous histories of those involved, together with innumberable aspects of the situation. A look at someone's most recent offence, or if necessary a broader examination of a whole series of offences, might reveal whether he or she is prone to act impulsively; or alternatively, betray a penchant for self-exposure to risks or a wish to compete against the odds of being caught.

Assessing impulsiveness

For the purpose of trying to help someone who would like to stop committing offences, it may be important in the present context to distinguish the person who tends to act without thinking and who is irrevocably drawn to 'where the action is' from the person who breaks the law out of a fondness for taking chances. While this may become abundantly clear following a scrutiny of offences, as just suggested, on some occasions further exploration will be necessary.

To clarify an individual's attitudes and motivations on this point a questionnaire like the one shown overleaf can be used. (The idea of this was drawn from the work of Kipnis (1971) though his impulsiveness scale is quite different in content and was used for a different purpose.) Its aim is to furnish a rough indication of someone's level of impulsiveness in a wide range of situations. It can be used either as a discussion starter, with a number of the items being taken separately and talked about for a few minutes each; or as the subject-matter for part of a one-to-one interview; or typed out and duplicated for completion by members of a group. Individuals are asked to put themselves in each of the imaginary situations described, and to say what they think they would do under the circumstances. For each item they are asked to say how likely they would be to take a certain course of action; their replies can be taken in their own words or recorded on a rating scale:

Absolutely certain	Very likely	Quite likely	Not very likely	Not at all likely

If you are having the questions typed out for repeated use, the scale could be inserted after each of the items.

As with other questionnaires presented elsewhere in the book, a rough-and-ready 'impulsiveness' index can be derived from the one above, by superimposing a five-point scale on individuals' responses (five = 'absolutely certain', four = 'very likely', and so on) and totalling their scores over all ten items. The primary use to which this could be put is as a topic for discussion, as a basis for comparisons between members if you are working with a group.

If an individual's reactions on this questionnaire, seen side-by-side with information from interviews, the '5-WH', or 'Action Replays', seem to confirm an overall tendency

---

Testing your reactions

How do you think you would react if any of the following things happened to you?

1. If you got an unexpected windfall of money – say £20 – from somewhere, how likely would you be to spend it fairly soon afterwards rather than hold on to it for a while?
2. If you saw something you wanted to buy, and had the cash on you at the time, how likely would you be to buy it rather than shop around to see if there's something even better?
3. In general, how likely are you to say what you think whenever it comes into your head, regardless of where you are or who is listening?
4. Suppose someone dared you to do something a bit dangerous, like climb up onto the roof of a two-storey house for instance, how likely would you be to try it?
5. If you are buying something secondhand (e.g. an amplifier, motorbike, TV set) and what looks like a real bargain turns up, how likely would you be to settle for it on the spot rather than wait to have it checked over?
6. Imagine you are talking to a group of friends who've all got more money than you. They are arranging to go together to a quite expensive club and want you to come too; how likely would you be to say you would?
7. You really need some money to pay off a few debts. In the pub one evening, a well-known local villain offers to lend you it interest-free, provided you 'do some work for him sometime'. Is it likely you would accept?
8. A group of friends turn up at your house one night with a car and invite you to go for a spin. You didn't even know any of them had a car. How likely would you be to just go?
9. Imagine that you are walking past a pub late at night when you notice that a side window has been left slightly open. How likely is it that you'd try to go in?
10. You are sitting at home watching television when suddenly you hear some sort of commotion going on a couple of streets away. How likely would you be to go around to find out what's happening?

---

to impulsiveness, the best strategy for such a person to adopt would probably be some form of self-control training; for example, thought stopping or the use of self-instructions.

Individual risk-taking

A habit of acting on impulse will however only explain the offence behaviour of a proportion of those who take risks: many others may do similar things, with the difference that they weigh up the odds very carefully beforehand, and *consciously decide* that a risk is worth taking. This may be absolutely manifest from their behaviour in general and the kinds of offences they have committed; some individuals seem to exude a 'gambler's instinct' from every pore. Nevertheless a proclivity towards brinkmanship can be just as much of a snare as being impulsive, having a violent temper, or being in the grip of any other obsession. In extreme cases it can be so strong as to assume the status of an addiction. The strength of an individual's compulsions to run risks can be appraised in a number of exercises.

Life styles

In some cases an underlying attraction to risk may be reflected in several aspects of a person's life style, and this can be explored in a straightforward way in interviews or group discussion. These might cover such questions as: Do individuals take part (or want to take part) in physically dangerous sports or other activities? Would they describe themselves as 'dare-devils'? Do they gamble? On horse racing, cards, in casinos, on any other events? How often and for how much money? Do they take risks in other ways – e.g., neglect relationships that are important to them, take little care over other things they say they value? What would an individual say was the riskiest thing he or she had ever done? How often does he or she take risks of any kind? Answers to these and other questions should reveal a great deal about the significance of risk in the different compartments of an individual's life.

Risk-taking dilemmas

The process of exploring risk can be made more searching and brought closer to offence behaviour by using a series of situations like those listed above for impulsiveness. In this exercise, however, individuals are asked to *think* about the risks involved and to say whether or not they would take them. The items listed overleaf can be used orally; or typed out separately on cards for distribution to a group; or presented together on a sheet as a kind of questionnaire.

Once again, if you are working with a small group, the responses made by members to each of the items could be compared and discussed. If any individual (either a member of a group or someone you are working with on his/her own) emerges from this as an attested risk-taker, he or she could be asked to think about the possible reasons for this. If it appears that risk-taking is part of a search for excitement or for something to do to pass the time, some of the suggestions in the next section of this chapter can be employed. If on the other hand an individual is attracted to risk-taking for its own sake and would prefer not to be, some exercises in self-control training would probably be more appropriate – and may indeed be the only course of action likely to offer the individual any real hope of solving the problem.

Levels of risk

Another exercise that could be used in addition to or as an alternative to the previous one is to ask individuals to identify a point at which the risks involved in an offence become unacceptable to them. This allows exploration both of their perceptions of riskiness (what seems like wariness to some might seem like foolhardiness to others), and of their appetite for taking risks even when the odds are stacked against them. For example, looking at the offence of shoplifting if individuals have been in trouble for this, they could be asked to say when they believe it is relatively more or less safe to commit the offence. Some of the things which might influence this include:

Size of store: small, medium, large, super-store
Level of security: whether there are cameras, detectives etc., and how many
Layout: arrangement of shelves or displays; access to doors etc.
Number of customers: time of day/week, affecting how busy the store is
Number of shoplifters: going on your own, in a small or large group, etc.

The purpose of this is not to persuade offenders that their chances of being caught are less if they shoplift in different circumstances; they will probably be well aware of this. It is rather to help them discover whether the factor of risk is an important one for them. Though the main reason underlying theft from shops may be economic, for some individuals the 'thrill' of it undoubtedly provides an extra inducement.

Another way to approach this would be to ask individuals to decide if they would commit an offence where there is a gradually accumulating risk of failure or detection.

Dilemmas

In each of the following situations you have to make a choice between playing safe and taking a risk. What would you do in each case?

Risk-taking in general

1. Some friends are going to a party in a town 40 miles away and they'd like you to go with them; one of them has a car. Your work starts early in the morning and you're already in trouble over time-keeping – you could be dismissed if you're late again. There's a reasonable chance you'd be back alright but sometimes these things can turn out quite different from the way they were planned. Would you go?

2. At the Job Centre you are told about a job as a hospital porter – work you've done before – and the clerk arranges an interview for you for the following week. On the way home you meet an old friend who has his own business, and he offers you a job working for him, also to start the following week. It would be a much better-paid job working for your friend; however he's been in business twice before and both times went bust. Would you start work for him on the Monday?

3. In the garage/filling station where you work, your work-mate is off sick and the boss has to go out over lunchtime. He asks if you will stay on the premises to keep the place open and keep an eye on things; you agree. But you know some friends of yours are meeting in a pub less than half a mile away; you could be there, have a drink and come back before your boss returns. Would you do it?

4. Several of your friends urge you to take a day off school; something you've done quite a few times before. However you've been given warnings by the headmaster and by your parents about what will happen if you do it again. You don't know how serious they are. Would you go anyway?

5. You are sitting at home feeling fed up; your parents have gone in some relatives' car over to their house for the afternoon. Their own car is in the garage, but they've warned you not to use it as you've already been fined for dangerous and careless driving. All the same, you'd like to see your boyfriend/girlfriend who lives on the other side of town; you could be there and back without your parents knowing. Would you try it?

In the following situations you have to decide whether or not you could get away with doing something that's against the law.

Risk-taking offences

6. Purely by mistake, you leave a shop without paying for an article which is in your hand or leave a café without paying. You think they may have noticed and may remember you; one of the staff was in your class at school. Do you think it would be safe *not* to go back?

7. Following an affray in a local pub, two friends of yours who were involved ask you to cover up for them by saying they were round in your house at the time. You are not sure who else might have seen them there. Would it be alright to give them an alibi if you were questioned about it?

8. A friend of yours who uses drugs quite a lot asks you to look after a large quantity of marijuana because he/she thinks the police are going to search his/her flat. You've never been in trouble over drugs yourself, but the Drug Squad have seen you with your friend in the past. Do you think you could risk looking after the stuff for your friend?

9. Not long after you stop claiming social security, another giro arrives which you didn't expect and you're not sure you're entitled to. Do you think it would be worth the risk to cash it anyway?

10. You are on a youth training scheme and some mates ask you to leave a window unlocked in the building where you're doing a placement. The staff of the scheme know you've been in trouble before. But your friends say they'll make it look like a real break-in. Do you think you could get away with it?.

Imagining for example that the offence is breaking into a warehouse, individuals could be offered a list like the following and asked whether they would be prepared to try:

An old and insecure warehouse, not well protected, with no burglar alarms.

An old, insecure warehouse, with no alarms, but surrounded by a high fence.

A new warehouse, with alarms of a known type in recognisable places.

A new warehouse, with alarms, and grounds and walls lit up at night.

A new warehouse, with alarms, well-lit grounds, etc., about a quarter of a mile from a police station.

A new warehouse, with alarms, grounds lit, etc., and security guards on the premises.

The increasing difficulty of such a break-in, and the progressively greater likelihood of detection, will be a deterrent to some, but a positive incitement and challenge to others. Of course, it all depends what is in the warehouse, and many other things besides; many who would not be drawn to the risk in itself, would nevertheless be prepared to take it if the potential rewards were high enough. A few, on the other hand, will be willing to court complete disaster just for the feelings of exhilaration this brings; they enjoy taking part in 'cliffhangers'. Of interest in the present context is the way the individual sees the risk alongside the various other elements as he or she decides whether or not to go through with the offence. Individuals could be asked to divide the above list into 'risks I'd take' and 'risks I wouldn't take', and to think about the reasons why some risks are admissible and others not. Their decisions could then be compared with what happened in actual offences they had committed; presumably, since they had been arrested and convicted on such occasions, their estimates of the riskiness of the situation must have been erroneous in some respect. Hopefully, if this were demonstrated, it might lead them to reappraise themselves in some way: to recognize their urge to take risks; or appreciate the extent to which their actions were governed by an attempt to escape boredom; or realize that they are much more likely to take risks when in the company of certain friends. The end product of this *might* be a resolve to take action to counter some of the self-damaging trends in their own behaviour.

All the sets of questions and discussion items listed above are designed first and foremost as devices to stimulate thought. Many offenders, despite having led lives consisting mainly of one blunder after another, have never spent more than a few seconds reflecting on the position they are in. Evidence suggests that a majority *do* at some stage think about the way their lives are going and become much less likely to get into trouble as a result. The object of the above exercises is to help to bring about this process sooner rather than later. None of the foregoing sets of questions is designed to be an accurate 'measure' of anything. All should be altered, embellished or simplified according to the kinds of individuals with whom you are working: their ages, offences, problems, level of ability, and interests. The usefulness of any exercise should be judged in terms of its capacity to help offenders to find things out about themselves, and make decisions about the future on the basis of what they have learnt.

Risk-taking in groups

The exercises we have looked at so far have all been about risk-taking as a kind of 'habit'; a tendency to succumb to the lure of risks, assumed to reside within individual offenders. A quite different sort of reason why risks are run was identified earlier: the fact that, other things being equal, groups are more likely to take risks than the individuals composing them. This is what is known as the 'risky shift' effect and it can be simulated if you are working with offenders in a group.

To do this, you have to create a situation in which individuals are asked to make decisions about a number of offences, thinking about them on their own or in a group, and then compare the individual and group decisions as to their riskiness. The exercise can be organized in one of several ways. All the members of a large group with which you are working can be asked to make individual decisions; after which they can be formed into small groups (say threes or fours) and asked to make the decisions, or comparable decisions, again. Alternatively, if you have two rooms, half of the group can work as individuals in one, while the other half works as a group (or a number of small groups) in the other. Two parallel series of offences to be given to individuals and groups are listed in the table below.

Individual decisions	*Group decisions*
1. You are the first customer to enter a pub after opening time; the place is deserted apart from you. The barman has to go downstairs to change the barrels. What are the chances that you could get away with taking something from behind the bar?	1. The group of you are the first customers in a pub after opening time; no-one else is in the pub. The The barman has to go downstairs to the barrels. What are the chances that you could get away with taking something from behind the bar?
2. You are thinking about shop-lifting in a big department store on on your own. What do you think are the chances that you could do it without getting caught?	2. You are all friends and you are thinking about shoplifting together in a big department store. What are the chances that you could do it without getting caught?
3. What do you think are the chances of breaking into a local, not very well protected shop, without being found out?	3. As a group you are thinking about breaking into a local, not very well protected shop. What are your chances of doing it without being found out?
4. Walking along a quiet, tree-lined street, you think about taking a car to drive to a disco a few miles away. What are your chances of getting away with it on your own?	4. Coming along a quiet, tree-lined street, a group of you think about taking a car to go to a disco a few miles away. What are your chances of getting away with it?
5. A friend of yours who's well-known for thieving asks if he can leave some stolen goods in your bed-sit. He says he will share some of the cash with you when he sells them. How good are the chances that you could do it without being caught?	5. You all share a flat and a friend of one of you wants to leave some stolen goods there; he promises a share of the proceeds when he sells them. What are the chances that you could do it without being caught?
6. A friend of yours asks if he can borrow your car one night to move some stuff that's been stolen from the docks and left somewhere to be picked up. What are the chances that you could do this and get away with with it?	6. You jointly own a car and a friend would like to borrow it one night to move some stuff that's been taken from the docks and left somewhere to be picked up later. What are the chances that you could do this and get away with it?

The task which individuals and groups are set is to evaluate what they think is the likelihood of successfully getting away with each offence in the list. Brief accounts of offences of the kind shown here are read out one at a time; and participants are asked to give the *odds out of ten* of avoiding being caught. For example, nine out of ten would mean an individual or group reckoned the chances of evading the law were very high; one or two out of ten, on the other hand, would mean they regarded detection as a near-certainty. Their decisions in each case should be written down; they could also be asked to record whether they would actually commit the offence in question. When all six offences have been dealt with in this way, comparisons can be made between the odds given by individuals and by groups.

For this purpose, an average should be taken of the odds out of ten given by individuals forming a group, and these juxtaposed, preferably on a large sheet or blackboard, with the odds given by the group for each offence in turn. If there are several groups this should be done separately for each group and its members. The net effect of all this should be that the group decisions are riskier – i.e., they give higher odds of success – than those made by individuals. Contrasts could be noted between the decisions made by different groups; by different individuals; and for each of the six offences.

The objective of this exercise is to impress upon individuals the fact that the 'risky shift' does occur; that the way they behave in groups is liable to be different from, and probably more perilous than, the way they would behave on their own. This is not to discourage them from joining groups; simply to alert them to the possible dangers. And it may, for some individuals, provide an explanation for a few of the things they have done and found difficult to understand. They may feel obliged to parade a certain bravado in front of particular people, for instance. There will probably be some groups, or some offences, for which the movement to risk fails to appear; the factors influencing this in different cases can also be valuable points of discussion.

The descriptions of offences given here should of course be changed and adapted to make them suitable for the groups with whom you are working; if necessary an entirely new list should be drawn up and substituted for this one. The only proviso is that the individual and group descriptions should be more or less equivalent in content. It may be useful to have additional details ready about each offence, to make it seem more lifelike, but as far as possible the same information should be supplied to both individuals and groups.

That groups more readily take risks than individuals may partially explain the familiar fact that a majority of offences, especially those committed by people under 20 years of age, take place in groups. But it also appears to be the case that offences committed by groups are more likely to be serious ones. Farrington, Berkowitz, and West (1982) found a number of differences between fights with only two combatants and those amongst larger groups. Group fights were more liable to involve the use of weapons and to result in injuries, and to take place after drinking. Whether this holds true for other kinds of offence remains a matter for future work.

In the discussion following this exercise, participants should be asked to relate it to their own experience. Does it appear as if the group risk effect is in part responsible for anything that has happened to them? Is there anything they could do about it? Social skills training to resist pressure might be one direction to take. Just being aware that the effect occurs, and learning to take evasive action when some kind of risk-taking seems imminent, might be another. A third potential answer to the whole question of risks and risk-taking might to be find non-criminal uses of time; it is to this possibility that we turn our attention next.

Spare time, boredom, and excitement

Without doubt, a very large number of offences, particularly (though by no means exclusively) those committed by younger offenders, are a product of the fact that individuals have little or nothing to do with their time, and in trying to find things to do, end up breaking the law. As Williamson (1978) has described, this might be a result of the pursuit of entertainment itself, or of the attempt, for example through the theft of money or the sale of stolen goods, to obtain the means of buying other forms of entertainment. While the best (some would say the only) answer to this problem lies in large-scale social action to provide higher incomes and better facilities for people in this position, there are still some things which it is feasible to do on a smaller scale with offenders with whom you are working.

Uses of time

The starting-point for this is an assessment of how individuals are currently using their time; how they would really like to use it; and whether there is any possible means of bridging the almost inevitable gap between the two.

Activity 'diaries'

As regards the first of these, individuals can be asked to survey how they fill their own time by compiling a kind of 'diary' for a selected period of their lives; a single week would do for this purpose. This could be the last week, which might still be fresh in their memories; or what they see as a 'typical' or 'average' sort of week; or perhaps the best or worst weeks they can remember – ones which they really enjoyed or found extremely boring respectively. It could be written in narrative form, like a real personal diary; or charted in a kind of timetable showing how individuals spent the mornings, afternoons, evenings and nights of each 24 hour period in the chosen week.

Subsequently, individuals should abstract some other information from the diaries they have prepared. How much time did they spend engaged in different kinds of activities? Some obvious categories could be used for this, like working, sleeping, or other essential chores like shopping, cooking or housework. Of prime interest however is how they used their 'spare' time; time not accounted for in these other ways. Did they take part in structured leisure activities, such as sports, or spend a lot of time just 'hanging about' hoping for something to happen? Total amounts of time falling under each of these headings could be obtained and comparisons made between members if you are working with a group. A second point of interest is how individuals felt about the week. What proportion of the time did they feel bored, excited, happy, or depressed? How much of the time would they consider they had spent purposefully, as opposed to just 'wasted away'? Are there any identifiable times when they feel they are more likely to get into trouble and is this related to a dearth of things which they would *like* to do and with which they could occupy themselves more constructively? All these questions should provide fruitful directions for further exploration and discussion.

Preferred activities

The other side of the issue of spare time is how individuals would prefer to spend it, assuming they are dissatisfied with the options open to them at the moment. To help them crystallize their ideas on this, they could be asked to complete a diary for another week: but this time to plan an ideal usage of their time, to imagine a week that is crammed full of activities they would like to take part in. People's initial attempts at this may take them into the realms of fantasy, jet-hopping between Caribbean islands or whatever; this is worthwhile in itself, as it may reveal something about their genuine interests. It is a long way from solving their immediate problems, of course; but can nevertheless be used as a marker to work backwards from, perhaps yielding some more viable suggestions in the process. They may eventually arrive at a more down-to-earth vision which only departs in a few respects from the pattern they are following at the present. The remaining differences might then be within a range they have the power to traverse through some more tangible course of action.

Alternatively, if individuals find it difficult to spell out their preferences in this way, they could be offered a long list, in verbal or written form, of possible spare-time activities. They could then give their views on each, or rate them or rank them in some sort of way which helped them clarify their views on what would be an enjoyable and/or profitable use of time. Two different methods can be used for doing this. In one, people are asked to locate activities on a continuum, say from *boring* to *exciting*, represented by a line like this:

Very, very   Very, very
boring   exciting

If they are then supplied with a list of perhaps twenty or more potential uses of time, the business of trying to arrange them in order on the line may elucidate where their true preferences lie. If the items are then subjected to the 'reality test' of whether they are within the reach – personal, geographical, and financial – of the individual concerned (or can be brought within it by some means), there may just emerge an idea which he or she had not considered before. Another method is to prompt individuals by asking them to complete a checklist of activities with a rating scale attached, for example:

Look at the list of activities below, and put a tick beside any you have taken part in yourself. Rate how enjoyable you found them on the scale on the right.		
	Don't enjoy this at all	Enjoy this very much
Playing sports		
Watching sports		
Dancing		
Playing an instrument		
Listening to music		
Going drinking		
Going to see a film		
Talking to people		
Watching television		

This list could be enlarged to include as many activities as you think might be useful. It should not only throw light on individuals' preferred uses of time, but also, if sufficiently long and varied, perhaps sow the seeds of ideas that have not occurred to them in the past. Once again, using either of these exercises with a group affords the additional opportunity to compare and discuss individuals' replies.

An extra dimension can be added to these exercises by including *offences* in the lists of activities provided; either as 'offending in general' or in the form of specific types of offence. This may show how enjoyable they are thought to be as compared with more conventional modes of entertainment; it may starkly uncover the fact that individuals really do turn to crime because their neighbourhoods are devoid of anything else to do;

or may carry the blunt message that some kinds of offences are perceived as gratifying in their own right.

Finding things to do

If the search for things to do constitutes part of the reason why some people offend then a proportion of them at least might be less likely to do so if other channels for their energies could be found. Having helped individuals look at what they do and what they would rather be doing, the logical next step is to cast a net as widely as possible in the hope of finding things they *can* do. None of the suggestions below is an assured means of solving the 'spare time' problem, still less the offending problem within it, but some of them could strike a chord with someone, open up new vistas, or give an impetus to existing feelings that there must be better ways of spending the time than in custody, on supervision, or under the glare of the local police.

Brainstorming

A first exercise, if you are working with a group, is to ask them to *brainstorm* the problems of time, boredom, or entertainment by generating a list of as many possible ideas as they can think of for passing the time enjoyably in their part of the world. The purpose of brainstorming is to churn out ideas, by temporarily forgetting about their quality – whether they are sensible, practicable, and so on – and concentrating on the process of amassing as many of them as possible that *might* be useful for attacking a given problem. One person in the group records the ideas put forward on a blackboard or large sheet of paper where everyone can see them. The rest of the group simply throw out ideas, letting themselves be as inventive and imaginative as they can, building on each other's suggestions, just mentioning anything at all even if its relationship to the problem seems quite remote. When you have tried this for ten minutes or so, or for longer if people are still going strong, review the items produced. Many will be obvious, some will be absurd; but a few may contain the germs of real possibilities which members of the group may be interested in following up.

'Official' sources

Sizeable quantities of information about local amenities are usually available from town halls, libraries, and other agencies in a particular area. Guidebooks, leaflets, maps, duplicated lists of places where different facilities can be found, and various other kinds of printed matter, can all be procured free or at very low cost, and direct advice pertaining to anything local can be obtained. Individuals, on their own or in small groups, can be asked to gather as much of this information as possible, or to go along with specific questions to ask council employees about provision of a particular kind in their locality. The material they collect may provide some individuals with suggestions, leads, and perhaps even actual contacts which will solve part of the problem of what to do with their time.

Speakers

The opposite of going out and getting information is having the information come to you; and if you are working with groups it is a sound principle to organize some informal sessions for visits by external speakers or 'experts'. Recreation officers, managers of local leisure centres or clubs, sports coaches of one sort or another, specialists in miscellaneous crafts or hobbies, local radio or television personnel, devotees of this or that offbeat pursuit – all will be willing to convey facts, and to stir up enthusiasm, about the benefits gained from participation in the activities for which they are responsible or to which they feel committed.

Group members

But inputs of information to a group need not come solely from 'experts'; many group members will themselves be perfectly capable of talking, and answering queries about, their own interests and pastimes. Other sessions could be organized then in which individuals who are happy to do so give brief (say five- or ten-minute) presentations on their favourite spare-time activities; pinpointing what they derive from them; how they got started; costs, venues, and other information as appropriate. This will be both a challenge to the presenters (and could be further enlivened by being recorded on video) and a useful fund of information and advice for the listeners.

Surveys

A fuller picture of what there is to do in a district can be put together by asking individuals or groups to undertake a survey. Taking their own knowledge of the area to begin with, or drawing on some official sources, they set out to assemble as comprehensive a list as possible of all the opportunities the local environment has to offer. But the survey can also be done in more depth by seeking additional detail about what is available: how many tables a snooker club has, for example, its opening times, entry fees, and other points where applicable. It need not be confined only to custom-built leisure venues like sports halls or discotheques, it could also look at good places to go for walks, where the cheapest pint of beer or cup of tea can be had, and so on. The results could be written up as a report, displayed on a map, compiled into a brochure, or recorded as a video documentary. Conversely, a quite different survey could be mounted which focused on what *is not* available; seeking the views of local citizens on the inadequacy of community provision; doing an exposé of the scarcity of resources for a particular age group; or photographing the desolation of the streets around group members' homes.

Organized events

A more traditional kind of exercise, with more immediate appeal perhaps to younger offenders, is the arrangement of excursions and other recreational events – usually undertaken partly to broaden the experience of participants, partly for sheer enjoyment, and partly to give them an interlude away from the situations in which most of their offences are committed. They vary from day trips or outings to places of interest, to camping or canoeing holidays spread out over one or two weeks. Such events may have more potential impact on offence behaviour if they are organized as 'tasters' of activities to which individuals could return of their own volition afterwards; or if they are planned and executed by individuals or groups themselves and illustrate to them that it is possible to track down more rewarding uses of time if they feel motivated to do so.

Projects

If, in the area in which offenders live, there really *is* a shortage of things to do, and if they feel strongly enough about it, one final suggestion might be that they embark on a project to improve local conditions. This could take many different shapes. They may try to fill the vacuum themselves by setting up their own club, contriving their own schemes for entertainment, or otherwise becoming 'recreation officers' in their own right. Alternatively, they may be interested in forming their own pressure group – to demand more and better services from the local authority, and make representations to the town hall, community council, or local press on this issue. A coterie of offenders proclaiming that they might be less likely to commit crimes if they were less bored could attract a great deal of publicity; and with an articulate spokesperson, a thoughtful strategy, and a set of concrete proposals, it might achieve some real success.

If you are working in a community-based setting (in field probation, day centres, hostels, or intermediate treatment, for example), the above exercises are all potentially fertile in so far as a majority of your clientele will be living in the same geographical district and will have access to (or will have been banned from) more or less the same facilities. If you are working in an institution (like a children's home with education, assessment centre, detention or youth custody centre, or prison) the issue may seem more problematic, in that your residents' eventual destinations may be geographically very dispersed. But it still makes sense, for those who are trying to tackle their own offending behaviour, for them to plan their future uses of time. Some of the foregoing exercises can still be run; group members can still pool their ideas; speakers on many topics can be invited in; occasional outside visits can be made from some institutions; projects can be carried on at a distance. It all depends on the needs of those taking part and what they believe might be useful and relevant to their own offence-related problems. A few other suggestions concerning spare time and how individuals might decide to use it are given elsewhere (McGuire and Priestley, 1981).

Thinking and decision-making

So far, we have looked at a number of different reasons why individuals may take the kinds of risks that are intrinsic to numerous sorts of offence. They may be temperamentally inclined to be impulsive; may enjoy risk for its own sake; may be borne along by the relative incautiousness of groups; or may be just trying to escape from the tedium of the lives which society has condemned them to lead. In all of these causes there can be discerned a common ingredient: that individuals have weighed the odds up wrongly somehow, and instead of getting what they want have ended up doing themselves more harm than good. This brings us to one other possible explanation for this ironic sequence of events; that many offences are the result of bad decisions, and that the latter are in turn brought about by offenders' lack of particular kinds of thinking and decision-making skills.

There are many examples of offences which appear to fall into this category. Individuals may fail to see a certain situation, like a confrontation, developing, and may find themselves ineluctably drawn into a fight. They may not take into account all the facts about a proposed theft, burglary, or fraud, with the result that they are discovered; had they been better apprised of the circumstances, they might have hesitated and perhaps changed their minds. People may not realize in advance the consequences of joining particular groups – that later on they will also be expected to join them in breaking the law. Or individuals who set out to commit minor offences may find that matters get out of control and they have actually done something much more serious. In all these instances, if individuals were absolutely determined to carry out the offences in question, there is probably very little we could do to stop them. But a fuller appreciation of the facts, or a greater ability to think things through, *might* make one or two pause for thought; might sap their determination and even make some offenders reconsider the whole business.

The last section of this chapter is based on this hypothesis. Two possible remedies for the ill-conceived and injudicious nature of some offences are prescribed – at least for 'experimental trials'. One is the idea of giving offenders more facts: about specific offences and their effects; about crime in general; about criminology, penology, and the law. Roughly speaking this could be dubbed a kind of 'crime education'. The other is the idea of teaching various cognitive skills, like the ability to think of alternatives, solve problems, and predict the consequences of your own actions.

Crime 'education'

It is beyond dispute that many offences are at least partly the result of ignorance. At the simplest possible level, some individuals may be quite unaware that certain things are against the law. More commonly, many offences are committed because individuals are quite badly informed, for example about the effects on them of alcohol or other drugs. It goes almost without saying that a majority of offenders remain completely in the dark about the impact of their offences on their victims.

An educational programme designed to make offenders more knowledgeable about various aspects of crime, therefore, might make a valuable contribution towards altering offence behaviour. By this we do not mean that they be sent on courses about housebreaking, safeblowing, embezzlement, disguise, etc. (the surest way to teach them some of these arts is probably to send them to prison). But a certain amount of information could be imparted which might help them to see offending in a different light.

There are in fact encouraging precedents for this suggestion. Robertson and Heather (1982), for example, designed a six-session 'alcohol education' course for offenders aged under 25 who had problems in this area and whose offences were described as 'alcohol-related'. The course includes basic information about alcohol; instruction in monitoring blood alcohol levels (see chapter six); and exercises in self-exploration and problem-solving training. Early evidence suggests that the course is enjoyed by its target group and that they find it useful; a longer term evaluation is also being carried out. In a different vein Crawford and Howells (1982) have piloted a sex education course for adolescents convicted of sex-related offences. This course lasts for eight sessions and centres around the showing of films followed by group discussions, covering such topics as sexual development, intercourse, contraception, sexual problems and childbirth. Preliminary research on reactions to this course suggests that it certainly increased participants' knowledge a great deal, and also helped to decrease their sexual anxieties and bring about improvements in self-image. These gains were still observable in one group of adolescents who were followed up for nine weeks after completion of the course.

Though the scale of these enterprises has so far been fairly modest, the idea seems a potentially useful one. There is no reason why similar courses should not be designed and implemented for other kinds of offence-related behaviour, and if you are working with groups of offenders this might be worthy of consideration.

Which themes could such a course encompass? The content would obviously have to be geared very closely to the interests and abilities of the likely audience, but some obvious topics for inclusion could be:

How different types of offences are defined.
Crime rates in different regions or countries, at different points in time and for various kinds of offence.
Detection rates.
Juvenile crime statistics and background data on young offenders.
The 'dark figure' of crime.
The costs of crime.

The idea of the 'criminal career' and evidence in support of it.
Different kinds of sentences; the idea of the 'tariff'.
The nature of imprisonment; life 'inside'.
The effectiveness of different kinds of sentences.
The history of punishment.
Crime as portrayed in the press and on television.
The work of the police.
'White-collar' crime.
Crime in the local area.
The effects of crime on its victims.
Theories about the origins of crime.

The list could obviously be expanded almost indefinitely. Much of the material for such a 'curriculum' can be found in standard criminology textbooks; though other segments would be spread more widely in books on history, law, sociology and related subjects. Should the idea of assembling such a mass of information seem too daunting to you, bear in mind that it can almost all be done by consulting 'experts' in the various specialisms. Parts of the course could be built around talks or question-and-answer sessions incorporating external speakers. Polite invitations will almost certainly secure the co-operation of many individuals, e.g.

> Police officer; probation officer; social worker; solicitor; barrister; prison officer; magistrate; judge; sheriff; children's panel member; journalist; shop-owner; ex-prisoners or other experienced offenders; ex-alcoholics or drug addicts; criminologist; community relations worker; victims of offences – if they are definitely willing, and are carefully and sensitively prepared beforehand.

The contributors you choose and the points you ask them to cover will of course depend on the field in which you yourself work and the kinds, ages, concerns and other features of the offenders with whom you happen to be working.

The patterning of these sessions should be as informal as possible, and the didactic 'classroom' style dispensed with completely; offenders are no more tolerant of lectures than anyone else (and may be much less so). In any case, you may not be able to run more than a few sessions along these lines, and they may need to be juxtaposed with other kinds of activities. A more lively element can be introduced into the programme by means of projects, in which rather than being fed information, individuals have to go and seek it out for themselves, or undertake some other kind of work. Some possible projects on a 'crime' or 'offending behaviour' course include:

- Information-gathering and/or report-writing on any of the topics mentioned above, perhaps with particular reference to the local area
- Surveys of attitudes to crime and offenders; to hanging, rehabilitation, or any other controversies – carried out by a group using a 'clipboard' questionnaire or with cassette or videotape recorders
- Debates: divide a group into two (or more) sub-groups who each have to prepare positions on specially chosen topics, present them to each other (face-to-face or on video), and then debate the various points raised. Possible starters for dissent might be: 'we need prisons', 'crime is caused by poverty', 'the police should be armed', etc.
- Community action projects: in which individuals take one problem or issue of importance in the immediate neighbourhood and attempt to explore it or influence it in some sort of way, e.g., by organizing a petition, arranging an event, setting up a voluntary service – all perhaps connected in as direct a manner as possible with offending behaviour
- Individuals attempt to find out more about a particular law, or a set of circumstances,

which affect them personally, and formulate some recommendations for changes they would like to bring about.

A few of the above suggestions could be acted upon by individuals working single-handed; others could only be done properly by a group. Each could be used on a 'one-off' basis or integrated into a balanced course with other kinds of factual or discussion sessions. They could if it seems appropriate be set alongside sessions on self-esteem, social skills, or self-control, fashioned to suit particular offenders' needs; and even structured into a timetable if this seems desirable and circumstances allow.

Training in thinking skills

A diet of factual information could have a limited impact on *what* some offenders think; however, if we would like to help them alter the *way* they think and make decisions, we will have to look elsewhere. 'In regard to delinquents . . . there is evidence that they are poor problem solvers in interpersonal situations' (Little and Kendall, 1979, 89). What may be at stake is the 'mental apparatus' individuals have at their disposal; not in any pejorative sense, but in the sense that they may be hindered in their decision-making by careless or maladaptive habits of thought. Yet just as it is possible for individuals to improve their social skills or attain self-control, so too they can learn to unravel knots in their own minds and 'think straight' about things.

Distinguishing facts from opinions

Most of the time, the bulk of the thinking we do consists of something of a muddle of facts, attitudes, beliefs, half-truths, of some opinions we are not sure about, and others of which we are unshakeably convinced. While attempting to extricate ourselves from this confusion (if we want to) usually takes longer than a lifetime, we can at least learn to recognize when our beliefs are based on facts, on the one hand, or on value-judgments and opinions on the other. An exercise which can be used to set this process in motion entails offering a series of statements like the following.

1. Most reported crime is committed by people under 21 years of age.
2. The number of people in prison in this country has been rising steadily for the last few years.
3. There are too many people in prison.
4. The amount of money lost through tax evasion each year is much more than the amount lost through social security fraud.
5. Violent crimes against women are the result of male attitudes to women in general.
6. Unemployment is a major cause of crime.
7. Whether or not you go to prison for some offences depends on which part of the country you commit them in.
8. People would be less likely to break the law if punishments were more severe.
9. The majority of juvenile delinquents come from working-class backgrounds.
10. Locking up offenders who are less than 17 years old is an injustice in itself.

In accordance with the theme of this book, the items listed here all have to do with aspects of offending behaviour, but more 'neutral' ground could be chosen instead. Individuals are asked to decide, not which of the statements are true and which false, but which are statements of fact and which statements of opinion. We could obviously enter into some deep philosophical arguments about this distinction, but for the moment and for the purpose of running this exercise the criterion used can be the common-sense notion of whether a statement could be corroborated by reference to available evidence. Factual statements (nos 1, 2, 4, 7, and 9) meet this criterion whereas opinion statements (nos 3, 5, 6, 8, and 10) do not; they *may* be true or false but at present we do not have enough information to decide. Of course some purportedly factual statements turn out on inspection to be wrong; and whether or not someone can identify a statement as 'factual' may depend on whether he or she knows anything about its subject-matter. The objective of the exercise, however, is to instil into individuals a spirit of inquiry about statements with which they are confronted. Is there any way of deciding, first, whether an utterance is a fact or just someone's personal opinion on something? And even if a statement does seem to be factual, is it actually correct? How this might apply to decisions individuals themselves have to make, especially as regards committing offences, can be useful topics for discussion.

Alternative thinking

The preceding exercise is designed to stimulate 'thinking about thinking'; to instigate a process in which individuals will re-examine bad decisions they have made in the past and perhaps discover where they made mistakes. This process can be continued with exercises which focus on some of the skills which, according to the research of Spivack and others cited earlier, differentiate some offenders from non-offenders.

The first of these is *alternative thinking:* the ability, when faced with a problem, to approach it in a flexible way and think of a range of things you could do about it. This may sound at first like a talent you either possess or don't possess; but in fact it is a skill, and like other skills it can be improved by means of training. The latter involves asking individuals to immerse themselves in some problems other than their own; to produce any ideas they can think of for solving them; to practise this with a series of related problems; and lastly to redirect their energies towards difficulties with which they themselves are beset.

To begin with, participants are presented with a number of hypothetical problems like ones they may have encountered themselves, and asked to formulate as many potential solutions as they can. The problems might be:

> Imagine that, for the sake of getting a job, you have moved to a town where you don't know anyone. You are living in lodgings and the only other person there is a lot older than you. What kinds of things could you do to meet new people or to fix up some sort of social life for yourself?

or:

> You have just finished a six-month prison sentence. Some old friends you used to get into trouble with but haven't seen since before you went inside leave a message at your house saying they'll be round to pick you up on Friday night. You know they'll expect you to go out with them but you'd rather steer absolutely clear of them. What could you do or say to avoid having to go with them?

Each of these problems permits of many possible solutions and the more ideas people can generate, the more likely it is that there will be an acceptable and workable one amongst them. Several methods for getting hold of ideas could be attempted:

> 1. Working singly or in groups, individuals could *brainstorm* the problem, i.e., concern themselves exclusively with the task of netting *any ideas whatever* that might constitute partial or even just fractional steps towards a solution (cf. p. 168 above).
> 2. With some problems (e.g., the first one mentioned above) individuals could undertake a *survey* to ascertain the kinds of things other people have done, or might do, when in that position.
> 3. Someone picks something at random (an object in the room; a word out of a book; an idea mentioned by someone else) which seems to have no connection whatever with the

problem they are analysing; and then tries to make connections, to find bridges between the two. The suggestions which then emerge might form the basis of quite novel solutions to the problem.

If individuals find it difficult to collect any ideas on problems like those above, they could take a step backwards to some simpler problems and try to develop greater 'mental fluency', or ability to produce ideas in quantity. One way to do this is to try what is known as *divergent thinking*; they are asked to think of as many uses as possible for a common everyday object, such as a brick, comb, or elastic band. At the first attempt most people seem able to think of only a few possibilities; when they have repeated the exercise a few times, however, they become more adept and can marshal ideas in considerable numbers. A second technique is to use *remote associations*; to give people two ideas which on cursory inspection have little to do with each other (e.g., *moon* and *bathtub; jungle* and *carburettor*) and ask them to form links between them. Again after some practice most people find they can become much better at this. If however they seem defeated even by these requests, you could prompt them with some ideas to help them on the way, and invite them to enlarge on them or devise similar ones of their own.

Distant though these exercises may seem from the business of solving real-life problems, the skill involved in each is essentially the same. If people repeat the above sequence of activities with several problems of a type they might have to deal with in their own lives, they are almost bound to be better able to think 'alternatively' than at the outset. The final stage of the process then is to address their attention to situations in their own experience. This could be done first retrospectively, by asking them to look back and think about other ways out of tight corners in which they have found themselves in the past; then prospectively, envisaging courses of action they could take in analogous circumstances in the future.

Means-end thinking

The ability to mobilize ideas will not in itself enable offenders to solve problems, however. They need to translate them into a form in which they can be used in the real world; they need to take into account various constraints which might be operating there, and find ways either to adjust to them or to circumvent them. This skill is called by Spivack et al. (1976) 'means-end thinking' and it consists of 'articulating the step-by-step means that may be necessary in order to carry out the solution to any interpersonal problem' (Spivack, *op. cit.,* 5). Exercising this skill can be conceived of as something akin to plotting a route on a map, except that in this case the 'terrain' is the social world of relatives, friends, acquaintances, neighbours, salespeople, employers, officials of this or that agency, representatives of authority, even the public as a whole.

Competence in this skill may be explored in exercises in which they are told the beginnings and endings of stories and asked to 'fill in the middle in their own words', i.e., to describe a succession of events which will explain why the story finished as it did. The 'stories' used for this purpose are not literary works but brief sketches of situations in which someone is pursuing a goal of some sort; almost any outline of a common everyday concern can be adapted for this purpose, such as the following:

> Liz wanted to move out of her parents' home and stay in a place of her own, though her parents were against it . . .
> . . . a few weeks later Liz moved into a flat she was going to share with some friends.

People are asked to say what they think might have happened between the opening and the close of the story in order for it to have culminated in this way. Some will have very little idea at all of how events might have unfolded; others will have ideas that are totally unrealistic. Effective means-end thinking has a number of elements: first, an ability to think of means themselves and how they are inter-related i.e., how they might be instrumental in bringing about the desired goal; second, a recognition of any obstacles that might be in the way and how they could be overcome; and third, an appreciation of the time-scale likely to be needed for the accomplishment of a given goal – e.g., you can't go out and find a flat one day (unless you just happen to be lucky), it usually involves a period of search followed by a further period of arrangement and negotiation.

If offenders have frequently made bad decisions and acknowledge that this may be because they have not thought things through sufficiently well, they can try to refine their skills in this area by taking some problems and thinking about them more systematically. The essence of this process is really nothing more than helping individuals to 'slow down' their reactions; to examine more thoroughly which kinds of things are likely to succeed or to fail when attempting to solve a given problem; and to practise this with a variety of difficulties in the hope that they will become more accustomed to approaching things in this way. As regards offences for example, someone may have broken the law in an attempt to deal with a problem which they did not know how to solve in any other way. Working with the individual, the objective then becomes to help him or her to look at the situation in more detail; to identify exactly why certain steps which were taken were the wrong ones; and to map out other possible routes to a solution which do not entail an offence along the way. This might reveal, for example, that the person had taken a risk which, viewed more detachedly, really had very little chance of paying off. The longer-term hope is of course that a habit of thinking about problems in a slightly more rational fashion will become established in the person's mind.

Perspective taking

A third skill identified by the Spivack et al. research as possibly absent or deficient in some offenders was perspective taking, or the ability to imagine how a situation appears from the standpoint of another person. This is part of the broader skill labelled by the Spivack group as 'social cause-and-effect thinking'. In extreme cases where individuals are highly egocentric, such a tendency may be very manifest and may require no further authentication. In other cases, though they may not seem 'selfish' in the conventional sense of the word, people may be genuinely handicapped in their thinking by a one-side approach to things. In clinical work, this blinkering of social perception has been assessed using a test (called the *Thematic Apperception Test*) consisting of a series of cards, on each of which there is a drawing depicting an interpersonal situation of some kind. This is what is known as a *projective* test, i.e., individuals are asked to say what they think is going on in each picture, to write or tell a story in which they surmise what might have led up to the situation shown; it is assumed that their comments indicate something about their own attitudes and preoccupations. To explore egocentrism, individuals can be asked to describe how the situation looks to each of the characters involved; the extent to which they can 'empathize' with different points of view supplies a rough-and-ready measure of perspective-taking skills.

That this skill has important implications for offending behaviour has been demonstrated by the work of Chandler (1973) to which reference was made earlier. Chandler attempted to counter egocentrism in young offenders, employing a method of 'multi-role-reversal'. Participants role-played situations which they found difficult to handle; the role-plays were video-recorded, played back, and discussed; then re-enacted with the 'actors' in different roles. As we saw in chapter five, significant reductions in recidivism were obtained when this method was used with groups of adolescents. An exercise based on this work is outlined in chapter three (48).

Consequential thinking

One other kind of problem-solving or decision-making skill has occasionally been found to be lacking in some offenders: the ability to anticipate the consequences of actions. If individuals' offence patterns show time and again that they have failed to think ahead or that their expectations as to the likely outcome of events have been somewhat erratic, then it may be worthwhile trying to orient their attention towards this aspect of their thinking. As with the skills already described, this too can be developed through training and practice.

The methods used to do this are fundamentally the same as those used to cultivate alternative thinking. Here, however, rather than trying to generate possible courses of action, participants are trying to estimate the likely results of each. This can be used to serve two slightly different purposes.

The first is the acquisition of what might be called 'foresight' in relation to the effects of one's own actions. Taking specific solutions put forward for a given problem, use brainstorming and/or other techniques mentioned above (p. 176) and try to accumulate as comprehensive a list as possible of the things that will flow from a particular decision someone might make. It may be useful to prefix this exercise with the question 'What would happen if . . .?'. Again the emphasis here is on quantity not quality; the idea is to predict *all* the consequences of acting in a particular way.

A second use is in decision-making, when people are trying to make a choice between different courses of action open to them. Concerning each possibility in turn, they should first aggregate all the probable consequences as before; they then need to compare the net value of each. To do this they could apply four 'qualitative' criteria to the choices that are available, by asking the following questions about each:

> What are its *advantages?* i.e., how many of its consequences are good ones?
> What are its *disadvantages?* How many of its consequences are bad?
> How *important* is each of the consequences in turn?
> How *likely* is each of them to happen?

Though this may prove very time-consuming, it may ensure that individuals inquire as exhaustively as possible into a decision, and may help them to make the right choice if it is a significant one. It could even prove to be a mechanism they might adopt for future use. As with all the previous exercises, however, the intention here is that they will realize the benefits of working out the consequences of their decisions in advance, and that this will eventually become a regular feature of their thinking.

Attempting to become a clearer thinker and better decision-maker is the final strategy for influencing offence behaviour with which the central section of this book has been concerned. It might be objected that, if we help offenders get better at calculating the effects of their decisions, are we not just helping them to become more sophisticated criminals? Indeed, looking back at previous chapters, if we help them to think more highly of themselves, become more socially skilled, and better controlled, will the end result not be – bigger and better crooks?

A number of replies can be made to this. The first is that the materials here are designed to aid those who wish to alter their own offending behaviour. There will be a real self-selection involved in this and it is unlikely that any dedicated criminals will turn up to see what they can rake off in the way of hints and tips.

The second reply is that *any* form of 'education' or 'training' or 'self-improvement' we might offer to offenders, or to anyone else for that matter, might create fresh opportunities for infringing the law. Teaching people to read and write enables them to forge cheques or engage in fraudulent transactions. Teaching them to drive opens up a number of opportunities for speeding, drinking and driving, ferrying stolen goods, manning getaway cars. No-one objects to these forms of learning, despite the risks involved, for they are seen to be worthwile in themselves and in some cases may prove passports to personal reform.

A third reply is slightly more damaging to the aims of the book. It is that the strategies described here are by no means foolproof, they cannot be guaranteed to work 100 per cent of the time; there may be some failure somewhere along the line. If this happens, as with numbers of offenders it assuredly will – and if they simply go relentlessly through the familiar cycle of trouble, arrest, conviction and sentence, it may be necessary to turn to some of the suggestions in chapter eight.

Part three

The offender and society

8 Coping with the system

When all else fails, and the offenders with whom you are working actually commit fresh offences, should you then just wash your hands of them and abandon them to the tender mercies of the legal and penal systems? It is the argument of this book that offenders can, if they so choose, use social skills and self-control methods to reduce the likelihood of their committing offences in the first place. The same methods are equally applicable in situations where the concern is to minimize the harmful and potentially criminogenic effects of the system itself as it operates on individual cases.

At the threshold of the system lies the initial police-offender encounter, which can be handled in ways that are either less likely to lead to arrest, or to the commission of further offences in the process of resisting the lawful authority of the constable.

Negotiating the subsequent criminal trial is something which offenders themselves should approach as carefully as any crafty lawyer, since it is their own liberty and well-being that is at stake. This will entail contacts with probation officers and lawyers prior to the hearing, appearing in court, making pleas of mitigation, suggesting realistic alternative sentences to courts, and making use of the appeals machinery if necessary.

After sentence, offenders will need help in getting through periods of supervision or probation or community service, or in the payment of fines or compensation orders, in ways which are as useful, or as little harmful to themselves as possible. Some of them will also need to be prepared for the rigours of captivity and to ward off the psychological, moral and physical damage it can undoubtedly do.

The exercises in this chapter are all designed to assist offenders in coping with these contingencies; giving them a fuller understanding of the great machine that has laid hold of them; retaining as much control over the proceedings as they can; resisting to the utmost the corrosive effects of convictions on their lives; and reducing the probability that they will commit even more, and more serious, offences after completing their sentences.

Police

Encounters between policemen and offenders, whether 'suspected' or otherwise, are fraught with difficulties and dangers for both parties. In theory the policeman is the embodiment of a disinterested code of criminal law, charged with its enforcement in an impartial manner. In theory, the offender will prove to be guilty as charged. In practice, both are parties to situations where things are rarely so clear cut as that.

Whatever the *facts* of any case, and there is enormous scope for doubt and dispute about them, the attitudes of the offender are likely to range from the submissive 'It's a fair cop', to the indignantly self-justifying, to the homicidally determined. Policemen too occupy a broad spectrum of intelligence and character; some can calm the most explosive situation; others are looking for a fight in which they can legitimately hand out some physical retribution to the 'enemy'. Behaviour in the police-offender encounter, then, is often balanced on two kinds of knife edge: the one between the police 'proceeding' and 'taking no further action', and the one between violent and non-violent outcomes. The two issues are intimately linked since the actual demeanour of the offender in a wide range of 'marginal' situations is what determines how the police officer uses his discretion to proceed or not with a particular case.

The exercises that follow are illustrations of things to do with offenders who wish to examine and do something about their attitudes and behaviour when confronted with police personnel in the real world. They are not meant to be foisted on offenders who have no wish to change their ways; and they do not imply that all the fault for bad relations lies on one or other side of the equation. They are based on the assumption that police-offender encounters are first and foremost examples of human interaction – specialized ones it is true, but still capable of being more or less under the control of the people directly involved in them.

It is usual for the police to use what amounts to social-skills methods during their basic training for the job: simulated incidents; role-play; practice and rehearsal, with and without feedback from observers and video playback. If it is good for the police, it will almost certainly be good for offenders.

Police contact checklist

Write in the box how many times any of the following have happened to you.

☐ Been 'verballed'*
☐ Assaulted by a policeman for no good reason
☐ Assaulted by a policeman acting in self defence
☐ Assaulted a policeman
☐ Asked to accept TICs** you didn't do
☐ Accepted TICs you didn't do
☐ Picked up at work by the police
☐ Kept overnight for questioning and then released without being charged
☐ Stopped and searched in the street by a policeman
☐ Made a complaint against a policeman
☐ Been refused bail because of police objections
☐ Been promised a light sentence if you will inform on somebody else
☐ Been promised a heavy sentence if you don't co-operate

How many times have you been –

For an offence	Questioned and arrested	Questioned and not arrested
you *did* commit		
you did *not* commit		

---

* *'verballed'* – falsely reported by the police to have confessed verbally to an offence
***'TICs'* – previous offences, not cleared up by the police, admitted by the offender and 'taken into consideration' in court

A good place to start is with some assessment of past police contacts – how often has the offender come up against the law; under what circumstances; and with what outcome? A questionnaire like the one on p. 182 could be used to explore this.

Attitudes towards the police; some general assessment methods

Here are some general topics for discussion and interview, some sentences to complete and a couple of exercises for eliciting other aspects of offender attitudes towards the police. The topics and wording can of course be added to or modified to suit your specific aims and circumstances.

Group discussion topics

The police. Why we need policemen. How successful are the police? Corruption in the police force. Do the police keep the crime rate down? Police and traffic matters. Why people become policemen.

Sentence completion

Policemen are . . .
Detectives are . . .
Some policemen are . . .
Bent policemen are . . .
My feelings towards the police are. . .
Whenever I see a policeman I . . .
You can tell a policeman out of uniform by . . .
Policeman pick on . . .
Policemen in court often . . .
Policemen get violent when . . .
I lose my temper when a policeman . . .
Policemen ignore . . .
If I was a policeman I would . . .
Policemen are necessary because . . .
If there weren't any policemen . . .
Ten questions I would like to ask a policeman . . .

Peer interviews

The worst policeman you ever met. The best policeman you ever met. Why you feel the way you do about the police. Being arrested.

Word picture

Write down ten words which best describe the police. Write down ten words a policeman might write down to describe offenders.

Advertising for policemen

A useful group or solo project can be launched with the following instructions:
'It is your job to make up an advertisement inviting men and women to join the police force. To do this properly you need to do three things:

  1. Write a job *specification*. What do policeman do?
     What skills do they need? What are the conditions of work?
  2. Compile a list of *'ideal'* qualities for a policeman.
  3. Make a list of the things which would *attract* people into the police force.

Using all this information write an advertisement which would attract the right people. You should also suggest which papers and magazines should be selected for the advert.'

The writing of a job specification can be based on the information in CODOT (1973) or on any advertising material and recruitment literature actually used by the police force.

When the advert is completed it should be written out on a flip chart and displayed on the wall for use in a group discussion about the role of the police and the kinds of people who apply to join.

A rating scale

Just as offences themselves may be committed because of the values or beliefs held by individuals, so their responses to representatives of the forces of law and order may be fashioned or influenced by the attitudes they have towards them. These attitudes can be tapped in all sorts of ways and are an interesting subject of study in their own right, i.e. independently of whether that leads to any change in them or not.

A simple but useful mechanism for recording attitudes towards the police is a rating scale using pairs of evaluative adjectives; e.g.

MY VIEW OF THE POLICE

FAIR	└──┴──┴──┴──┘	UNFAIR
VIOLENT	└──┴──┴──┴──┘	NON VIOLENT
PLEASANT	└──┴──┴──┴──┘	UNPLEASANT
HOSTILE	└──┴──┴──┴──┘	FRIENDLY
HUMOROUS	└──┴──┴──┴──┘	HUMOURLESS
STRAIGHT	└──┴──┴──┴──┘	BENT
BAD	└──┴──┴──┴──┘	GOOD
SLAPDASH	└──┴──┴──┴──┘	THOROUGH
CONCERNED	└──┴──┴──┴──┘	UNCONCERNED
VINDICTIVE	└──┴──┴──┴──┘	'LIVE AND LET LIVE'
HONEST	└──┴──┴──┴──┘	DISHONEST
CUNNING	└──┴──┴──┴──┘	STRAIGHTFORWARD
BORED	└──┴──┴──┴──┘	INTERESTED
INTELLIGENT	└──┴──┴──┴──┘	UNINTELLIGENT
. . . . . .	└──┴──┴──┴──┘	. . . . . .
. . . . . .	└──┴──┴──┴──┘	. . . . . .
. . . . . .	└──┴──┴──┴──┘	. . . . . .

This form can be used to rate individual police officers or the police in general. Add any other pairs of adjectives which occur to you in the spaces provided. You can also rate yourself and see how you compare.

The rating sheet can be used in a number of ways. One is that of comparing views in a small group; all the members complete a sheet and connect all the points to make a profile. The profiles can be collated and averaged out to give a 'group' profile, with which individuals can compare their own ratings. Sheets can also be completed at intervals to measure any changes which may or may not be taking place in a person's perception of policemen.

'What would you do?' situation cards

Type out the following situations onto cards, together with the options for action.

SITUATION 1

You walk round a corner and see five youths beating up a policeman in a shop doorway. He is getting the worst of it and as he goes down they are beginning to put the boot into him. There is no-one else about.

WHAT WOULD YOU DO?

_____   Walk away and forget it?
_____   Go and help the policeman?
_____   Go and help the youths?
_____   Shout at them to stop because a police car is coming?
_____   Find a phone and ring the police for help?

SITUATION 2

You have had four pints of light split, three double whiskies and a rum and coke. You are driving a friend home. You see a car that has run off the road ahead; there is somebody lying on the grass verge either dead or unconscious; a man, bleeding badly from face wounds flags you down. There is no-one else around and not much traffic. The man says, 'Can you get the police and an ambulance and help me with my wife, she's in a bad way?'

You have previous convictions for traffic offences. Your friend cannot drive.

WHAT WOULD YOU DO?

_____   Do as he says?
_____   Say you will fetch help, drive off and forget it?
_____   Drive on, ring 999, then drive off without leaving your name?
_____   Leave your friend on the scene and disappear?

SITUATION 3

You are driving at 50 mph in a built up area. A patrol car stops you. The PC, who knows you, says 'You were speeding'. You have two previous convictions for speeding. You need a driving licence to keep your job as a van driver. You ask him not to book you; to give you a break. He says 'What's it worth?' You are not sure if he is serious.

WHAT WOULD YOU DO?

_____   Give him a fiver?
_____   Give him a fiver – and then report him?
_____   Ask him if he is serious?
_____   Ask him how much he wants?
_____   Make no reply?
_____   Tell him to stick it?

SITUATION 4

You have been offered a job at a holiday camp. You pack a suitcase and set off to walk to the nearest motorway to hitch a lift. A patrol car stops you and two policemen get out. They ask who you are and where you are going. You tell them. They ask to look in your case. They tip the contents all over the pavement and then walk away.

WHAT WOULD YOU DO?

_____   Say nothing?
_____   Protest politely?
_____   Write to the chief constable?
_____   Shout at them?
_____   Hit the smaller one?

Distribute the cards to individuals or small groups of offenders and ask them 'what they would do?' Discuss the different responses of the individuals or groups.

If these situations or responses do not seem appropriate to the people with whom you are working, devise different ones.

Arrest!

Offenders faced with imminent arrest (let us assume that they have committed an offence) can make use of preparations they have made in two areas: a knowledge of rights to which they are entitled, and a behavioural strategy for securing them and avoiding violent confrontation or the commission of further offences like 'resisting arrest' or obstructing the police. To some young men, any strategy that falls short of instant, total and violent opposition to all members of the police force is a sign of personal weakness. Others recognize that the price they pay for such self-indulgence is too high, and that the system ends up winning anyway, whatever minor damage they may manage to inflict on its individual representatives. With them it is possible to work in a constructive way, to handle police – offender encounters more subtly – and, from their own point of view, more effectively.

Rights

In the presence of a constable intent on arrest there is virtually nothing the citizen can do except comply, i.e. 'go quietly'. But:

1. You need not accompany the constable to the police station if you do not wish to unless he says you are under arrest. In that case you *must* be given the reason for your arrest.
2. You need not answer questions of any kind.
3. You can ask to see a friend or relative or legal adviser; but you may not get to see any of them if the police consider it will hinder their inquiries.

These may seem simple points, both to know and to act upon, but it may be beyond many people to put them together in the heat of the moment. Role-played practice of coolness under fire can help the tongue-tied individual speak his/her lines more confidently; for example:

'Are you arresting me?' 'Would you mind telling me what for?'
'I am not going to say anything until I have seen my solicitor/friend/parent.'
'I have made a note of your number and I shall be making a complaint.'

The 'P.O.W.' tactic

Some offenders are consumed with hatred for any officer of the law, to an extent that makes unrealistic any attempt to train them in effective interactive skills. One 'least-worst' tactic, designed to minimize the harmful effects of verbal or physical outbursts during an arrest, is to invite the offender to see him/herself as a 'prisoner-of-war', captured by the enemy, and obliged under the terms of the Geneva convention to give only name, rank and number. Translated into civilian terms, this means giving name, age and address to the arresting officer, and refusing to say anything else whatsoever. A nice touch might be for the offender to memorize and offer his/her CRO number as a part of the permitted package. Repeating this information under realistically simulated conditions will prepare the offender for dealing with real-life encounters in this way: 'My name is John H. Smith; I live at 32, Acacia Avenue, Surbiton, Surrey. My date of birth is 15.12.59, and my CRO number is . . . . This is all I am willing to say at this stage, until I have seen my legal adviser.'

Behaviour in the police interview

Like many of the situations dealt with in the chapters on 'social skills' and 'self-control' the police/offender encounter is a potential explosion, cocked on a hair-trigger. A look, a smile, a wrong word or gesture on either side can initiate physical action and reaction. From where the offender stands, the less aggravation the better. A policeman who is determined to provoke a physical response will almost certainly succeed in the end, if only in self-defence against an unwarranted beating. From the offender's point of view, behaviour in this situation has to be dignified and self-possessed, unflustered and civil, but not subservient. It is the mid-point between 'passive' and 'aggressive', which is 'assertive'.

Invite the group you are working with to re-create an incident between an offender and a policeman – which might be one personally experienced or witnessed in the past – in which things went awry, *either* because the offender was too passive, *or* too aggressive. Record it if possible on video tape. Replay the tape, stop it at critical junctures in the development of the incident and discuss how it might have been done differently. Gather suggestions for alternative strategies, *plus* examples of actual words to say at that point. At the end, invite the 'actors' to replay the action, this time making use of the suggestions and with the benefit of hindsight and subsequent discussion. Tape the result, replay that, and assess its effectiveness in procuring the desired result. (In groups of 'juveniles' a greater degree of verisimilitude can be achieved by having adults – preferably strangers to the participants – play the role of the police.)

> *Example* Gary was a prisoner about to be released. He had previous experience of conflict with the police and feared his ability to control his temper and his lip in future meetings with his friends in blue. The prison officers running the pre-release group to which he belonged, and its other members, helped him to recreate role-played versions of the kinds of incidents and situations he feared. He practised keeping his cool under the most extreme provocation. After his release, it came to pass as he had predicted, and a pair of policemen did their utmost to provoke him into retaliation – searching him and his bags in public in an ostentatious and unpleasant manner. Using his newly acquired skills he refrained from hitting either of the constables, *and* lived to fight another day. They tired of the sport and drove off leaving him at liberty, the beginning of the longest such period in his life.
>
> Had he not been able to keep quiet he could well have been back inside for assaulting a policeman. But *he* had decided that he wished to act differently in those circumstances, and with the help of others had practised being able to do so.

Police decision-making

So far as the individual offender is concerned, the most important decision the police make is whether to proceed with a prosecution or not. The exercise of this discretion is strictly limited (although not by law) in adult cases – it is most often used for road traffic or similar 'administrative' offences. But it is standard practice in juvenile cases – i.e., those under 17 who would appear in the juvenile courts – for the police to carefully consider whether to prosecute or to caution an offender.

This exercise, which can be done by individuals or on a group basis, presents a hypothetical set of cases to a hypothetical set of juvenile bureau officers. In each case a caution/prosecute decision has to be made.

Cautioning juveniles. Instruction sheet

When children under the age of 17 are caught by the police commiting an offence, a decision has to be made whether to take them to court or to give them a caution – a formal telling off in the presence of their parents given by a senior police officer.

Following the 1969 Children and Young Persons Act the police have been encouraged to deal with more and more children in this way. More than half the children who come to the notice of the police for offences are cautioned and the other half prosecuted.

Most police forces have set up special Juvenile Bureaux whose officers have to decide which children to prosecute and which to caution.

As a general rule police forces claim that their first duty is 'the prevention of crime' but officers who deal with juveniles are concerned to protect 'the interests of the child' as well.

A decision-making exercise

Five typical juvenile cases, some of them involving more than one offender, have to be decided in this exercise. Read each one carefully and decide, if you were the police, whether you would prosecute or caution the child in question. Mark an answer on the DECISION FORM and then say briefly why you made that decision.

You can compare your decisions with those made by practising policemen about these cases.

CAUTIONING JUVENILES
Decision form

	C	P	Reason
Terence Wayne			
John Strode			
Leroy Curtis			
Lucinda Curtis			
William Ellis			
Lorraine Smigielski			
Elaine Smigielski			
Anita Lewis			
Philip Goodman			
Anthony Murphy			
Robert Coombs			

C = Caution   P = Prosecute

Case 1

OFFENCE

The oldest boy Terence Wayne took a car without the owner's consent from a car park and picked up the other children in the street. They were caught later by a mobile police patrol. The car was undamaged.

OFFENDERS

1. TERENCE WAYNE. Age 16.

Offence: Taking away a vehicle without owner's consent.
Driving under age.

Took the car from the car park. Living at home with his parents, and three brothers and two sisters, all younger than himself. Home conditions are reasonable and the parents concerned. He has worked as a butcher's apprentice since leaving school.

Previous convictions: Taking a car six months ago – fined £15
Damage to windows, three years ago – conditional discharge.

2. JOHN STRODE. Age 14.

Offence: Driving under age.

Was driving the car when stopped by the police. Parents separated. He lives with his mother who has a job as a barmaid. Children left to their own devices a good deal. Home conditions are materially good. Two years ago all the children were taken into voluntary care for a period of six months due to Mrs Strode's depression. John gets on well at school where he is in an academic stream but sometimes becomes rather aggressive when frustrated.

No previous convictions.

3. LEROY CURTIS. Age 14.

4. LUCINDA CURTIS. Age 13

Offence: Being carried

Brother and sister living at home with mother and step-father, both working. Two other children working in this country, two younger children in Jamaica. Stepfather is a labourer. Home conditions are average for the area. No special problems at school.

Previous convictions: *Leroy* – Riding as an unauthorized passenger on a friend's
moped, a year ago – caution.
Lucinda – not previously known to police.

5. WILLIAM ELLIS. Age 10

Offence: Being carried

Lives with his parents and an 8 year old sister. Father is a clerk with the local authority and Mrs. Ellis has a part-time job as a school meals supervisor. Father spends most of his spare time tending his allotment.

Case 2

OFFENCE

Whilst truanting, three girls went on a shop-lifting spree stealing clothes, cosmetics and jewellery from five separate stores including Woolworths, Boots, and W.H. Smith to a total value of £32.16.

OFFENDERS

1. LORRAINE SMIGIELSKI. Age 14

2. ELAINE SMIGIELSKI. Age 10

Both girls live at home with their parents and an older sister. Father, who is of Polish extraction, works as an engineering fitter. Home conditions are excellent and both parents are concerned at the girls' involvement in this offence. Family relationships appear good on the whole. They feel that Lorraine may have been influenced by Anita and have stopped the association. They have been experiencing some difficulty lately in controlling Lorraine who has become moody and rude. Her teachers say she is average at school and presents no particular problems.

Elaine, on the other hand, is docile and rather immature for her age. Her parents are not sure she knew what was happening.

3. ANITA LEWIS. Age 15

Anita lives at home with her parents, an older brother, and two younger brothers. Home conditions are very poor. Mr Lewis has just been released from prison, following a six months' sentence for stealing metal. He is at present unemployed, drinks heavily, and seems to resent the presence of the children. Anita has been a great help to her mother during this period of stress and the offence came immediately after her father's return home. At school she is thought to have ability which is not used. Her behaviour is good.

Previous conviction: Shoplifting, 18 months ago.

Supervision Order for two years to the Local Authority.

Case 3

OFFENCE

Boy driving a 250 c.c. motor cycle, under age, without 'L' plates, excise licence or MOT certificate, collided with a stationary car, causing damage to the value of £130. The boy fractured his knee cap.

OFFENDER

PHILIP PAUL GOODMAN Age 16

Lives at home with his parents and younger sister in a privately owned semi-detached house, with high material standards. His father is a buyer for a supermarket chain. Philip left school recently and is working as a clerk in a building society office. He is passionately interested in motor bikes and has come to police notice on three previous occasions.

Previous convictions: Similar offence, 6 months ago – fined £35.

Riding as an unauthorized passenger, 13 months ago – conditional discharge.

Riding as an unauthorized passenger, 2 years ago – Police caution.

Case 4

OFFENCE

Whilst left alone in a neighbour's house, took £27 from a drawer which he forced open with a screwdriver.

OFFENDER

ANTHONY JOHN MURPHY Age 16

An only child. His parents were divorced three years ago and Anthony has lived since then with his father, who is an engineering shift worker and not at home a great deal in the evenings. Relations between them are good, however, and they sometimes go fishing together at weekends. His mother, now remarried, lives in London and sees Anthony only three or four times a year.

Anthony has had three jobs since leaving school, where he was considered to be of average ability although lazy. He is currently working for a roofing contractor earning high wages and he can give no explanation for the offence and will not say what has happened to the money which has not been recovered. His father, who has already repaid the money, thinks that he may have spent it on records.

He is not previously known to the police.

Case 5

OFFENCE

Set fire to a hay barn causing damage to the value to £2,300.

OFFENDER

ROBERT CHARLES COOMBES Age 13

Robert, an only child, lives at home with his parents. His father is registered as disabled and his mother works part time as a telephone operator. The home is comfortably furnished and well kept. Robert was a delicate child and missed a lot of schooling in earlier years. His educational level is still low for his age. He tends not to have friends and to spend his time going on long bicycle rides to collect newts and frogs. Has been attending the Child Guidance clinic for the past two years, but lately has not been keeping appointments. He left a note at the scene of the crime which said, 'The Bloody Red Baron strikes again.'

Not previously known to the police.

Decisions made on these 'cases':				
	By 11 Juvenile Bureau Officers		By 9 Offenders (ages 17-30)	
Case	Caution	Prosecute	Caution	Prosecute
Terence Wayne	0	11	0	9
John Strode	4	7	7	2
Leroy Curtis	7	4	8	1
Lucinda Curtis	10	1	9	0
William Ellis	11	0	8	1
Lorraine Smigielski	7	4	7	2
Elaine Smigielski	11	0	8	1
Anita Lewis	5	6	2	7
Philip Goodman	0	11	0	9
Anthony Murphy	9	2	7	2
Robert Coombs	5	6	2	7

When the individuals/teams have considered the cases, made their decisions and recorded them on the sheet provided, together with some indication of the reasons for making that particular decision, the results can be discussed – looking at similarities and differences, and comparing totals for a whole group with the decisions made by 11 serving juvenile bureau officers presented with these identical cases (shown above).

An extension of the exercise, which nicely illustrates the contingent nature of legal decision-making, is to appoint three groups to act as (a) the juvenile bureau, (b) the probation service or social services department, and (c) a juvenile court panel, respectively. The police decide whether to prosecute or not; the probation officers or social workers, acting on the assumption that the cases *will* be prosecuted, make recommendations to the court as to the sentences they think appropriate in each case; and finally the juvenile bench deal with the cases as they see fit when they arrive in court. To help the probation officers and social workers and the juvenile court magistrates it may be necessary to display a list of possible sentences:

Absolute discharge
Conditional discharge
Fine
Community service
Supervision (with or without a condition of 'intermediate treatment' (or 'supervised activity').
Attendance centre
Youth custody order
Disqualification (in RTA offences only)

Some of the qualifications and implications of these sentences can be discussed before the decision-making starts. Cases similar to these can easily be compiled for use with adult offenders; and prisoners could simulate decisions on parole applications.

Many groups of offenders, given decisions like these to take, turn out to be more punitive than law and order professionals, a surprising finding in view of their frequent and bitter attacks on the injustices they claim to have suffered personally at the hands of the system.

That is a major point for the discussion that follows the exercise; as is the fact that cases which would almost certainly attract cautions in real life end up with supervision order recommendations and sometimes custody orders *if* it is assumed that they have been prosecuted. Nothing could more clearly illustrate the contingencies and inconsistencies to which legal and penal decision-making is so prone.

Making a complaint

In the case of wrongful arrest the citizen has the right to sue the police for damages for wrongful arrest. This is a strictly legal proceeding best left alone by amateurs. For advice see a solicitor or consult a neighbourhood law centre.

When the citizen is aggrieved by the manner or behaviour of the police, for whatever reason, the only means of redress is appeal to the internal complaints procedures operated by police departments themselves. There are many unsatisfactory aspects to these proceedings, but since they are all that is available, some offenders will wish to

---

32, Field Lane,
GARFORTH.

Monday 14th June.

Dear Sir,

I wish to make a formal complaint about one of your officers, PC E.B. Mottram, number 105A who was on duty in the Castletown area last Thursday night, the 10th of June.

At about 10 pm I was driving home from the Elephant public house, where I had drunk two half pints of beer shandy. PC Mottram stopped me and asked to see my driving licence. I said I did not have it with me but could produce it at the police station the following day. He then smelt my breath and asked me to blow into a breathalyser, which I did, with negative results.

At this point PC Mottram became abusive and told me to 'get out of the f - - - - motor.' He then ordered me to turn out my pockets. I asked him what for.

He swore at me again and punched me several times in the ribs and stomach and kidneys. I did not hit him back in case he arrested me for assaulting a policeman.

Eventually I turned out my pockets, and he then searched the inside of the car and the boot. He found nothing there and then walked off.

At no time did I do or say anything to provoke this violent behaviour on PC Mottram's part.

The Chief Constable,
Police HQ,   Yours faithfully,
County Hall,   *J. Connor*
GARFORTH.   John Connor.

---

avail themselves of them. Actually making a complaint might in fact be a good project for a group to engage in, helping one of their number to formulate one and press it home through the proper channels.

In the first instance, this might take the form of writing out a formal statement of complaint. A simulated reply from the officer involved could also be written; and members of the group – or outsiders – could be called on to adjudicate in the case by calling the complainant and the constable to separate hearings. Examples of a letter and of a constable's response to it are shown opposite and below.

COMPLAINTS PROCEDURE.
OFFICER'S STATEMENT.   PC E.B. MOTTRAM. 105A. C Division. 16th June.

At 10.05 pm on the evening of the 10th of June this year whilst on foot
patrol in the Castletown area I observed a white Ford Zephyr motor car,
registration number VYA 223 B being driven along the London Road in an
erratic manner. I stopped it and asked the driver for his name and
address which he gave as John Connor, 32, Field Lane, Garforth. I
asked him to show me his driving licence which he said he did not have
with him. His manner was surly and truculent and I asked him to get
out of the car. His breath smelt of alcohol and I invited him to take
a breathalyser test. He did so but with negative results. When he
had finished breathing into the bag, he held it up, said 'F - - -
you copper' and threw it on the floor. As he tried to get back into
his car he threw the door open in a violent way so that I had to jump
out of the way. I fell against him and some jostling took place. It
is possible that my elbow may have come into contact with his side.
I warned him about his behaviour and searched his pockets and the car,
both inside and in the boot. I then continued my patrol. Connor
made no complaint about my behaviour at the time. There were no
witnesses.

Signed. *E. B. Mottram*

Witness. *J. B. Salmon*

Detective Chief Inspector Salmon.

Police co-operation

The value of any work you do on police/offender relations can be considerably enhanced by the presence of real-life police officers. Getting them to come along and take part in whatever activities you have planned may not be easy, and there is a tendency for police forces who do decide to co-operate to nominate a cheerful and avuncular community constable who is not all that typical of some of his colleagues on the beat or in the CID. A somewhat harder and less friendly representative, or one capable of convincingly portraying those qualities, may be of more use to groups of offenders who have difficulties in their dealings with police.

The simplest way of using a live policeman is to prepare some questions beforehand for group members to ask and discuss during the session. This will demand sensitive and sometimes firm handling on the part of the worker, if the proceedings are not to become merely a rehearsal and reinforcement of entrenched attitudes on both sides.

If the constable is willing, he can be asked to play the part of a policeman in typical arrest situations – either ones nominated by group members from their own knowledge or experience, or proposed by the policeman.

If he is even more willing, the roles can be reversed so that the offender plays the part of the police constable, and the constable that of an offender – a mutually educational experience in many cases.

Other possibilities for work with the police: a visit to the police station; a ride in a squad car; joint sessions with police cadets; an explanation of police paperwork and prosecutions; instruction in motor-bike riding.

None of these activities are designed to gloss over the very real antagonisms that exist at street level between young people and the police, nor to suggest that responsibility for this state of affairs can be laid at the feet of lawless youth alone. They are intended instead to provide some insights into the organization and procedures deployed by the police in their work and to provide some opportunity for representatives of the two factions to talk together out of normal context – it is surprising how few of either have ever done so.

In court

Even the most casual observer of court proceedings of any kind, from juvenile to grown-up, can hardly fail to be struck by the proportion of defendants who appear to be confused and over-awed by what is going on around them. First-timers are at a particular disadvantage in this respect, but experience seldom brings assurance to any but the most self-possessed. Given the absolutely central role of the accused in criminal trials this lack of comprehension and failure to contribute has several serious consequences. One is that defendants are unable to defend themselves as well as justice may assume and expect. They are of course, in more serious cases, represented by learned counsel, but what may seem legally expedient does not necessarily coincide with what defendants with their wits about them would wish to say on their own behalf. As a result undoubted injustices occur, both as to conviction and as to sentence.

Preparing offenders to face criminal proceedings should be undertaken with these aims in mind: first to familiarize them with what is likely to happen in court; and secondly to equip them to make the most positive contribution of which they are capable before any decisions are reached affecting their own future lives and liberties.

Understanding court procedure

Workers in the criminal justice system are in a privileged position to experience and understand its workings, and to pass on their knowledge and insights to those who are about to be tried. They can do this by simple exposition and discussion, by showing relevant films, distributing written accounts, inviting other court officials to give talks, or by any other educational means.

The exercises that follow suggest additional and alternative ways in which knowledge and skill can be acquired or improved.

Devising a guide to defendants' rights

One way of learning about something is to attempt to teach it to others; for example, a group of offenders could work together over a period to devise a guide to defendants' rights. This would entail deciding on the major areas to be covered, seeking out and making sense of all the relevant information, translating it into simple and intelligible language, designing a format and layout, drawing illustrations and actually producing something in a form that could be given to other offenders facing court proceedings.

The following three items are taken from a *Defendant's Handbook* devised by a local group of Radical Alternatives to Prison (RAP).

a) Flowchart summarising the contents of the *Handbook* (see overleaf)

b) Extract from the *Handbook* (numbers refer to boxes in the flowchart):

28. *Remand for Reports*. This can be from old records or an interview with the Probation Service, the Welfare or a Doctor.

29. *Remand for further inquiries*. The police can make cases last six months. Usually they hope to pin some spare unsolved crimes on you. If the trial has started they will find a new date to suit the same magistrates.

30. *Probation Service*. Not all Probation Officers think you should be boiled in oil. Some very quickly despair of their well meaning efforts to help you and get very unhappy if you turn up in Court again. Can be useful for jobs and lodgings. It is best to string along with them, in fact you can be charged if you don't.

c) The Court Room – an illustration:

Courtroom simulation

A courtroom simulation serves a number of purposes:

1. Giving information about court procedures and familiarizing those taking part with what happens.

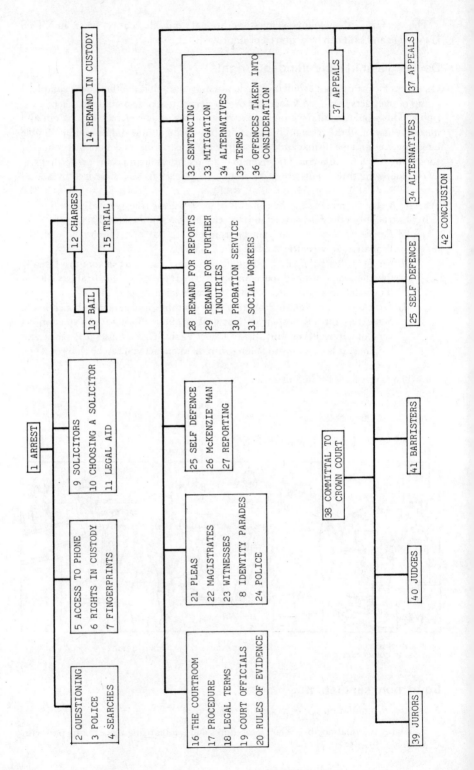

2. Creating role reversals which promote insights into the proceedings from different perspectives, e.g. those of the police, the magistrates, social workers, probation officers.
3. Providing practice in presenting a case in court; making a plea of mitigation, etc.

Depending on the number of people taking part, roles should be allocated as follows:

MAGISTRATES At least two and preferably three magistrates who should be briefed with a description of their duties: listening to the evidence, asking the defendant and his/her parents questions, retiring to consider a verdict – guilty or not-guilty – and reaching decisions as to sentence and communicating them to defendants.
DEFENDANT(S) The defendant may act as him/herself or be provided with a starting point, e.g.
'You are Adam Smith, 15, charged with breaking and entering the premises of F.W.Woolworth in Stepney High Road at 10.00 pm on Friday the . . .' Details of home background, previous convictions, etc., may also be provided.
POLICE PROSECUTOR The job of the prosecutor, usually a senior police officer, is to present the case against the defendant in as factual and detailed a way as possible. In contested, i.e., 'not guilty' cases the prosecutor has to cross-examine witnesses, both for the prosecution and for the defence, and also the defendant.
PARENT(S) The defendant's parents who should have the same basic detail about home circumstances.
SOCIAL WORKER/PROBATION OFFICER . . . whose task is to write and present a report on the defendant to the court. Some guidance may be needed about the likely contents of such reports.
COURT CLERK An important role which requires the knowledge of procedure and of possible sentences; best taken by a staff member.
Lesser roles may be allocated if numbers allow: court usher, defending solicitor, educational welfare officer, co-defendants, local press.

Preparation time should be allowed for all the participants to absorb the information on their role briefings.

After the simulation has been run there should be a general discussion about the conduct of the case and its relevance to the real-life experiences of those taking part. A video recording might be helpful to look back at particular performances, especially those of defendants.

The realism of the simulation can be heightened by securing permission to stage the proceedings in an actual court-room – juvenile or adult – and by enlisting the aid of a proper clerk to the court, and even of magistrates themselves. None of these is essential, and their presence should not be used to deny offenders the possibility of themselves sitting on the bench in judgment over their fellow-delinquents.

Pleas in court

Appearing in court, even for those with previous experience, is an ordeal. Being the focus of attention; the possibility of cross-examination by clever lawyers; and above all the uncertainty about the verdict and about the nature and length of any subsequent sentence – all combine to undermine the self-confidence of all but a fortunate minority. The end result is that most offenders say nothing in court except in response to the charge(s) being put to them, or to direct questions from counsel or the bench. They hardly ever volunteer information about themselves, ask questions of the prosecution witnesses, or make pleas which might mitigate the sentence of the court. In those rare cases where defendants do speak up for themselves, there is a chance and it is no more than that – that they will succeed in affecting the final decision.

The aim of a defendant in making a personal plea to the court will depend on the nature of the offence and his/her previous record, and on a realistic estimate of the likely outcome of the case. Someone who is clearly destined to go to prison may want to make a case for a shorter rather than a longer period inside. In more marginal cases the plea may be for a non-custodial rather than a custodial disposal.

Whatever the defendant decides to attempt, preparation and practice are the keys to any success with which their efforts may be rewarded.

The deferred sentence provision brought in by the Court Act 1973 presents the best opportunity for creative submissions to courts regarding alternative sentences. If the offender works out in advance a clear plan of action, the chances of success may be surprisingly high. The plan might be to engage in two kinds of activity – *firstly*, ones related to the offender as an individual, such as attending meetings of Alcoholics Anonymous, undergoing medical treatment for depression, joining a discussion group run by a local voluntary organization, taking specific steps to pay off debts, mend relationships, sort out personal problems; and *secondly*, ones related to the offences committed and to their victims – under this heading might come offers of direct compensation to the losers, either in cash or in kind, or an indirect form of restitution through the completion of a prearranged programme of volunteer activity for local organizations.

Once the plan has been prepared, and the written consents of relevant agencies and individuals have been secured, the next stage is to practise presenting it to the court. This may be done in writing, or verbally, or both.

The worker's role in all this is to point out some of the possibilities, lend a helping hand in the formulation of a plan, and provide opportunities for role-played rehearsals of the submission. A friendly presence in court during the making of the actual plea can also be reassuring.

Inside!

A sentence of imprisonment, or of detention, or even of consignment to a community home with education on the premises (CHE) might appear to be the end of the road so far as the worker with the delinquent in the community is concerned. But for the prospective captive, it is only the beginning of a journey beset with unknown dangers, both physical and mental. Part of the luggage a person should carry into such an experience is some preparation for the vicissitudes of institutional life. This preparation might contain a number of elements, depending on the sex, age and sophistication of the offender – all related to the likely form of custodial sentences he or she will receive at the conclusion of a court case. They could include an introduction to the idea of an inmate subculture and all that it entails for new arrivals on the scene; some orientation to the official prescriptions for 'doing time'; and some strategies for resisting the twin threats of institutionalization and criminalization. All these are best thought of in terms of *institutional career planning* or *counselling*.

Institutional career plans

A career plan for a young person setting out to work for a firm or organization would be concerned with maximizing his/her potential within the possibilities set by the aims and structure of the enterprise. It would consider factors such as the intelligence and past achievements of the person concerned, his or her strengths and weaknesses, interests, aptitudes, skills etc. – all related to the opportunities for training and self-development that exist within the environment of the job or career in question. Applied to 'doing time' a career plan would be concerned in the first place, not with *maximizing* potential, but with *minimizing* the damage that prison or borstal or detention does to someone. This might mean making plans to combat the passivity and boredom that can otherwise characterise a long sentence; it might mean taking up new mental and physical activities – deciding to do some 'O' levels or 'A' levels, or an Open University course; becoming a weight-lifter or a gymnast; developing some craft, skill or pastime; a programme of personal reading or writing in any of a million fields of interest; the cultivation of yoga or transcendental meditation; it might mean making use of whatever training, educational and recreational facilities are offered by the official regime.

A different aspect of the problem of separation from society is the welfare of those who are left behind: family, lovers, friends. Something can be done to keep up old ties via letters and visits, but these are limited, and perhaps best concentrated where priorities are highest. In the case of people with family responsibilities these questions are posed in their most acute form: how to go on being a mother or a father to children you see only once a month, or even less often. It is not a problem unique to someone in prison, but the latter is an additional and complicating factor since some of the stigma of conviction may rub off on immediate kin, and kids may be labelled at school by staff or other children. Then there are financial problems, and the corroding anxiety about sexual fidelity that can burn through the strongest and most carefully tied lifelines to sanity.

There are no general answers to any of these difficulties. They need to be thought of and thought through in each case, discussed with involved parties, and made subject to a number of contingency arrangements.

Finally, there is the question, 'Release – what then?' Life sentence, or very long sentence, offenders may feel this to be an academic area, but having some ideas and taking some action in preparation for the day, however distant, is part of the purpose of career planning for institutional life. It keeps hope alive – an eye on the horizon where one day the shoreline of freedom will loom out of a sea-fret of seemingly interminable time.

Career plans can be constructed by someone working alone, simply thinking about the issues and answering some basic self-set questions; or as a collaboration between the person concerned and a worker; or as the end-product of some group deliberation in which other offenders participate.

If you are working with offenders who are not imminently faced with incarceration, the idea of institutional career planning can be introduced on a hypothetical basis by asking them to work in pairs or small groups to help each other formulate plans for keeping mentally and physically intact during three lengths of sentence: six weeks in a detention centre; two years in a youth custody institution; and a life sentence with a minimum recommendation of fifteen years to serve in a maximum security prison.

Compare and discuss the resulting plans.

Prison simulation

In a famous simulation, Philip Zimbardo arbitrarily divided a group of psychology students into 'guards' and 'prisoners' and simulated a prison in the departmental basement (Haney, Banks, and Zimbardo 1973; Zimbardo 1973). 'Prisoners' were locked in cells by the 'guards' and an institutional regime evolved. Zimbardo called a halt to the experiment when relations between the two groups degenerated into violence – a telling demonstration of the power of role-play, and a warning against lightly undertaking exercises with such serious themes.

But a shorter-term and more straightforward simulation can serve to give 'a taste of prison' to those who have never been there. The procedures of reception, the daily routines, relations between staff and inmates, rules, discipline, punishments – these and many more scenes from institutional life can be reproduced in the relative safety of the worker's office or the project meeting-room. If the worker lacks the experience or the knowledge necessary for a proper degree of realism, it is not too difficult to recruit someone who possesses it; former inmates of most types of penal establishments abound in most settings where work with offenders is undertaken.

Sensory deprivation

Solitary confinement under certain conditions – monochrome walls, constant artificial light, effective sound-proofing, or the hooding of captives who are subjected to constant unpleasant noise levels – are well tested mechanisms for producing the symptoms of psychological disorder in those who are subjected to them. Ordinary imprisonment or detention is unlikely to approach these extremes, but there is inherent in all captivity an element of sensory deprivation (Cohen and Taylor, 1972; Solomon et al., 1965).

Individuals who face the prospect of incarceration, whether imminently or not, can be given a taste of these conditions to see how they stand up to them. Total sensory deprivation is extremely difficult and expensive to arrange – it entails immersion in blood-temperature fluid with piped air and an absence of all light and noise. Under *these* conditions hallucinations and other signs of disturbance are commonly experienced. Less drastic and more realistic, people can be shut into small bare rooms with no furniture except a block of wood on which to sit, and with the window(s) obscured to allow in a very subdued level of light.

How long can the individual endure sitting in the room without asking to be released? How did it feel? What did he/she think about? Results for several people can be compared and discussed, together with ideas for combatting the conditions – not unlike some police cells, or the 'chokey' block of prisons and youth custody institutions. Traditional methods of coping include a mixture of physical (where permissible) and mental activity. At the least, isometric exercises would be possible whilst sitting on a seat. Relaxation and meditation are other tactics that might be tried. Mental exercise can take any of a multitude of forms. Counting in long series. Recalling minute detail from memory e.g., trying to remember *all* the people you know, or have ever met. Recalling areas of knowledge gained at school or elsewhere. Writing verse in one's head. Remembering the details of one's life, of any period, and in any desired depth of detail. Engaging in fantasy of all sorts.

The experiment can then be repeated and reports gained on the utility of the different methods discussed.

Inmate sub-cultures

It is a well-attested fact that inside residential institutions of all sorts, from schools to hospitals to prisons – there exist what have come to be called 'inmate subcultures' (Giallombardo, 1966; Morris and Morris, 1963; Social Science Research Council, 1960; Sykes, 1958).

These subcultures are characterized by a number of common features:

- a sense of 'us-and-them' between inmates and staff,
- a set of informal values which prescribe an 'ideal type' of fellow inmate,
- an informal code of conduct regulating relations between inmate and inmate, and between inmates and staff,
- specialised role positions within the inmate social structure, differentiated by function,
- an informal hierarchy of status positions,
- mechanisms for subverting or counteracting official policies and practices and for re-

distributing material and moral resources within the inmate group,
- tacit accommodations between inmate and staff interests designed to protect the interests of both, and sometimes leading to corruption,
- a special terminology which designates some of these roles and rules.

Old institutional hands assume and fit into these rules, roles and values as though they were familiar pairs of gloves. New entrants to life inside may experience some difficulty in recognising and adapting to the subculture of the place to which they have been committed.

Preparation for this aspect of life inside might consist of general talk about the phenomenon of the subculture; about leaders, 'bullies' and 'daddies'; about the special language of the school or the prison or whatever; and about inmate/staff relations and how they are best handled by newcomers to the system.

Eliciting the social structure of the prison

If you are working with people in prison, one of the most important sets of influences on the quality of their daily lives is that provided by their fellow-prisoners. There is a voluminous literature devoted to the topic of the 'inmate sub-culture', in which students of the prison have discerned and described a variety of roles filled by individual prisoners. Some of these are 'instrumental', i.e., concerned with the trading that goes on around the supply of tobacco or drugs, the distribution of privileges and food, the passing of illicit messages, and the suborning of subordinate discipline staff. Some of them are 'expressive' i.e., related to the status which accrues to some inmates because of their manifest personal qualities or their previous criminal activities.

Finding out about these informal social structures can be an arduous and time-consuming business, but the outlines of the system can be elicited quite rapidly for discussion purposes by the use of 'pattern notes' (Buzan, 1974). This is a form of personal brainstorming described by Tony Buzan in his book *Use your Head*. The basic idea is to follow divergent thought patterns outwards from a topic or title written in the centre of a page, rather than working from top to bottom and left to right, as in conventional note-taking. An example of pattern notes completed by one long-term prisoner on the subject of 'other men in prison' is shown overleaf.

An analysis of pattern notes completed by ten long-term prisoners produces a list of roles or role-types, together with some of their associated characteristics:

Model prisoners: institutionalized. Vegetating, unable to cope, prison pallor, deprived, deterioration.
Loners:depressives. Lack of interest, frustration, no-hopers, depressed state, humble, timid.
Complainers. Welfare moaners, family problems, tobacco problems, petty-minded, no character, no courage, always blame others, 'innocent'.
Foolers. Idiots, time wasters, parasites, trouble-makers, mentally depraved.
Self-centred. Selfish, mean, jealous, indifferent, deceit, failures.
Con-men. Misleading, cheats, liars, world of fantasy, never tell truth, dreamers, can be funny, better educated.
Bullies. Emotional, extrovert, barons, swindlers, dealers, drug-addicts, dangerous, unreliable.
Rebels. Trying to retain individuality.
Sex-cases. Unclean inmates, rapist, necrophiliac, mentally sick, sodomites, can corrupt young children, very bad against children, always get parole first time.
Hobbyists. Matchsticks, reading, TV, classes, soon get tired, always sleeping.
True friends. Nice people, a few, feeling.

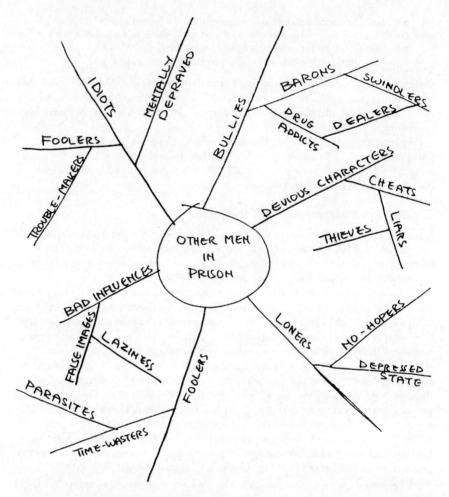

The most striking feature of this collective portrait of people in prison is the negative and derogatory view the men have of each other. Of the 11 categories, 8 are pejorative; rebels and hobbyists are painted in neutral shades; and only the 'true friend' offers anything positive in relations between prisoners. These are of course the views of one group of men in one long-term prison. Conducted with other groups of residents, inmates or prisoners, the exercise should reveal different patterns for discussion and reflection.

The web of circumstances: 'me' in prison

A similar procedure can be used to help individuals identify some aspects of their personal situations in prison. In the centre of a sheet of paper, the person concerned depicts him or herself behind a barred window (see opposite).

Radiating out from this window are lines along which the consequences of an offence, a conviction, and a custodial sentence are spelled out for the individual concerned and for significant others: parents, victims, wives, lovers, children.

The results can be displayed and discussed, and common themes drawn out by the worker.

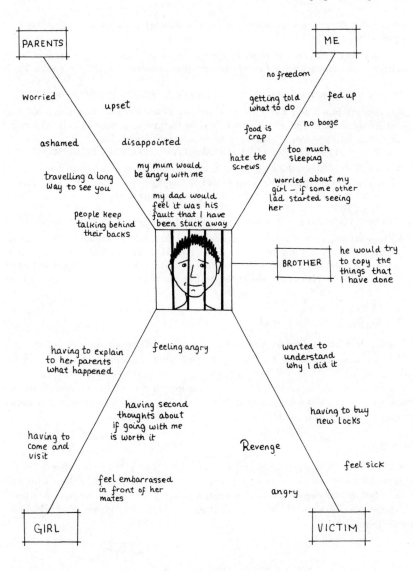

PARENTS

ME

no freedom

Worried

upset

getting told
what to do

fed up

ashamed

disappointed

food is
crap

no booze

travelling a long
way to see you

my mum would
be angry with me

hate the
screws

too much
sleeping

people keep
talking behind
their backs

my dad would
feel it was his
fault that I have
been stuck away

worried about my
girl – if some other
lad started seeing
her

BROTHER

he would try
to copy the
things that
I have done

having to explain
to her parents
what happened

feeling angry

wanted to
understand
why I did it

having second
thoughts about
if going with me
is worth it

having to buy
new locks

having to
come and
visit

Revenge

feel sick

feel embarrassed
in front of her
mates

angry

GIRL

VICTIM

Staff versus inmate values: a test of conformity

Given that institutions are split social structures with an *official* and an *unofficial* culture, it is possible to locate individual inmates at points along a line that leads from total conformity to staff values at one end, to total conformity to inmate values at the other. This could be done by simply marking a point on a scale, but it can be tested more specifically, and in a form that lends itself to comparisons between people and over time, by using this situation test. It is based on the work of Stanton Wheeler in American prisons (Wheeler, 1961; Priestley, 1980).

Here are some stories of incidents in prison life. Under the first three are the statements STRONGLY APPROVE; APPROVE; DISAPPROVE; STRONGLY DISAPPROVE. For each of the incidents 1, 2 and 3, underline the statement which is nearest to the way you feel about what the prisoner has done. For incident number 4, underline the statement you agree with.

1. A prisoner is put on a work party at a flat rate wage. Some of the other men on the party criticize him because he does more work than anybody else. He works as hard as he can.
STRONGLY APPROVE   APPROVE   DISAPPROVE   STRONGLY DISAPPROVE

2. Prisoners Bluett and Parks are good friends. Bluett has a £5 note which has been smuggled into the prison. He tells Parks that the staff are suspicious and asks him to hide the money for a few days. Parks takes the money and carefully hides it.
STRONGLY APPROVE   APPROVE   DISAPPROVE   STRONGLY DISAPPROVE

3. A prisoner, without thinking, commits a minor offence against prison discipline. An officer who sees him puts him on report for it. Later, three prisoners are talking about it. Two of them criticize the officer. The third prisoner defends the officer and says he was only doing his duty.
STRONGLY APPROVE   APPROVE   DISAPPROVE   STRONGLY DISAPPROVE

4. Two prisoners are planning an escape. They threaten to beat up another prisoner unless he steals a chisel for them from a workshop. He is afraid of them and whilst trying to smuggle the chisel into the wing is caught by an officer. He is put on report and stands to lose remission. He can get off the charge if he blames the other two prisoners. Should he:

A.   Make a statement about the other two?
B.   Keep quiet and take the blame?

Conformity/non-conformity scores can be obtained by giving each of the four answers to questions 1, 2 and 3, a score from 1 to 4, where 1 is a non-conformist response and 4 is conformist.

Wheeler used an instrument like this to explore and confirm the hypothesis that prisoners were at their most anti-staff in the middle periods of their sentences and at their most conformist just after reception and just before release.

Release

Re-entering the community after a period of incarceration presents the offender with a set of problems for which intensive preparation ought to be offered by those who work in custodial institutions. But that is another field altogether which we have dealt with elsewhere (McGuire and Priestley, 1983; Priestley, McGuire, Barnitt, Flegg, Hemsley and Welham, 1984).

9 Beyond the individual

Most of this book has been about working face to face with offenders, individually or in groups, and its contents have been designed for those who are engaged in such work on a day-to-day basis, and who probably earn their living by it. In the penultimate chapter, however, we made a slight change of emphasis, to look at problems arising in the relationship between offenders and the 'system' of legal, penal and welfare agencies with which they have to contend.

In this final chapter, we would like to change the emphasis again, and address the still wider issue of the relationship betwen that 'system' and crime considered in more general or abstract terms. For beyond a certain point, there is only so much that can be achieved by approaching offence behaviour at the individual level. In a number of important ways criminal behaviour *is* a product of the society in which it occurs. Identification of these may provide some cues for possible action that could be taken at a level 'beyond the individual'.

The first of them is that there are strong associations between offence behaviour and various aspects of the way society is organized. Adjudicated offenders more often come from the disadvantaged strata of society, according to economic, educational and other indicators of 'social status'. Recorded crime is correlated with lower incomes, poor housing, family disruption, residence in deteriorating urban areas, and numerous other indices of deprivation (Rutter and Madge, 1976). This may be because such factors directly or indirectly 'cause' crime, or at least bring about the conditions in which it will probably appear. On the other hand it may be because there is built into the operation of the law a bias against some segments of society. Which of these is more likely to be correct is a point of disagreement amongst commentators; there is probably quite a lot of truth in both of them.

Another way in which society very obviously produces crime is that criminal acts are 'defined' by society in the literal sense that they are acts forbidden by its rules. This might seem a trivial piece of semantics were it not for the fact that such definitions and rules serve a number of different purposes within a society – not least, that of preserving the existing social order. 'There is no behaviour which is always and everywhere criminal' (Phillipson, 1971, 5); and the kinds of behaviour most commonly judged to be criminal reflect something about a society's structure and the power of different interest groups within it. Even allowing that the criminal law usually (though not always) corresponds with moral strictures broadly accepted within a society, laws can still be unjust, can be out of step with behaviour which is for the most part tolerable or causes no great harm, and can thus 'create' offences unnecessarily – in some instances causing society more overall inconvenience than the offences themselves.

A third way in which society contributes to crime is in its reaction to it. This takes two forms. One is the way offenders are dealt with; there seems little doubt that the essentially punitive basis of much sentencing is as likely to incline the individual to re-offend as it is to deter him or her; and in any case the 'labelling' of offenders and their excommunication from society further reinforce their position as deviants. The other is the manner in which crime is represented by the media; apart from the crude medievalism of the morality enshrined in most newspaper reporting, and the atmosphere this helps to nurture, there is evidence that press hysteria can 'amplify' particular patterns of criminality over a period of time (Cohen and Young, 1973).

Finally, it may be that society helps to perpetuate criminality within itself because the very foundations of its response to offending are themselves utterly misguided. Once an offence has been committed, the momentum of the criminal justice machine carries it onward towards the fulfilment of a single aim: the apprehension, scrutiny, and processing of the offender. The other party involved in the offence – the victim – is almost entirely absent from the scene. Accustomed as we are to this state of affairs, it is diffcult even to perceive how unnatural it is. Our whole conception of what it means to break the law and what should happen afterwards is cast in terms of it; and its influence on what we do with offenders, and thereby on their subsequent behaviour, must be both pervasive, and profound.

In what follows here, we consider each of these factors in turn, to see if there are any respects in which, by manipulating them in a particular direction, we might entertain some hope of having an impact on offending behaviour.

Social change

The first kind of contribution that societies make towards the maintenance of criminality, is the physical conditions in which large numbers of citizens are expected to live. There is little the present book can say about this subject. Crime is just one amongst many ailments with which contemporary society is afflicted – alongside inequalities of considerable magnitude in material circumstances, wide disparities in status and power, racial tensions, chronic levels of unemployment, and the intensification of all these ills in particular inner-city 'ghettos'. The increasing crime-rate is just one symptom of a deeper economic and social malaise. Criminologists amongst others have pointed to the need to redress some of these injustices if there is to be any possible chance of controlling the incidence of crime. In many cases a way out of the imbroglio has been seen in types of 'community action' directed at specific urban districts where crime and other problems are at their worst. Of necessity, however, these are limited in scope and restricted to the neighbourhoods with which they are concerned; many are overwhelmed by the sizeable organizational task of trying to co-ordinate the work of agencies with different and sometimes conflicting interests; and there has been no clear evidence that they have an impact on offending in any case.

Dismayed by the failure of these and other initiatives, some workers have adopted a stance which can be described as 'non-intervention'. In its crudest form, as advocated by some, this view implies that the step-by-step build-up of problems and the slow but inexorable accretion of social unrest will one day result in a political explosion. Any attempt to interfere with this process by mitigating the plight of individuals is somehow a betrayal of the revolutionary cause – the only way of bringing about change in people's lives that is real and not illusory. This may be a historically 'correct' analysis, but it lacks that humanity which is not only the starting-point but also the proper end of the revolutionary impulse. Servants of historical 'inevitabilities' often tend to be blind to the passing needs of their fellow human beings, and seem willing to sacrifice the relief of present suffering on the altar of a theoretical model of social and political development.

A more compassionate position was expressed by Schur (1973), with special reference to the problem of juvenile delinquency. His view was that society should "accommodate . . . to the widest possible diversity of behaviours and attitudes' and that we should move towards a situation in which '. . . the basic injunction for public policy becomes: *leave kids alone wherever possible*' (Schur, *op. cit.*, p. 154, 155, italics in original). 'If the choice is between changing youth and changing the society (including some of its laws), the radical non-interventionist opts for changing the society' (*ibid.*, 155). Yet for Schur this did not mean that work with individuals should be abandoned; he still saw room for this, provided it was undertaken on a voluntary basis, and preferably outside institutions. Use of the materials in this book would not be incompatible with this conception. Many offenders do see their own offending behaviour as a problem; aiding them in the process of doing something about it *when this is what they want to happen* is quite consistent with the notion of 'intervening' in their lives to the minimum extent possible.

This still leaves unanswereed the question of changing society. The problem is primarily a political one, and political means the only means by which it can be properly dealt with. Whether individuals wish to engage in political activity (of whatever kind) is obviously dependent on many other aspects of their opinions and beliefs apart form their approach to offending as such. While the abolition of the gross distortions of our society would almost certainly lead to a reduction in many kinds of offence, the extent to which individuals take action to secure this is entirely a matter of personal choice. However, even for those who are reluctant to participate in politics in the larger sense, there are still many things that can be done within the legal and penal spheres themselves; in the remainder of this chapter we look at what some of these things might be.

Working for change in the legal and penal systems

The attitudes of those who work in the law and order field range from the most entrenched conservatism to violent radicalism. But between them lies a middle ground where a great agenda of amendments to the legal and penal systems waits to be agreed and acted upon. Common sense suggests what many of these items are, and a sense of natural justice provides all the justification they need. In this context two sorts of responsibility devolve upon workers in the system. The first is a habit of watchfulness; a vigilance on behalf of civil liberties and a willingness to speak out and act against abuse and cruelty, both as individuals and via membership of professional organisations. At a time of growing tensions between certain segments of society and the agencies of control, such scrutiny is especially necessary. Some of it is best done by outsiders, by pressure groups, but those who work inside the system have a privileged view of what is going on and a greater opportunity to have their voices heard. A second responsibility is for raising one's sights from immediate issues of civil liberty, to wider questions of policy as they affect the legal and penal systems. In the paragraphs that follow we make some suggestions about possible and relevant campaigns and related activities. They are neither comprehensive nor exhaustive, but even a small additional expense of effort in directions like these would soon yield practical dividends in the shape of changes for the better.

Observing the system

Monitoring the police

Street encounters between police officers and members of the public define the front-line in what is increasingly represented in the press and popular mythology as the 'war against crime'. The use of martial metaphor to depict these events has accompanied a 'tooling-up' on both sides; a classic process of escalation in a conflict which has only tenuous roots in the real world. The police are persuaded that crime is getting out of control, and that the answer lies in wider powers and more equipment. Offenders and others, increasingly convinced that policemen are engaged in a public vendetta against them, react with mounting anger and violence against what they perceive as 'provocative' police activity. The first, and worst casualties of these transactions, are not the broken heads of the participants, but the civil liberties of everyone else; the bystanders and non-combatants, whose interests and privacies are in danger of being swept aside in the drive to secure more control and more convictions.

Offenders themselves are the most frequent witnesses to the way in which these conflicts are worked out in practice, but because of the stigma which attaches to them after legal proceedings, their views are the least likely to command public attention or approval. Probation officers, social workers, prison officers and other professional groups on the other hand are respectable and respected voices in debates on these matters. They can raise them therefore in defence of all our freedoms by reporting what appear to them to be abuses of police power and by working for the greater accountability of police forces to the communities they are supposed in theory to serve. Representatives of different agencies might collaborate in the work of pooling the information they gain and presenting it, first of all to the relevant police authorities and chief constables, and secondly to the local media. These activities should be directed towards a kind of quality control of the activities of the local constabulary.

'Courtwatch'

Another aspect of the 'system' which could be monitored is the court itself. This could even be done by offenders, working on a rota basis to cover and observe all of the magistrates' courts proceedings for a particular area, noting the decisions which are made; whether legal aid or bail applications are granted or refused; what proportion of people are given custodial or non-custodial sentences; whether custodial sentences are given with or without the bench seeing social inquiry reports; whether defendants are represented or not; whether they speak up in their own defence or not; whether they are treated with courtesy and consideration by court staff; how convenient the waiting and other facilities are for defendants and their friends and supporters, and for witnesses.

With a supply of accurate data gathered over a period in which, say, one hundred cases have been adjudicated, it is quite possible to say something about the quality of justice being dispensed in that particular court, and to publicize the results in the local media so as to bring about changes which seem desirable.

An extension of 'courtwatch' would be to offer advice about legal aid and assistance to defendants; to offer McKenzie services; and to help some defendants make pleas for alternative and non-custodial sentences.

The politics of penal reform

'Law and order' rides high in the list of popular motions for debates at the annual conferences of the Conservative and Unionist party. It is clear, from what delegates say in support of these motions, that 'law and order' is seen as a punitive antidote to the 'crime and disorder' caused partly by a general breakdown of respect for authority and partly by the ministrations of those to whom they refer scathingly as 'do-gooders', i.e., individuals and groups who take a liberal stance on sentencing policy and penal practice. Curiously, given the direction in which many of these aspersions are cast, the

Labour party has never taken more than a passing interest in the problems of crime and its 'treatment'. Its annual conferences have little time for the subject, and Labour governments in power have only ever conceived and passed *one* major legislative measure to bring about radical change in the way that offenders are dealt with. That measure was the Children and Young Persons Act 1969. It became law at precisely the moment when Labour was passing out of office and its key sections were simply never implemented by the new Conservative administration. Nor were they brought in by the next Labour government of 1974-9.

There is scope therefore for supporters and activists in both of the major parties to propose and press for the inclusion in party policy of more rational and humane measures; and for supporters of neither to bombard both with fact and opinion designed to do likewise.

Paradoxically, the prospects for radical change are brighter when governments of the right are in power. The only moderately reformist measure brought in since the war, and concerned with adult offenders, was R. Maudling's Criminal Justice Act of 1972 which introduced community service orders, day training centres, and added emphasis on the payment of compensation to victims. Moves towards decarceration in the United States have prospered under state administrations pursuing tight fiscal policies, for whom the financial savings have outweighed a natural reluctance to do anything which might appear to be 'soft' on crime. The same is true in this country, where the virtual dismemberment of the traditional 'approved school/community home' system has been brought about by budgetary rather than ideological pressures.

A double strategy which stresses concern for the victim and for restitution and conciliation, yoked with financial savings, might well appeal to conservative politicians in power. The liberal left, on the other hand, still tends to cling to an essentially 'treatment'-oriented approach to crime, believing that the caught criminal needs expensive and time-consuming re-education and therapy before being returned to the community. But for all practical purposes, Labour Party policy on crime and related matters is a blank page waiting to be written on (Taylor, 1981).

Individuals who work with offenders, in any capacity, are particularly well placed to contribute to political debate about penal policy and practice; to supply ammunition for use in such debates in the form of factual analysis and reportage of current conditions and trends, *and* in the form of ideas and schemes to remove injustices and promote better ways of responding to crime. Several possibilities might be pursued in this respect.

De-criminalization

An obvious target for change concerning offence behaviour is the criminal law itself. There is no doubt that certain kinds of behaviour currently defined as offences, or which lead ultimately to individuals appearing in court, could either be 'de-criminalized' completely, or dealt with in some other way. 'De-criminalization' means that a form of behaviour ceases to be regarded as an offence. A number of what are now regarded as offences merit consideration for this course of action, and in some instances there are pressure groups in existence trying to achieve this goal. The most conspicuous and frequently recited examples are prostitution (soliciting) and possessing cannabis. But to these could be added drunkenness, which could be more appropriately dealt with, in many cases, through some formal non-criminal (perhaps medical or social work) procedure. A case could be made for altering the law with regard to unlawful sexual intercourse, particularly where the offender and victim are of similar age. Also with respect to the young, it may be that truancy could (and should) be taken out of the jurisdiction of the juvenile court. The list could be much longer; indeed Nietzel (1979) discusses a list of upwards of twenty 'illegitimate activities' which could justifiably be decriminalized. While the exact revisions to be made to the law would obviously have to be a matter for wide-ranging public debate, there is no doubt that for many kinds of behaviour, more harm than good is done by charging individuals with offences, subjecting them to the rigours of court appearances, and imposing upon them convictions, fines, or sentences of imprisonment.

Sentencing practice

In relation to many other offences, and to the practice of the courts in general, there is little doubt that the way offenders are dealt with is liable to increase rather than decrease the total amount of offending behaviour in the community. In some instances, the reaction of the 'system' is nothing less than an injustice in itself. A number of areas call for attention and exploration here.

Inconsistencies in sentencing

Parliament may pass laws, but in criminal matters they are administered by the courts. There is ample and accumulating evidence that the administration of justice in the lower courts of England and Wales – to look no further afield – is riddled with anomalies and local variations which together constitute what amounts to a state of injustice. The variations are plainly visible in the annual supplementary criminal statistics published by the Home Office. One of the most striking concerns the proportions of adult male offenders, convicted of indictable offences, who are sentenced to immediate imprisonment. In 1981, for example, this proportion varied from a high of 13.23 per cent in the county of Dorset, to a low of 4.14 per cent in Warwickshire. Committing an offence in Dorset therefore, an individual might be three times more likely to be sent to prison than if he were to commit the same offence in Warwickshire. These differences have been the subject of critical commentaries published by Radical Alternatives to Prison, a pressure group, since 1972. But they were evident as long ago as the early sixties in the work of Hood (1962) who looked at a batch of anonymous English courts, and have been confirmed in more recent studies of sentencing in magistrates' courts (Tarling, 1979). These are not however the only inconsistencies in the administration of justice. Inequalities in the granting of legal aid, for example, have been brought to public notice by the Legal Action Group. Successive national officers appointed to stand surety for the fairness and integrity of our legal and penal systems (Lord Chancellors and Home Secretaries), have reacted to these continuing disclosures with vain appeals for more rational sentencing.

But that does not mean that there is nothing to be done. The 'Ball and Chain Awards' presented each year to the most punitive bench by Radical Alternatives to Prison (RAP) appear to have had some effect on at least two magistrates' court areas.

Gloucestershire magistrates

Year	% imprisoned	Position in RAP table
1977	13.83	1
1978	12.11	3
1979	9.50	11
1980	7.73	26

(Radical Alternatives to Prison, 1982)

Both Bristol and Gloucestershire have in the past headed the league tables of rates of imprisonment for male adult offenders. Both have responded to adverse publicity by substantially and permanently reducing the use they make of sentences of imprisonment.

Such changes are not of course automatic; but the effort is clearly worth making, and not only at county level, but in particular local courts where sentencing patterns may be yet more idiosyncratic.

Lengths of sentences and the use of imprisonment

Apart from these variations, another valid criticism of current sentencing practices revolves around the extent to which sentences of imprisonment are used in general. Concern over this issue derives from the fact that the United Kingdom is second top in a European 'league table' of use of imprisonment (beaten into first place by West Germany; Taylor, 1981). Further, our prison population continues to rise. In October, 1976, prisons in England and Wales held 42,000 adults, a hitherto unsurpassed number and one which '. . . had previously been identified by the Home Secretary as being that point at which conditions in the prison system would approach the intolerable' (Tutt, 1978, 14). Yet in July 1981 the prison population arrived at 45,500, a figure *8,500 above* 'normal certified accommodation'; at the same time the average length of prison sentence stopped falling, as it had been doing for a few years up until then (*Guardian*, 9/9/82). Repeated exhortations from Home Secretaries, Lord Chief Justices and Appeal Court judges to dispense shorter sentences have been to no avail.

Unless some really effective action is taken the prison population will go on rising still further. However a number of possible remedies have been proposed by different parties to this debate and they could form the basis for more concerted political lobbying. They include:

- Lengths of sentence to be reduced on a statutory basis, i.e. maximum sentences are designated for particular offences, and written into an Act of Parliament.
- Removal from magistrates' courts of the power to send people to prison, more serious offenders being sent automatically to Crown court.
- Abolition of the sentence of imprisonment as a penalty for certain offences, e.g. drunkenness, non-payment of fines.
- The introduction of 'partial imprisonment' or 'semi-custody' as practised in some other countries, i.e. offenders are allowed day release for work or are in custody only at weekends, provided this were used as an *alternative* to full time custody.
- Lowering of the 'threshold' for parole, making many more prisoners eligible for earlier discharge from custody.

Enactment of any of these suggestions could reduce the prison population dramatically. The continued use of imprisonment for many offenders is little short of pointless. The available evidence forces on us the conclusion that the basis on which imprisonment is retained for a large number of offences is not a rational one; a majority of prisoners could be dealt with in other ways without creating any additional 'menace to society'.

Decarceration

The most radical initiative of all of course would be the complete dismantling of some of our penal institutions. Such a move might seem like an enormously risky one for any society to take, fraught with incalculable dangers and threatening to bring to life the most nightmarish visions of streets overrun by criminals. Yet in a number of communities, steps in this direction have been taken, and the chaos prophesied by some has failed to materialize. The farthest-reaching and best known example of this is in the state of Massachusetts, where over a period of just a few months in 1971-2, all the training schools (the United States equivalent of Community Homes with Education) were closed down, and more than a thousand young offenders were transferred to other forms of supervision. Similar innovations, though phased more gradually, have also been introduced in California and Florida. In Massachusetts, despite widespread misgivings and much media-led controversy, it has proved possible to establish community programmes for juveniles convicted even of the most serious offences (Rutherford, 1978), and rates of recidivism and of crime in general have not been adversely affected by the change. Clearly, it is quite feasible to manage the vast majority of younger offenders, and probably a larger proportion of adult offenders, without recourse to the unnecessary and ineffectual measure of incarceration.

Arguing for alternatives

Discussion of the discontinuance of custody as a sentence is intimately bound up with the question of alternatives to it. In Massachusetts, California and Florida extensive use has been made of other facilities in the community, and many special schemes have been set up to absorb the numbers no longer being placed in confinement. They include various kinds of residential group programmes lasting short periods (for juveniles requiring different kinds of help or supervision); placement in ordinary boarding schools; an increase in the use of foster care; an assortment of non-residential group programmes; and community supervision ranging in formality from the 'high-level surveillance' of serious offenders by detached workers, to a system in which offenders are paired with interested and committed members of the public and supplied with the financial means to go on a trip somewhere (Rutherford, 1978). In the case of Massachusetts all these resources are co-ordinated in such a way that they are flexible enough to produce a 'package' matched to the needs of individual offenders; indeed the whole approach '. . . assumes the active involvement by the individual youth in the selection of services and programmes' (Rutherford, *op. cit.*, 113).

While a number of 'alternatives to custody' for both adolescent and adult offenders are now fairly well established in the United Kingdom, for the most part the capacity they have for bringing about a complete change in the balance of our penal system remains under-exploited. Despite the existence of community service, intermediate treatment, hostels, day centres, and other options, the numbers of offenders of all ages who continue to be locked up remains unacceptably high. The promise of intermediate treatment, for example, has not yet been fulfilled. According to Thorpe (1978) for example, '. . . it is possible to construct a programme of intermediate treatment which would theoretically provide community-based supervision for virtually the full range of juvenile delinquents, leaving only those who require highly skilled attention in institutions, primarily because their behaviour is such as to constitute a serious danger to others' (*op. cit.*, 79). Similarly, there is massive potential in the proliferation of probation-run day centres with activities and programmes structured to varying degrees. While a certain amount of ground has been gained through these measures, too many offenders are still lost to the more punitive end of the sentencing spectrum. The most widely adopted and frequently used substitute for custody continues to be community service (Harding, 1978), though doubts have been voiced about whether it operates as a genuine 'alternative', i.e., whether those sentenced to it would otherwise have been given terms of custody. Doubts have been expressed too about whether other means of dealing with offenders, such as 'diversion' schemes which are intended to protect individuals from being processed by the judicial system, merely represent a widening of the net of social control (Morris, 1978).

Nevertheless, there continues to be a great deal of room for expansion of all these services, and for experiment with novel combinations of activities within them. It appears increasingly less likely that the impetus to explore these and other possibilities will come from the higher ranks of the judicial and penal establishment; more pressure still needs to be exercised from individuals working within the system who confront the issues daily.

New Careers

The New Careers movement has a long and honourable history in the United States, where hundreds of thousands of members of dispossessed groups – the poor, blacks, ex-prisoners – have been trained for work in the welfare agencies on which many of them had hitherto depended for material assistance and other supports – agencies whose working styles were previously characterized by bureaucratic remoteness and a certain air of distance from the real lives and concerns of those who came to patronize their services. New Careers started from the idea that the consumers of these services could be trained to work within the agencies that supplied them, initially in ancillary roles but increasingly with access to fully fledged occupational/professional positions and status, with career opportunities to match. The benefits of these arrangements for the new careerists are self-evident, but one of the spin-offs for the employing agencies was the possibility of bringing about qualitative changes in the services they provided. Workers with close ethnic and cultural ties to the populations they served were *more* rather than less likely to act with courtesy and tolerance and understanding towards them.

In this country only one centrally funded programme along the lines of New Careers has operated (since 1972, at Filton Road, Bristol) (Briggs, 1975; Millham, Bullock, and Hosie, 1978; Priestley, 1974; Seddon, 1979). It has demonstrated that the progression from prisoner to probation officer is not only possible but positively desirable, and yet it has not been followed by similar projects. The principle has however been accepted by a number of probation areas, and offenders have been employed in a variety of settings as ancillary workers (typically financed by special employment projects), and it has ceased to be a matter of surprise that ex-prisoners and other convicted offenders should secure employment in hostels and as probation aides or in community service schemes. But there is scope for a dramatic increase in New Careers style programmes, for both young offenders – where funding could come under Youth Training Scheme initiatives – and for older offenders where it could be seen as a fruitful adjunct to prison education and vocational training programmes, or as part of a 'direct recruitment' process in the probation service.

The various initiatives which have been discussed so far for monitoring and attempting to alter the way 'the system' works are just a few of the directions which could be pursued. There are many others besides. The whole area of preventive work as applied to populations of potentially 'at risk' juveniles merits considerable attention and there are already useful precedents for undertaking it; based, for example on the use of modelling (Harris, 1973; Vriend, 1969), or on variant forms of training in self-control (deCharms, 1972). Again, the development and expansion of self-help groups for offenders – for example along the lines of Richard Hauser's work in Wandsworth prison which led to the formation of Recidivists Anonymous – was another departure with many possibilities which were under-exploited. And linked to all of this, the production of what might be termed 'positive publicity' by the agencies involved in work with offenders, might also rectify some of the more serious distortions in the way 'crime' is generally perceived. This could include both the advertising of the kinds of work which such agencies carry out, together with a broader educational effort designed to correct some of the more bizarre images of crime and criminality presented in the pages of our popular newspapers.

Victim-offender relations: an alternative to the criminal law?

In the chapter on 'Values', the victim-offender relationship was introduced in the context of challenging individual offenders to look at some of the consequences of their behaviour in the lives of others. To conclude the book this connection is proposed as a possible alternative organizing principle for the whole of the criminal law (Priestley, 1977).

In so-called simpler societies one of the main functions of law and of the customary procedures through which it is expressed, is to repair the damage done to the social fabric by the commission of an offence. This repair may be done symbolically as in the North American Indian ceremony of renewing the sacred medicine arrows (Adamson Hoebel, 1954), or it may be done more practically by the payment of compensation directly to the victim, or to the victim's surviving relatives in the case of killings. A recent upsurge of interest in victims and victim-offender relations in the United States and this country holds out, for the first time in a thousand years, the prospect of fundamental change in the Anglo-Norman-American tradition of criminal law.

It is still a *prospect*, and a distant one at that, but there are sound reasons for not dismissing the whole notion at the outset as utopian nonsense. Firstly, redressing the balance in favour of the victim makes sense at all sorts of levels. The victim is clearly better off if more resources – time, attention, money, etc. – are devoted to his/her needs and interests. The offender is clearly better off if society bends its best efforts towards restitution and reconciliation rather than the imposition of pain and suffering in the shape of punishment. Society is clearly better off if both these things happen as part of a wider concern to restore to the offender more of the responsibility for his/her criminal activity, rather than seeking to treat him/her as a kind of moral object lesson for the rest of society. The appeal on all three levels is to common sense and to standards of fair play which would be outraged, if the true outlines of the criminal law could be seen beneath the accretion of several centuries of custom and usage, and of an elaborate theory that places the law in the realm of metaphysics, above mere reason and certainly above politics.

The present *system* for dealing with offenders has clearly failed in nearly all of the tasks it sets itself. It succeeds to some extent in protecting the public from the harmful behaviour of those it holds in custody for given periods of time; but it fails both to deter others from doing likewise, since they go on committing offences apparently in ever greater numbers, *and* it does not seem to have much of an impact on the subsequent behaviour of the offenders who are subjected to it. It is costly in financial and human terms and it continues to exist and to expand mainly on the grounds that no one can think of anything better. A response based on the victim-offender relationship *is* something better.

Informal contacts between offenders and their victims could constitute a complete alternative to police action in the first instance. Community based services could deal with admitted cases where both parties consented, without the police being notified at all. Where consent was witheld, or in cases of a prescribed seriousness, the process of victim-offender restitution and conciliation could form an alternative to police cautions, diversion to community schemes, prosecution and conviction, or the serving of any kind of sentence imposed by a court.

With the exception of cases in which offenders pose a continuing physical threat to other members of the community, victim-offender proceedings could – as confidence was gained in their use, as limitations and difficulties were perceived and remedied, as public support increased – gradually supplant the use of the criminal law as society's principal response to the commission of offences. Such a shift would require little in the way of legislation; would restore to the community, and the individuals who compose it, a major share of the responsibility for coping with the consequences of offending in their midst. Such a community would, in the process of time, become *self-policing*; a place, that is, where crime was relegated to its rightful and relatively minor role in the matrix of social and co-operative relationships that make up civil society.

And it would become a society in which all the ugly apparatus of repression and punishment would find no place except as museum exhibits of man's historical inhumanity to man.

References

Adamson Hoebel, E. (1954). *The Law of Primitive Man*. Cambridge, Mass.: Harvard University Press.

Alexander, J.F. and B.V. Parsons (1973). Short-term behavioural intervention with delinquent families: impact on family process and recidivism. *Journal of Abnormal Psychology*, 81, 219-225.

Argyle, M. (1969). *Social Interaction*. London: Tavistock.

Argyle, M. (1975). *Bodily Communication*. London: Methuen.

Armor, D.J., J.M. Polich, and H.B. Stambul (1976). *Alcoholism and Treatment*. Santa Monica, Cal.: Rand Corporation.

Aronson, E. and D.R. Mettee (1968). Dishonest behaviour as a function of differential levels of induced self-esteem. *Journal of Personality and Social Psychology*, 9, 121-127.

Athens, L.H. (1980). *Violent Criminal Acts and Actors*. London: Routledge and Kegan Paul.

Atrops, M.E. (1978). Behavioural plus cognitive skills for coping with provocation in male offenders. Unpublished doctoral dissertation, Fuller Theological Seminary.

Bailey, W. (1966). Correctional outcome: an evaluation of 100 reports. *Journal of Criminal Law, Criminology and Police Science*, 57, 153-160.

Baldwin, J., A.E. Bottoms, and M.A. Walker (1976). *The Urban Criminal: a study in Sheffield*. London: Tavistock.

Bandura, A. (1973). *Aggression: a Social Learning Analysis*. Englewood Cliffs, N.J.: Prentice-Hall.

Bandura, A. (1977). *Social Learning Theory*. Englewood Cliffs, N.J.: Prentice-Hall.

Bandura, A. and R.H. Walters (1967). *Social Learning and Personality Development*. New York: Holt, Rinehart, and Winston.

Barlow, D.H., G.G. Abel, E.B. Blanchard, A.R. Bristow, and L.D. Young (1977). A heterosocial skills behaviour checklist for males. *Behavior Therapy*, 8, 229-239.

Baxter, J.C. (1970). Interpersonal spacing in natural settings. *Sociometry*, 33, 444-456.

Beck, A.T., A.J. Rush, B.F. Shaw, and G. Emery (1979). *Cognitive Therapy of Depression: a treatment manual*. New York: Guilford.

Becker, H.S. (1953). Becoming a marijuana user. *American Journal of Sociology*, 59, 41-58.

Becker, H.S. (1963). *Outsiders: Studies in the sociology of deviance*. New York: Free Press.

Bentham, J. (1791). *Panopticon*.

Bennett, L.A. (1974). Self-esteem and parole adjustment. *Criminology*, 12, 346-360.

Berg, N.L. (1971). Effects of alcohol intoxication on self-concept. *Quarterly Journal of Studies on Alcohol*, 32, 334-453.

Berne, E. (1968). *Games People Play*. Harmsondsworth: Penguin Books.

Blackburn, R. (1978). Psychopathy, arousal, and the need for stimulation. In R.D. Hare and D. Schalling (Eds.), *Psychopathic Behavior: Approaches to Research*. New York: Wiley.

Blackburn, R. (1980). Still not working? A look at recent outcomes in offender rehabilitation. Paper presented at the Scottish Branch of the British Psychological Society Conference on 'Deviance', University of Stirling.

Bond, I.K. and H.C. Hutchison (1960). Application of reciprocal inhibition therapy to exhibitionism. *Canadian Medical Association Journal*, 83, 23-25.

Bottoms, A.E. and W. McWilliams (1979). A non-treatment paradigm for probation practice. *British Journal of Social Work*, 9, 159-202.

Bowlby, J. (1946). *Forty-four Juvenile Thieves*. London: Bailliere, Tindall and Cox.

Bowman, P.C. (1978). A cognitive-behavioral treatment program for impulsive youthful offenders. Unpublished manuscript, Virginia Commonwealth University.

Braukmann, C.J., D.L. Fixsen, E.L. Phillips, M.M. Wolf, and D.M. Maloney (1974). An analysis of a selection interview training package for predelinquents at Achievement Place. *Criminal Justice and Behavior*, 1, 30-42.

Briggs, D. (1975). *In Place of Prison*. London: Maurice Temple Smith.

Brim, O.G. and S. Wheeler (1966). *Socialisation after Childhood: Two Essays*. New York: Wiley.

Brody, S.R. (1976). *The Effectiveness of Sentencing – a review of the literature*. Home Office Research Study No. 35. London: HMSO.

Brown, G. (1975). *Microteaching: A programme of teaching skills*. London: Methuen.

Bugental, J. and S. Zelen (1950). Investigations into the self-concept – the W-A-Y technique. *Journal of Personality*, 18, 483-498.

Burgess, R., R. Jewitt, J. Sandham, and B.L. Hudson (1980). Working with sex offenders: a social skills training group. *British Journal of Social Work*, 10, 133-142.

Buzan, T. (1974). *Use Your Head*. London: BBC Publications.

Camp, B.W. (1966). WISC performance in acting-out and delinquent children with and without EEG abnormality. *Journal of Consulting Psychology*, 30, 350-353.

Camp, B.W. (1980). Two psychoeducational treatment programs for young aggressive boys. In C.K. Whalen and B. Henker (Eds.), *Hyperactive Children: The social ecology of identification and treatment*. New York: Academic Press.

Camp, B.W., G.E. Blom, F. Hebert, and W.J. van Doorninck (1977). "Think Aloud": a program for developing self-control in young aggressive boys. *Journal of Abnormal Child Psychology*, 5, 157-169.

Cannon, W.B. (1942). Voodoo death. *American Anthropologist*, 44, 169-181.

Cannon, W.B. (1957). Voodoo death. *Psychosomatic Medicine*, 19, 182-190

Cavior, H.E. and A. Schmidt (1978). A test of the effectiveness of a differential treatment strategy at the Robert F. Kennedy Center. *Criminal Justice and Behavior*, 5, 131-139.

Chandler, M.J. (1973). Egocentrism and anti-social behavior: the assessment and training of social perspective-taking skills. *Developmental Psychology*, 9, 326-332.

Chaney, E.F., M.R. O'Leary, and G.A. Marlatt (1978). Skill training with alcoholics. *Journal of Consulting and Clinical Psychology*, 46, 405-415.

Chesterton, G.K. (1922). *Eugenics and Other Evils*. Cassell.

Cloward, R.A. and L.E Ohlin (1960). *Delinquency and Opportunity*. New York: Free Press.

Coche, E. and A.A. Douglas (1977). Therapeutic effects of problem-solving training and play-reading groups. *Journal of Clinical Psychology*, 30, 820-827.

Coche, E. and A. Flick (1975). Problem-solving training groups for hospitalized psychiatric patients. *Journal of Psychology*, 91, 19-29.

CODOT: Classification of Occupations and Directory of Occupational Titles, (1972), 3 Vols. London: HMSO.

Cohen, A.K. (1955). *Delinquent Boys: the Culture of the Gang*. New York: Free Press.

Cohen, S. and L. Taylor (1972). *Psychological Survival: the Experience of Long-term Imprisonment*. Harmondsworth: Penguin Books.

Cohen, S. and J. Young (1973). *The manufacture of news. Social problems, deviance and the mass media*. London: Constable.

Copemann, C.D. (1973). Aversive counterconditioning and social re-training: a learning theory approach to drug rehabilitation. Unpublished doctoral dissertation, State University of New York at Stony Brook.

Crawford, D.A. and J.V. Allen (1979). A social skills training programme with sex offenders. In M. Cook and G. Wilson (Eds.), *Love and Attraction*. Oxford: Pergamon.

Crawford, D.A. and K. Howells (1982). The effect of sex education with disturbed adolescents. *Behavioural Psychotherapy*, 10, 339-345.

Criminal Injuries Compensation Board (1982). *Report for 1981.* Cmnd. 8401. London: HMSO.

Criminal Injuries Compensation Board (1983). *Report for 1982.* Cmnd. 8752. London: HMSO.

Culbertson, F.M. (1957). Modification of an emotionally held attitude through role playing. *Journal of Abnormal and Social Psychology,* 54, 230-233.

Curran, J.P. (1975). Social skills training and systematic desensitization in reducing dating anxiety. *Behaviour Research and Therapy,* 13, 65-68.

Davidson, W.S. and E. Seidman (1974). Studies of behavior modification and juvenile delinquency: a review, methodological critique, and social perspective. *Psychological Bulletin,* 81, 998-1011.

Davies, D.L. (1962). Normal drinking in recovered alcohol addicts. *Quarterly Journal of Studies on Alcohol,* 23, 94-104.

Davies, P.T. (1982). The pattern of problems. In M.A. Plant (Ed.), *Drinking and Problem Drinking.* London: Junction Books.

deCharms, R. (1972). Personal Causation Training in the schools. *Journal of Applied Social Psychology,* 2, 95-113.

Deitz, G.E. (1969). A comparison of delinquents with nondelinquents on self-concept, self-acceptance, and parental identification. *Journal of Genetic Psychology,* 115, 285-295.

Deschner, J.P. (1984). *The Hitting Habit: anger control for battering couples.* New York: Free Press.

Dinitz, S., W.C. Reckless, and B. Kay (1958). A self gradient among potential delinquents. *Journal of Criminal Law, Criminology and Police Science,* 49, 231.

Dinitz, S., F.R. Scarpitti, and W.C. Reckless (1962). Delinquency vulnerability: a cross group and longitudinal analysis. *American Sociollogical Review,* 27, 515-517.

Douglas, J.W. B., J.M. Ross, and H.R. Simpson (1968). *All Our Future.* London: Peter Davies.

Downes, D. (1966). *The Delinquent Solution.* London: Routledge and Kegan Paul.

Dyck, R.J. and B.G. Rule (1978). Effect on retaliation of causal attributions concerning attack. *Journal of Personality and Social Psychology,* 36, 521-529.

Eitzen, D.S. (1976). The self-concept of delinquents in a behavior modification treatment program. *Journal of Social Psychology,* 99, 203-206.

Ellis, A. (1962). *Reason and Emotion in Psychotherapy.* New York: Lyle Stuart.

Emmons, T.D. and W.W. Webb (1974). Subjective correlates of emotional responsivity and stimulation seeking in psychopaths, normals, and acting-out neurotics. *Journal of Consulting and Clinical Psychology,* 42, 620.

Erikson, K.T. (1966). *Wayward Puritans: a study in the sociology of deviance.* New York: Wiley.

Evans, D.R. and M.T. Hearn (1973). Anger and systematic desensitization: a follow-up. *Psychological Reports,* 32, 569-570.

Eysenck, H.J. (1964). *Crime and Personality.* London: Routledge and Kegan Paul.

Falloon, I.R.H., P. Lindley, R. McDonald, and I.M. Marks (1977). Social skills training of out-patient groups: a controlled study of rehearsal and home-work. *British Journal of Psychiatry,* 131, 599-609.

Farber, I.E. (1963). The things people say to themselves. *American Psychologist,* 18. 185-197.

Farley, F.H. and S.V. Farley (1972). Stimulus-seeking motivation and delinquent behaviour among institutionalized delinquent girls. *Journal of Consulting and Clinical Psychology,* 39, 94-97.

Farrington, D.P. (1978). The family backgrounds of aggressive youths. In L. Hersov, M. Berger, and D. Shaffer (Eds.), *Aggression and Anti-social Behaviour in Childhood and Adolescence.* Oxford: Pergamon.

Farrington, D.P., L. Berkowitz, and D.J. West (1982). Differences between individual and group fights. *British Journal of Social Psychology,* 21, 323-333.

Farrington, D.P., L. Biron, and M. leBlanc (1982). Personality and delinquency in London and Montreal. In J. Gunn and D.P. Farrington (Eds.), *Abnormal Offenders: Delinquency and the Criminal Justice System.* Chichester: Wiley.

Fawcett, B., E. Ingham, M. McKeever and S. Williams (1979). A social skills group for young prisoners. *Social Work Today*, 10, 16-18.

Folkard, M.S., D.E. Smith and D.D. Smith (1976). *IMPACT. Intensive matched probation and after-care treatment. Vol.II. The results of the experiment.* Home Office Research Study No.36. London: HMSO.

Foucault, M. (1979). *Discipline and Punish. The Birth of the Prison.* Harmondsworth: Penguin Books.

Fowles, A.J. (1978). *Prison welfare: an account of an experiment at Liverpool.* Home Office Research Study No.45. London: HMSO.

Foy, D.W., R.M. Eisler, and S. Pinkston (1975). Modeled assertion in a case of explosive rages. *Journal of Behavior Therapy and Experimental Psychiatry*, 6, 135-138.

Foy, D.W., P.M. Miller, R.M. Eisler, and D.H. O'Toole (1976). Social-skills training to teach alcoholics to refuse drinks effectively. *Journal of Studies on Alcohol*, 37, 1340-1345.

Frease, D.E. (1973). Delinquency, social class, and the schools. *Sociology and Social Research*, 57, 443-459.

Frederiksen, L.W., J.O. Jenkins, D.W. Foy and R.M. Eisler (1976). Social-skills training to modify abusive verbal outbursts in adults. *Journal of Applied Behavior Analysis*, 9, 117-125.

Frederiksen, L.W. and N. Rainwater (1981). Explosive behavior: a skill development approach to treatment. In R.B. Stuart (Ed.), *Violent Behavior: Social learning approaches to prediction, management and treatment.* New York: Brunner/Mazel.

Freedman, B.J., L. Rosenthal, C.P. Donahoe, D.J. Schlundt, and R.M. McFall (1978). A social-behavioral analysis of skill deficits in delinquent and nondelinquent children. *Journal of Consulting and Clinical Psychology*, 46, 1448-1462.

Fry, P.S. (1975). Affect and resistance to temptation. *Developmental Psychology*, 11, 466-472.

Galaway, B. and J. Hudson (Eds.) (1978). *Offender Restitution in Theory and Action.* Lexington, Mass.: D.C. Heath.

Giallombardo, R. (1966). *Society of Women: a study of a women's prison.* New York: Wiley.

Glueck, S. and E. Glueck (1950). *Unravelling Juvenile Delinquency.* Cambridge, Mass.: Harvard University Press.

Goldfried, M.R. (1979). Anxiety reduction through cognitive-behavioral intervention. In P.C. Kendall and S.D. Hollon (Eds.), *Cognitive-Behavioral Interventions: Theory, Research, and Procedures.* New York: Academic Press.

Goldfried, M.R. and M. Merbaum (Eds.) (1973). *Behavior Change through Self-control.* New York: Holt, Rinehart and Winston.

Goldstein, A.P. (1981). Social skill training. In A.P. Goldstein, E.G. Carr, W.S. Davidson II, P. Wehr and others, *In Response to Aggression.* New York: Pergamon.

Goldstein, A.P. and A.W. Goedhart (1973). The use of Structured Learning for empathy enhancement in paraprofessional psychotherapist training. *Journal of Community Psychology*, 1, 168-173.

Goldstein, A.P., M. Sherman, N.J. Gershaw, R.P. Sprafkin, and B. Glick (1978). Training aggressive adolescents in prosocial behaviour. *Journal of Youth and Adolescence*, 7, 73-92.

Goldstein, A.P., R.P. Sprafkin, and N.J. Gershaw (1976). *Skill Training for Community Living.* New York: Pergamon.

Goldstein, N. (1974). Reparation by the offender to the victim as a method of rehabilitation for both. In I. Drapkin and E. Viano (Eds.),. *Victimology: A New Focus.* Vol. II. Lexington, Mass.: D.C. Heath.

Gordon, A. and S. Williams (1977). Social skills training with a sexual offender population. Paper submitted to Canadian Psychological Association Convention. Unpublished manuscript, Regional Psychiatric Centre, Kingston Penitentiary.

Graf, R.G. (1971). Induced self-esteem as a determinant of behavior. *Journal of Social Psychology*, 85, 213-217.

Green, R.A. and E.J. Murray (1973). Instigation to aggression as a function of self-disclosure and threat to self-esteem. *Journal of Consulting and Clinical Psychology*, 40, 440-443.

Greenberg, S.W. (1981). Alcohol and crime: a methodological critique of the literature. In J.T. Collins (Ed.), *Drinking and Crime: Perspectives on the relationships betwen alcohol consumption and criminal behaviour*. London: Tavistock.

Guardian newspaper. 'Figures deal blow to base of penal policy' (by M. Dean). 9th September 1982.

Guardian newspaper. 'Alarm at gun toll in US'. 23rd November 1982.

Gutride, M.E., A.P. Goldstein, and G.F. Hunter (1973). The use of modeling and role playing to increase social interaction among asocial psychiatric patients. *Journal of Consulting and Clinical Psychology*, 40, 408-415.

Hall, P.M. (1966). Identification with the delinquent subculture and level of self-evaluation. *Sociometry*, 29, 146-158.

Haney, C., C. Banks, and P.G. Zimbardo (1973). Interpersonal Dynamics in a simulated prison. *International Journal of Criminology and Penology*, 1, 69-97.

Hannum, J.W., C.E. Thoresen, and D.R. Hubbard (1974). A behavioral study of self-esteem with elementary teachers. In M.J. Mahoney and C.E. Thoresen (Eds.), *Self-control: Power to the Person*. Monterey, Cal.: Brooks/Cole.

Harding, J. (1978). The development of Community Service. In N. Tutt (Ed.), *Alternative Strategies for Coping with Crime*. Oxford & London: Basil Blackwell & Martin Robertson.

Harding, J. (1982). *Victims and Offenders*. London: Bedford Square Press.

Harris, G.G. (1973). The use of modeling procedures to modify vocational aspirations of potential high school dropouts. *Journal of Community Psychology*, 1, 298-301.

Hauser, R. and H. Hauser (1962). *The Fraternal Society*. Oxford: Bodley Head.

Hay, W.M., L.R. Hay, and R.O. Nelson (1977). The adaptation of covert modeling procedures to the treatment of chronic alcoholism and obsessive-compulsive behavior: Two case reports. *Behavior Therapy*, 8, 70-76.

Hearn, M.T. and D.R. Evans (1972). Anger and reciprocal inhibition therapy. *Psychological Reports*, 30, 943-948.

Heather, N. (1981). Relationships between delinquency and drunkenness among Scottish young offenders. *British Journal on Alcohol and Alcoholism*, 16, 50-61.

Heather, N. and I. Robertson (1981). *Controlled Drinking*. London: Methuen.

Hedberg, A.G. and L. Campbell III (1974). A comparison of four behavioural treatments of alcoholism. *Journal of Behavior Therapy and Experimental Psychiatry*, 5, 251-256.

Hensman, C. (1969). Problems of drunkenness amongst male recidivists. In T. Cook, D. Gath, and C. Hensman (Eds.), *The Drunkenness Offence*. Oxford: Pergamon.

Her Majesty's Stationery Office (1969). *The Sentence of the Court. A Handbook for Courts on the Treatment of Offenders*. London: HMSO.

Hersen, M. (1979). Modification of skill deficits in psychiatric patients. In A.S. Bellack and M. Hersen (Eds.), *Research and Practice in Social Skills Training*. New York: Plenum Press.

Hersh, R.H., J.P. Miller, and G.D. Fielding (1980). *Models of Moral Education: An Appraisal*. New York: Longman.

Hewitt, J.P. (1970). *Social Stratification and Deviant Behaviour*. New York: Random House.

Hirschi, T. and M.J. Hindelang (1977). Intelligence and delinquency: a revisionist review. *American Sociological Review*, 42, 571-587.

Hoghughi, M. (1983). *The Delinquent: Directions for Social Control*. London: Burnett.

Holborn, J. (1975). Casework with short-term prisoners. Part II of *Some Male Offenders' Problems*. Home Office Research Study No.28. London: HMSO.

Hollon, S.D. and P.C. Kendall (1981). *In vivo* assessment techniques for cognitive-behavioral processes. In P.C. Kendall and S.D. Hollon (Eds.), *Assessment Strategies for Cognitive-Behavioral Interventions*. New York: Academic Press.

Honderich, T. (1976). *Punishment: the supposed justifications*. Harmondsworth: Penguin Books.

Hood, R. (1962). *Sentencing in Magistrates' Courts*. London: Stevens.

Hood, R. and R. Sparks (1970). *Key Issues in Criminology*. London: Weidenfeld and Nicolson.

Horton, A.M. and C.H. Johnson (1977). The treatment of homicidal obsessive ruminations by thought stopping and covert assertion. *Journal of Behavior Therapy and Experimental Psychiatry*, 8, 339-340.

Hosford, R.E., C.S. Moss, and G. Morrell (1976). The self-as-a-model technique: helping prison inmates change. In J.D. Krumboltz and C.E. Thoresen (Eds.), *Counseling Methods*. New York: Holt, Rinehart and Winston.

Howe, P. (1979). Intermediate treatment: The development and operation of a 'social skills' group. Mimeo, the Barton Project, Oxford.

Howells, K. (1976). Interpersonal aggression. *International Journal of Criminology and Penology*, 4, 319-330.

Hudson, J. and B. Galaway (Eds.) (1980). *Victims, Offenders, and Alternative Sanctions*. Lexington, Mass.: D.C. Heath.

Ickes, W. and M.A. Layden (1978). Attributional styles. In J. Harvey, W. Ickes, and R. Kidd (Eds.), *New Directions in Attribution Research*. (Vol. 2). Hillsdale, N.J.: Lawrence Erlbaum Associates.

Ignatieff, M. (1978). *A Just Measure of Pain: the Penitentiary in the Industrial Revolution 1750-1850*. London: Macmillan.

Ivey, A.E. and J. Authier (1978). *Microcounseling*. Springfield, III.: Charles C. Thomas.

Jackson, B. (1972). Treatment of depression by self-reinforcement. *Behavior Therapy*, 3, 298-307.

Jacobs, P.A., M. Brunton, M.M. Melville, R.P. Brittain, and W.F. McClement (1965). Aggressive behavior, mental subnormality, and the XYY male. *Nature*, 208, 1351-1352.

Jacobson, E. (1938). *Progressive Relaxation*. Chicago: University of Chicago Press.

Jellinek, E.M. (1960). *The Disease Concept of Alcoholism*. New Haven, Conn.: Hillhouse Press.

Jensen, G.F. (1973). Inner containment and delinquency. *Journal of Criminal Law and Criminology*, 64, 464-470.

Jesness, C.F. (1975). Comparative effectiveness of behavior modification and transactional analysis programs for delinquents. *Journal of Consulting and Clinical Psychology*, 43, 758-779.

Johnson, K. and K. Morrow (1979). *Approaches*. Cambridge: Cambridge University Press.

Johnson, R.E. (1979). *Juvenile Delinquency and its Origins: an integrated theoretical approach*. Cambridge: Cambridge University Press.

Joplin. G.H. (1972). Self-concepts and the Highfields program: Recidivists versus non-recidivists. *Criminology*, 9, 491-495.

Kaplan, H.B. (1975). *Self-attitudes and Deviant Behavior*. Pacific Palisades, Cal.: Goodyear.

Kaplan, H.B. and J.H. Meyerowitz (1970). Social and psychological correlates of drug abuse: a comparison of addict and non-addict populations from the perspective of self-theory. *Social Science and Medicine*, 4, 203-225.

Keltner, A.A., P. Marshall, and W.L. Marshall (1981). The description of assertiveness in a prison population. *Corrective and Social Psychiatry and Journal of Behavior Technology Methods and Therapy*, 27, 41-47.

Kendall, P.C., A.J. Finch, V.L. Little, B.M. Chirico, and T.H. Ollendick (1978). Variations in a construct: quantitative and qualitative differences in children's locus of control. *Journal of Consulting and Clinical Psychology*, 46, 590-592.

Kendall, P.C. and S.D. Hollon (Eds.) (1979). *Cognitive-Behavioral Interventions: Theory, Research, and Procedures*. New York: Academic Press.

Kifer, R.E., M.A. Lewis, D.R. Green, and E.L. Phillips (1974). Training predelinquent youths and their parents to negotiate conflict situations. *Journal of Applied Behavior Analysis*, 7, 357-364.

Kingsmill, J. (1854). *Chapters on prisons and prisoners*. London:Longman.

Kinzel, A.F. (1970). Body-buffer zone in violent prisoners. *American Journal of Psychiatry*, 127, 99-104.

Kipnis, D. (1971). *Character Structure and Impulsiveness*. New York: Academic Press.

Kirchner, E.P., R.E. Kennedy, and J.G. Draguns (1979). Assertion and aggression in adult offenders. *Behavior Therapy*, 10, 452-471.

Kitwood, T. (1980). *Disclosures to a Stranger*. London: Routledge and Kegan Paul.

Klein, N.C., J.F. Alexander, and B.V. Parsons (1977). Impact of family systems intervention on recidivism and sibling delinquency: a model of primary prevention and program evaluation. *Journal of Consulting and Clinical Psychology*, 45, 469-474.

Kuhn, M.H. and T.S. McPartland (1954). An empirical investigation of self-attitudes. *American Sociological Review*, 19, 68-76.

Lanyon, R.I., R.V. Primo, F. Terrell, and A. Wener (1972). An aversion-desensitization treatment for alcoholism. *Journal of Consulting and Clinical Psychology*, 38, 394-398.

le Bow, M.D. (1981). *Weight Control: the behavioral strategies*. New York: Wiley.

Lefcourt, H.M. (1976). *Locus of Control: Current Trends in Theory and Research*. Hillsdale, N.J.: Lawrence Erlbaum Associates.

Lefkowitz, M.M., L.D. Eron, L.O. Walder, and L.R. Huesmann (1977). *Growing Up to be Violent: a Longitudinal Study of the Development of Aggression*. New York: Pergamon.

Lesser, G.S. (1959). The relationships between various forms of aggression and popularity among lower-class children. *Journal of Educational Psychology*, 50, 20-25.

Levenson, H. (1981). Differentiating among internality, powerful others, and change. In H.M. Lefcourt (Ed.), *Research with the Locus of Control Concept: Vol. 1: Assessment Methods*. New York: Academic Press.

Lewin, K. (1951). *Field Theory in Social Science*. New York: Harper.

Lindsay, W.R., R.S. Symons, and T. Sweet (1979). A programme for teaching social skills to socially inept adolescents: description and evaluation. *Journal of Adolescence*, 2, 215-228.

Linehart, M.M. and K.J. Egan (1979). Assertion training for women. In A.S. Bellack and M. Hersen (Eds.), *Research and Practice in Social Skills Training*. New York: Plenum Press.

Lipton, D., R. Martinson, and J. Wilks (1975). *The Effectiveness of Correctional Treatment: a survey of treatment evaluation studies*. New York: Praeger.

Loeb, A., S. Feshbach, A.T. Beck, and A. Wolf (1964). Some effects of reward upon the social perception and motivation of psychiatric patients varying in depression. *Journal of Abnormal and Social Psychology*, 68, 609-616.

Lombroso, C. (1895). *The Female Offender*. New York: Appleton.

Lowe, P. and C. Stewart (1983). Women in prison. In S. Spence and G. Shepherd (Eds.), *Developments in Social Skills Training*. London: Academic Press.

MacAndrew, C. and R.B. Edgerton (1969). *Drunken Comportment: a social explanation*. London: Nelson.

MacShane, D. (1979). *Using the Media*. London: Pluto Press.

Mahoney, M.J. and C.E. Thoresen (Eds.) (1974). *Self-control: Power to the Person*. Monterey, Cal.: Brooks/Cole.

Malamuth, N.M. and S. Feshbach (1972). Risky shift in a naturalistic setting. *Journal of Personality*, 40, 38-49.

Maloney, D.M., T.M. Harper, C.J. Braukmann, D.L. Fixsen, E.L. Phillips, and M.M. Wolf (1976). Teaching conversation-related skills to predelinquent girls. *Journal of Applied Behavior Analysis*, 9, 371.

Marlatt, G.A. (1979). Alcohol use and problem drinking: a cognitive-behavioral analysis. In P.C. Kendall and S.D. Hollon (Eds.), *Cognitive-behavioral Interventions: Theory, Research, and Procedures*. New York: Academic Press.

Marshall, W.L., M.M. Christie, and R.D. Lanthier (1979). Social competence, sexual experience and attitudes to sex in incarcerated rapists and pedophiles. Report to the Solicitor General of Canada. Unpublished manuscsript, Ontario Regional Psychiatric Centre, Kingston.

Martinson, R. (1974). What works? – questions and answers about prison reform. *The Public Interest*, 10, 22-54.

Marzagao, L.R. (1972). Systematic desensitization treatment of kleptomania. *Journal of Behavior Therapy and Experimental Psychiatry*, 3, 327-328.

Mathiesen, T. (1974). *The Politics of Abolition*. London: Martin Roberston.

Mayers, M.O. (1980). *The Hard-Core Delinquent*. Farnborough: Saxon House.

McClintock, F.H. and N.H. Avison (1968). *Crime in England and Wales*. London: Heinemann.

McCullough, J.P., G.M. Huntsinger, and W.R. Nay (1977). Self-control treatment of aggression in a 16-year-old male. *Journal of Consulting and Clinical Psychology*, 45, 322-331.

McGuire, J. and P. Priestley (1981). *Life After School: a social skills curriculum*. Oxford: Pergamon.

McGuire, J. and P. Priestley (1983). Life skills training in prisons and the community. In S. Spence and G. Shepherd (Eds.), *Developments in Social Skills Training*. London: Academic Press.

McGuire, J., P. Priestley and C. Thomas (1984). *Video on Video* (tape and notes). London: Tavistock.

Meichenbaum, D.R. (1977). *Cognitive-behavior Modification: an integrative approach*. New York: Plenum Press.

Meichenbaum, D.R. (1980). Self-instructional methods. In F.H. Kanfer and A.P. Goldstein (Eds.), *Helping People Change*. New York: Pergamon.

Meichenbaum, D.R. and R. Cameron (1973). Training schizophrenics to talk to themselves: a means of developing attentional controls. *Behavior Therapy*, 4, 515-534.

Meichenbaum, D.R. and J. Goodman (1971). Training impulsive children to talk to themselves: a means of developing self-control. *Journal of Abnormal Psychology*, 77, 115-126.

Melzack, R. and P.D. Wall (1982). *The Challenge of Pain*. Harmondsworth: Penguin.

Meyers, A., M. Mercatoris, and A. Sirota (1976). Use of covert self-instructions for the elimination of psychotic speech. *Journal of Consulting and Clinical Psychology*, 44, 480-483.

Miller, W.B. (1958). Lower class culture as a generating milieu of gang delinquency. *Journal of Social Issues*, 14, 5-19.

Miller, W.R. and R.F. Munoz (1976). *How to control your drinking*. Englewood Cliffs, N.J.: Prentice-Hall.

Millham, S., R. Bullock, and K. Hosie (1978). Another try. In N. Tutt (Ed.), *Alternative Strategies for Coping with Crime*. Oxford & London: Basil Blackwell & Martin Robertson.

Minkin, N., C.J. Braukmann, B.L. Minkin, G.D. Timbers, B.J. Timbers, D.L. Fixsen, E.L. Phillips, and M.M. Wolf (1976). The social validation and training of conversational skills. *Journal of Applied Behavior Analysis*, 9, 127-139.

Morris, A. (1978). Diversion of juvenile offenders from the criminal justice system. In N. Tutt (Ed.), *Alternative Strategies for Coping with Crime*. Oxford & London: Basil Blackwell & Martin Robertson.

Morris, T. and P. Morris (1963). *Pentonville: a Sociological Study of an English Prison*. London: Routledge and Kegan Paul.

Mulligan, G.M. (1979). Self-esteem: Its measurement, correlates and change among institutionalised young offenders. Unpublished doctoral dissertation, Queen's University of Belfast.

Nasby, W., B. Hayden, and B.M. DePaulo (1980). Attributional bias among aggressive boys to interpret unambiguous social stimuli as displays of hostility. *Journal of Abnormal Psychology*, 89, 459-468.

National Association of Victim Support Schemes (1982). *Second Annual Report*. London: NAVSS.

Nickel, T.W. (1974). The attribution of intention as a critical factor in the relation between frustration and aggression. *Journal of Personality*, 42, 482-492.

Nietzel, M.T. (1979). *Crime and its Modification: a Social Learning Perspective*. New York: Pergamon.

Novaco, R.W. (1975). *Anger Control: The development and evaluation of an experimental treatment*. Lexington, Mass.: D.C. Heath.

Novaco, R.W. (1977). Stress inoculation: a cognitive therapy for anger and its application to a case of depression. *Journal of Consulting and Clinical Psychology*, 45, 600-608.

Novaco, R.W. (1978). Anger and coping with stress: cognitive behavioral interventions. In J.P. Foreyt and D.P. Rathjen (Eds.), *Cognitive Behavior Therapy*. New York: Plenum Press.

Novaco, R.W. (1979). The cognitive regulation of anger and stress. In P.C. Kendall and S.D. Hollon (Eds.), *Cognitive-behavioral Interventions: Theory, Research, and Procedures*. New York: Academic Press.

Novaco, R.W. (1980). Training of probation counselors for anger problems. *Journal of Counseling Psychology*, 27, 385-390.

Nowicki, S. and B.R. Strickland (1973). A locus of control scale for children. *Journal of Consulting and Clinical Psychology*, 40, 148-154.

Oden, S. and S.R. Asher (1977). Coaching children in social skills for friendship making. *Child Development*, 48, 495-506.

O'Donnell, C.R. and L. Worell (1973). Motor and cognitive relaxation in the desensitization of anger. *Behaviour Research and Therapy*, 11, 473-481.

Ollendick, t.H. and M. Hersen (1979). Social skills training for juvenile delinquents. *Behaviour Research and Therapy*, 17, 547-554.

Ost, L., A. Jerremalm, and J. Johansson (1981). Individual response patterns and the effects of different behavioral methods in the treatment of social phobia. *Behaviour Research and Therapy*, 19, 1-16.

Owen, R. (1816). *A New View of Society*. London: Longman.

Parsons, B.V. and J.F. Alexander (1973). Short-term family intervention: a therapy outcome study. *Journal of Consulting and Clinical Psychology*, 41, 195-201.

Patrick, J. (1973). *A Glasgow Gang Observed*. London: Eyre Methuen.

Pattison, E.M., M.B. Sobell, and L.C. Sobell (1977). *Emerging concepts of Alcohol Dependence*. New York: Springer.

Pechacek, T.F. and B.G. Danaher (1979). How and why people quit smoking: a cognitive-behavioral analysis. In P.C. Kendall and S.D. Hollon (Eds.), *Cognitive-behavioral Interventions: Theory, Research, and Procedures*. New York: Academic Press.

Phillipson, M. (1971). *Sociological Aspects of Crime and Delinquency*. London: Routledge and Kegan Paul.

Phillpotts, G.J.O. and L.B. Lancucki (1979). *Previous convictions, sentence and reconviction: A statistical study of a sample of 5000 offenders convicted in January 1971*. Home Office Research Study No.53. London: HMSO.

Piliavin, I. and S. Briar (1964). Police encounters with juveniles. *American Journal of Sociology*, 70, 206-214.

Platt, J.J., W.C. Scura, and J.R. Hannon (1973). Problem-solving thinking of youthful incarcerated heroin addicts. *Journal of Community Psychology*, 1, 278-281.

Platt, J.J., G. Spivack, N. Altman, and D. Altman (1974). Adolescent problem-solving thinking. *Journal of Consulting and Clinical Psychology*, 42, 787-793.

Polich, J.M., D.J. Armor, and H.B. Braiker (1980). *The Course of Alcoholism: Four Years After Treatment*. Santa Monica, Cal.: Rand Corporation.

Prentice, N.M. and F.J. Kelly (1963). Intelligence and delinquency: a reconsideration. *Journal of Social Psychology*, 60, 327-337.

Priestley, P. (1974). New Careers: power sharing in social work. In H. Jones (Ed.), *Towards a new social work*. London: Routledge and Kegan Paul.

Priestley, P. (1977). Victims: the key to penal reform. *Christian Action Journal*, Summer, 12-13.

Priestley, P. (1980). *Community of Scapegoats: The segregation of sex offenders and informers in prisons*. Oxford: Pergamon.

Priestley, P., D. Fears, and R. Fuller (1976). *Justice for Juveniles*. London: Routledge and Kegan Paul.

Priestley, P. and J. McGuire (1983). *Learning to Help: basic skills exercises*. London: Tavistock.

Priestley, P., J. McGuire, D. Flegg, V. Hemsley, D. Welham and R. Barnitt (1984). *Social Skills in Prisons and in the Community*. London: Routledge and Kegan Paul.

Priestley, P., J. McGuire, D. Flegg, V. Hemsley, and D. Welham (1978). *Social Skills and Personal Problem Solving*. London: Tavistock.

Rackham, N. and T. Morgan (1977). *Behaviour Analysis in Training*. Maidenhead: McGraw-Hill.

Radical Alternatives to Prison (1982). *'A scandal within a scandal . . .': Rates of imprisonment in Magistrates' Courts: England and Wales 1980*. 70, Novers Park Road, Bristol BS4: RAP.

Radical Alternatives to Prison (n.d.). *Defendants' Handbook*. 70, Novers Park Road, Bristol BS4: RAP.

Radzinowicz, L. and J. King (1977). *The Growth of Crime: the International Experience*. London: Hamish Hamilton.

Rahaim, S., C. Lefebvre, and J.O. Jenkins (1980). The effects of social skills training on behavioral and cognitive components of anger management. *Journal of Behavior Therapy and Experimental Psychiatry*, 11, 3-8.

Reckless, W.C., S. Dinitz, and B. Kay (1957). The self component in potential delinquency and non-delinquency. *American Sociological Review*, 22, 570.

Reckless, W.C., S. Dinitz, and E. Murray (1956). Self-concept as an insulator against delinquency. *American Sociological Review*, 21, 744-746.

Rimm, D.C., J.C. deGroot, P. Boord, J. Heiman, and P.V. Dillow (1971). Systematic desensitization of an anger response. *Behaviour Research and Therapy*, 9, 273-280.

Rimm, D.C., G.A. Hill, N.N. Brown, and J.E. Stuart (1974). Group-assertive training in treatment of expression of inappropriate anger. *Psychological Reports*, 34, 791-798.

Rimm, D.C. and J.C. Masters (1979). *Behavior Therapy: Techniques and Empirical Findings*. New York: Academic Press.

Roberts, J. (1972). *Self-image and Delinquency: A study of New Zealand adolescent girls*. Wellington: Research Series No.3, Research Section, Department of Justice, New Zealand.

Robertson, I.H. and N. Heather (1982). An alcohol education course for young offenders: A preliminary report. *British Journal on Alcohol and Alcoholism*, 17, 32-37.

Rogers, C.R. (1957). The necessary and sufficient conditions of therapeutic personality change. *Journal of Consulting Psychology*, 21, 95-103.

Rosenbaum, M.E. and R. deCharms (1960). Direct and vicarious reduction of hostilities. *Journal of Abnormal and Social Psychology*, 60, 54-61.

Rosenberg, M. (1965). *Society and the Adolescent Self-image*. Princeton, N.J.: Princeton University Press.

Rotter, J.B. (1966). Generalized expectancies for internal versus external control of reinforcement. *Psychological Monographs*, 80 (Whole No.609).

Rutherford, A. (1978). Decarceration of young offenders in Massachusetts. In N. Tutt (Ed.), *Alternative Strategies for Coping with Crime*. Oxford & London: Basil Blackwell and Martin Robertson.

Rutter, M. (1978). Family, area and school influences in the genesis of conduct disorders. In L. Hersov, M. Berger, and D. Shaffer (Eds.), *Aggression and Anti-social Behaviour in Childhood and Adolescence*. Oxford: Pergamon.

Rutter, M. and N. Madge (1976). *Cycles of Disadvantage: a review of research*. London: Heinemann.

Rutter, M., B. Maughan, P. Mortimore, and J. Ouston (1979). *Fifteen Thousand Hours: Secondary schools and their effects on children*. London: Open Books.

Sarason, I.G. (1968). Verbal learning, modeling, and juvenile delinquency. *American Psychologist*, 23, 245-266.

Sarason, I.G. (1978). A cognitive social learning approach to juvenile delinquency. In R.D. Hare and D. Schalling (Eds.), *Psychopathic Behavior: Approaches to Research*. New York: Wiley.

Sarason, I.G. and V.J. Ganzer (1973). Modeling and group discussion in the rehabilitation of juvenile delinquents. *Journal of Counseling Psychology*, 20, 442-449.

Saskatchewan Newstart (1969). *Life Skills Coaching Manual*. Prince Albert, Sask.: Training Research and Development Station, Department of Manpower and Immigration.

Scarpitti, F.R. (1965). Delinquent and non-delinquent perceptions of self, values, and opportunity. *Mental Hygiene*, 49, 399-404.

Scarpitti, F.R., E. Murray, S. Dinitz, and W.C. Reckless (1960). The 'good' boys in a high delinquency area: Four years later. *American Sociological Review*, 25, 555-558.

Schrader, C., J. Long, C. Panzer, D. Gillet and R. Kornblath (1977). An anger control package for adolescent drug abusers. Unpublished manuscript, Long Island Jewish-Hillside Medical Center, Glen Oaks, New York.

Schrag, C. (1954). Leadership among prison inmates. *American Sociological Review*, 19, 37-42.

Schur, E.M. (1973). *Radical Non-Intervention: Rethinking the Delinquency Problem*. Englewood Ciffs, N.J.: Prentice-Hall.

Schwartz, M. and S.S. Tangri (1965). A note on self-concept as an insulator against delinquency. *American Sociological Review*, 30, 922-926.

Scopetta, M.A. (1972). A comparison of modeling approaches to the rehabilitation of institutionalized male adolescent offenders implemented by paraprofessionals. Unpublished doctoral dissertation, University of Miami.

Seddon, M. (1979). Client as social worker. In D. Brandon and W. Jordan (Eds.), *Creative Social Work*. Oxford: Basil Blackwell.

Shaw, M. (1974). *Social Work in Prison: An experiment in the use of extended contact with offenders*. Home Office Research Study No.22. London: HMSO.

Shaw, S. (1982). What is problem drinking? In M.A. Plant (Ed.), *Drinking and Problem Drinking*. London: Junction Books.

Sheldon, W.H. (1949). *Varieties of Delinquent Youth*. New York: Harper.

Sherwood, J.J. (1965). Self-identity and referent others. *Sociometry*, 28, 66-81.

Shore, M.F. and J.L. Massimo (1979). Fifteen years after treatment: a follow-up study of comprehensive vocationally-oriented psychotherapy. *American Journal of Orthopsychiatry*, 49, 240-245.

Shore, M.F., J.L. Massimo, and R. Mack (1965). Changes in the perception of inter-personal relationships in successfully treated adolescent delinquent boys. *Journal of Consulting Psychology*, 29, 213-217.

Shore, M.F., J.L. Massimo, and D.F. Ricks (1965). A factor analytic study of psychotherapeutic change in delinquent boys. *Journal of Clinical Psychology*, 21, 208-212.

Sinclair, I.A.C., M. Shaw, and J. Troop (1974). The relationship between introversion and response to casework in a prison setting. *British Journal of Social and Clinical Psychology*, 13, 51-60.

Smith, M.H. (1933). *The Psychology of the Criminal*. London: Methuen.

Sobell, M.B. and L.C. Sobell (1978). *Behavioral Treatment of Alcohol Problems*. New York: Plenum Press.

Social Science Research Council (1960). *Theoretical Studies in Social Organisation of the Prison*. New York: SSRC.

Solomon, P. and others (1965). *Sensory Deprivation: A Symposium*. Cambridge, Mass.: Harvard University Press.

Spence, A.J. and S. Spence (1980). Cognitive changes associated with social skills training. *Behaviour Research and Therapy*, 18, 265-272.

Spence S. (1979). Social skills training with adolescent offenders: a review. *Behavioural Psychotherapy*, 7, 49-56.

Spence, S. (1980). *Social Skills Training with Children and Adolescents: A Counsellor's Manual*. Windsor: National Foundation for Educational Research.

Spence, S. (1981). Validation of social skills of adolescent males in an interview conversation with a previously unknown adult. *Journal of Applied Behavior Analysis*, 14, 159-168.

Spence, S. (1983). Adolescent offenders in an institutional setting. In S. Spence and G. Shepherd (Eds.), *Developments in Social Skills Training*. London: Academic Press.

Spence, S. and J.S. Marzillier (1979). Social skills training with adolescent male offenders: I. Short-term effects. *Behaviour Research and Therapy*, 17, 7-16.

Spence, S. and J.S. Marzillier (1981). Social skills training with adolescent male offenders: II. Short-term, long-term and generalized effects. *Behaviour Research and Therapy*, 19, 349-368.

Spivack, G. and M. Levine (1963). *Self-regulation in acting-out and normal adolescents*. Report M-4531. Washington, D.C.: National Institute of Health.

Spivack, G., J.J. Platt, and M.B. Shure (1976). *The Problem-solving Approach to Adjustment*. San Francisco: Jossey-Bass.

Staats, A.W. and W.H. Butterfield (1965). Treatment of non-reading in a culturally deprived juvenile delinquent: an application of reinforcement principles. *Child Development*, 36, 925-942.

Stephan, C., S. Stephano, and L. Talkington (1973). Use of modeling in survival skill training with educable mentally retarded. *Training School Bulletin*, 70, 63-68.

Stewart, C.H.M. and D.R. Hemsley (1979). Risk perception and likelihood of action in criminal offenders. *British Journal of Criminology*, 19, 105-119.

Sumpter, G.R. (1972). The youthful offender: a descriptive analysis. *Canadian Journal of Criminology and Corrections*, 14, 282-296.

Sykes, G.M. (1958). *Society of Captives: A Study of a Maximum Security Prison*. Princeton, N.J.: Princeton University Press.

Sykes, G.M. and D. Matza (1957). Techniques of neutralization: a theory of delinquency. *American Sociological Review*, 22, 664-670.

Tangri, S.S. and M. Schwartz (1967). Delinquency research and the self-concept variable. *Journal of Criminal Law, Criminology, and Police Science*, 58, 182-190.

Tarling, R. (1979). *Sentencing Practice in Magistrates' Courts*. Home Office Research Study No. 56. London: HMSO.

Taylor, I. (1981). *Law and Order: Arguments for Socialism*. London: Macmillan.

Taylor, I., P. Walton, and J. Young (1973). *The New Criminology: For a social theory of deviance*. London: Routledge and Kegan Paul.

Thelen, M.H., R.A. Fry, S.J. Dollinger, and S.G. Paul (1976). Use of videotaped models to improve the interpersonal adjustment of delinquents. *Journal of Consulting and Clinical Psychology*, 44, 492.

Thompson, B. (1974). Self-concepts among secondary school pupils. *Educational Research*, 17, 41-47.

Thorpe, D. (1978). Intermediate treatment. In N. Tutt (Ed.), *Alternative Strategies for Coping with Crime*. Oxford & London: Basil Blackwell & Martin Robertson.

Tifft, L. and D. Sullivan (1980). *The Struggle to be Human: Crime, Criminology, and Anarchism*. Orkney: Cienfuegos Press.

Timms, P. and E. Noyes (1982). Trying to comprehend the rapist's trauma. *Guardian*, April 2nd.

Toch, H. (1969). *Violent Men: An inquiry into the psychology of violence*. Chicago: Aldine.

Todd, F.J. (1972). Coverant control of self-evaluative responses in the treatment of depression: a new use for an old principle. *Behavior Therapy*, 3, 91-94.

Turk, D.C. (1978). Cognitive behavioral techniques in the management of pain. In J.P. Foreyt and D.P. Rathjen (Eds.), *Cognitive Behavior Therapy*. New York: Plenum Press.

Tutt, N. (1978). Introduction. In N. Tutt (Ed.), *Alternative Strategies for Coping with Crime*. Oxford & London: Basil Blackwell & Martin Robertson.

Twentyman, C.T. and R.M. McFall (1975). Behavioral training of social skills in shy males. *Journal of Consulting and Clinical Psychology*, 43, 384-395.

Vriend, T.J. (1969). High-performing inner-city adolescents assist low-performing peers in counseling groups. *Personnel and Guidance Journal*, 47, 897-904.

Wahler, R.G. and H.R. Pollio (1968). Behavior and insight: a case study in behavior therapy. *Journal of Experimental Research in Personality*, 3, 45-56.

Wallach, M.A., N. Kogan, and D.J. Bem (1962). Group influence on individual risk-taking. *Journal of Abnormal and Social Psychology*, 65, 75-86.

Warren, M.Q. (1977). Correctional treatment and coercion: The differential effectiveness perspective. *Criminal Justice and Behavior*, 4, 355-376.

Watts, W. and L.A. Free (1978). *State of the Nation III*. Lexington, Mass.: D.C. Heath.

Wehman, P. and S. Schleien (1980). Social skills development through leisure skills programming. In G. Cartledge and J.F. Milburn (Eds.), *Teaching Social Skills to Children: Innovative Approaches*. New York: Pergamon.

Werner, J.S., N. Minkin, B.L. Minkin, D.L. Fizsen, E.L. Phillips, and M.M. Wolf (1975). "Intervention package": An analysis to prepare juvenile delinquents for encounters with police officers. *Criminal Justice and Behavior*, 2, 55-84.

West, D.J. and D.P. Farrington (1973). *Who Becomes Delinquent?* London: Heinemann.

West, D.J. and D.P. Farrington (1977). *The Delinquent Way of Life*. London: Heinemann.

Wheeler, S. (1961). Socialisation in correctional communities. *American Sociological Review*, 26, 697-712.

Whitehill, M.B., M. Hersen, and A.S. Bellack (1980). Conversation skills training for socially isolated children. *Behaviour Research and Therapy*, 18, 217-225.

Whiteley, J.S. (n.d.). *Out of Step: The psychopath and society*. London: British Medical Association and National Association for Mental Health.

Whyte, W.F. (1943). *Street Corner Society*. Chicago: Chicago University Press.

Wickramasekera, I. (1968). The application of learning theory to the treatment of a case of sexual exhibitionism. *Psychotherapy: Theory, Research, and Practice*, 5, 108-112.

Williams, A.F. (1965). Self-concepts of college problem drinkers: (1) A comparison with alcoholics. *Quarterly Journal of Studies on Alcohol*, 26, 589-594.

Williams, D.Y. and T.J. Akamatsu (1978). Cognitive self-guidance training with juvenile delinquents: applicability and generalization. *Cognitive Therapy and Research*, 2, 285-288.

Williams, S.M. (n.d.). Personality differences between rapists, pedophiles and normals. Unpublished manuscript, Kingston Penitentiary and Queen's University.

Williamson, H. (1978). Choosing to be a delinquent. *New Society*, 46, 333-335 (November 9th).

Wolpe, J. (1958). *Psychotherapy by Reciprocal Inhibition*. Stanford, Cal.: Stanford University Press.

Worchel, P. (1960). Status restoration and the reduction of hostility. *Journal of Abnormal and Social Psychology*, 63, 443-445.

Yule, W. (1978). Behavioural treatment of children and adolescents with conduct disorders. In L. Hersov, M. Berger, and D. Shaffer (Eds.), *Aggression and Anti-social Behaviour in Childhood and Adolescence*. Oxford: Pergamon.

Ziller, R.C. (1973). *The Social Self*. New York: Pergamon.

Zimbardo, P.G. (1973). The mind is a formidable jailer: a Pirandellian prison. *New York Times Magazine*, April 8th.

Zuckerman, M. (1971). Dimensions of sensation seeking. *Journal of Consulting and Clinical Psychology*, 36, 45-52.

Zuckerman, M. (1978a). Sensation seeking and psychopathy. In R.D. Hare and D. Schalling (Eds.), *Psychopathic Behavior: Approaches to Research*. New York: Wiley.

Zuckerman, M. (1978b). Sensation seeking. In H. London and J.E. Exner (Eds.), *Dimensions of Personality*. New York: Wiley.

Index